LETTING

LETTING GOD

SCOTT'S CHOICE

ELAINE BREWSTER

HOUNDSTOOTH
PRESS

SCOTT'S CHOICE
Letting Go and Letting God

ISBN   978-1-5445-2384-2 *Hardcover*
          978-1-5445-2382-8 *Paperback*
          978-1-5445-2383-5 *Ebook*
          978-1-5445-2640-9 *Audiobook*

DEDICATED TO MY CHILDREN,

SARA, BEN, JACOB, AARON, MATTHEW, AND KATIE,

AND THEIR FAMILIES—MY REASONS

FOR BEING.

CONTENTS

PART TWO

Imagine yourself as a living house.

God comes in to rebuild that house.

At first, perhaps,

you can understand what He is doing.

He is getting the drains right and stopping the leaks in the roof

and so on; you knew that those jobs needed doing

and so you are not surprised.

But presently He starts knocking the house about

in a way that hurts abominably

and does not seem to make sense.

What on earth is He up to?

The explanation is that He is building quite a different house

from the one you thought of—

throwing out a new wing here, putting on an extra floor there,

running up towers, making courtyards.

You thought you were going to be made

into a decent little cottage,

but He is building a castle.

—C. S. Lewis, *Mere Christianity*

INTRODUCTION

Cancer is so much more than a suspicious spot on a scan. It's insidious and lasting. The damage stretches far beyond the patient. Family members, friends, and loved ones all feel the effects throughout their lives. The sweeping nature of cancer demands a comprehensive approach to healing.

As with most families around the world, my family has been devastated by cancer more than once in the last twenty years. We've celebrated milestones, big and small, lifted each other in dark moments, and consoled each other in the hardest ones. It was during these difficult periods when I realized something more had to be done. For my family, for myself.

Integrative or alternative medicine has been an interest of mine for as long as I can remember. Thinking about the body as a beautiful, complete system rather than disparate parts is my preferred way of approaching healing.

Alternative medicine is designed to balance the body. With the help of tools that range from health magnets and oils to sound and light waves to the foods we eat, integrative health focuses on the needs of the entire body. The aim is to cleanse the body, restore its internal frequencies, and realign it with the earth, air, and sun energy. Here, the body is in an excellent position to *heal itself*.

When Barbara, my caring and thoughtful sister, was facing her second fight with cancer, I knew that we, as a family, needed to look further than the options Western medicine provided us. The constant cycle of chemotherapy, surgery, and radiation was not only insufficient for what we were facing, but also created additional problems inside her body that could have been avoided. I dove into research to find answers that might help us in our newest fight.

I read books, listened to practitioners, and connected with other integrative medicine patients to learn everything I could. I compiled a folder of all the most promising information, hoping that something would jump out to my sister. I kept "waving my arm" from the sidelines, hoping that she would consider any of the options I'd found for her.

I even went so far as to put her on a call with a Mexican surgeon who co-owned a clinic in Tijuana. In a gentle voice, which Barbara loved, he explained the philosophy of his clinic. He explained that it was not enough to simply attack the cancer. He said, "We do things to build up the body, while at the same time we work to eliminate the cancer. Using only chemotherapy or radiation destroys the immune system." The whole point of what the clinic was working on was summed up in one magical word: "immunity." His voice took on a reverent quality when he smiled. "Immunity—*that's* the horse we're counting on."

My sister was a teacher who was curious about new things, but she was deeply entrenched in Western teachings. While she listened, and even asked a few questions, ultimately, she decided to go a more traditional route. She endured multiple rounds of chemotherapy and radiation with the support of all of us around her. But, heartbreakingly, Barbara died just ten days into her third round of chemotherapy.

As devastating as my sister's battle with cancer was, nothing could have prepared me for the shock of losing my wonderful husband, Scott, the same way. At the beginning of his journey, we weren't overly worried. We knew much more about the best holistic methods used for healing cancer diagnoses. Scott was positive, persistent, and faithful. His perspective was so contagious that I began journaling our journey with the goal of helping others who might face the same situation.

After his last breath, when I realized our holistic plans did not work, I planned to toss out my notes, assuming that if anyone knew his end result, they would want to run in the other direction! It was my sister-in-law Kelly, a psychologist, who said our difficulties were part of the tale. She said everything, from finding the right treatment for Scott to finding the right time for those treatments, was all helpful. Each detail helps others feel less alone and introduces them to a new way of thinking about healing. With that hopeful thought, I began crafting our story again. Through my writing, I realized that Scott's story merely *starts* with alternative and energy methods, but then progresses through emotional growth and, finally, spiritual growth to lead him to God. It *is* a story worth telling and worth learning from.

My ultimate goal is to inspire you to investigate your own body's healing. Whether you are interested in every part of integrative medicine or are just hearing about it for the first time, I invite you to listen to our story. Learn from it, and take what you need to keep your body healthy and in full alignment.

It is also my hope that this story honors my husband—a good man who was ever ready to learn, grow, and do; a man who accepted change by moving forward with enormous determination and vigor.

—Elaine Carr Brewster, 2021

PART ONE

CHAPTER 1

SOMETHING ON YOUR LIVER

DECEMBER

It was 6:00 a.m. on Sunday, December 1, 2002. His dark hair tousled, my slender husband, Scott, nudged me awake, saying, "Let's go to the emergency room. I want them to give me something to take away this pain." I looked up at him. His handsome features were scrunched up with some agony that had been hurting terribly for the past few days. Last night he'd tossed in bed all night. Now, preparing to get up, he sat on the edge of the bed and rubbed the heel of his right hand against his right rib cage, attempting to push back that hurt. Later I remembered often seeing this action, long before December.

My fifty-one-year-old husband was concerned about the pain because of a blood clotting condition he'd just discovered he had. On a recent long trip to Australia, he had developed a large blood clot and had found that it was due to a hereditary disorder called factor V Leiden. Factor V is a mutation of one of the clotting factors in the blood that can increase the chance of developing abnormal blood clots. It can even cause death.

Hospital personnel were not so ready to dispense either a blood thinner or pain medication. "We need to find out what this is before we prescribe something for you," they said. They sent him to have a chest angiography (to check the blood vessels in the chest) and then a CT scan (to check cross-sections of bones as well as soft tissues). Both procedures were more detailed than X-rays.

After a while, the doctor on call came back. Folding his hands behind him, he said, "Well, there's good news and bad news. The pain is not caused by a blood clot."

Scott tangibly relaxed over this good news and smiled thinly.

The doctor went on: "But there's something on your liver that shouldn't be there."

I caught my breath, and Scott unconsciously leaned backward, our world suddenly collapsed to a small, white-sheeted cubicle. Wasn't the emergency room doctor supposed to wait for the primary care physician or someone else to tell us something unexpected like this? Wasn't there some way to prepare us? This was not at all why we thought we'd come. What could it be?

Thus started our four-month quest for a cure for the "something" on his liver. Early on, during a phone conversation with my daughter-in-law, Lindsey, two phrases popped unbidden into my mind with a sort of flicker that felt like a déjà vu:

"Scott will make a choice; once chosen, it will be irrevocable."

Throughout my life, words or ideas occasionally appear in my mind that I know are not of my own making; they don't emanate from my brain. The earliest one I recall was the day of my first singing contest when I was seventeen years old. My first thought of the morning came with absolute clarity: I would win the contest. The notion made me neither arrogant nor flippant; it just made me glad. I went about my day happily knowing that I would win and was delighted, but not surprised, when I did. Who knows? Maybe it was that very idea that someone in Heaven dropped into my head that made me sing in such a way that I *did* win the contest.

These particular phrases about Scott came from that same heavenly source and stood out with such clarity that I wrote my short experience of receiving them in my journal. Thereafter, I treated them as a portent, paying close attention to see what choices Scott would make, but I never told anyone those two phrases. I figured the words meant that Scott would make a choice of treatment, and the treatment would lead toward a certain path, presumably with a healthy outcome. Those words from God's Spirit, in addition to what Scott asked of me, helped to define our different roles in this venture: mine was to research choices of treatment; his was to choose and, hopefully in the choosing, to get better!

∼

The "something" was a big something—nine centimeters by four centimeters, or roughly four and a half inches by two inches. The doctors undoubtedly had a frame of reference for this, but we did not. I didn't understand that it wasn't just big; it was *huge*! I would not gain a perspective of its enormity until three months later.

Something that big would surely be a tumor, but not a single doctor could or would say if it was cancer. I suspect every one of them thought it was cancer, but in our politically correct world, and with the inherent careful nature of doctors, they didn't say a thing. They did begin a battery of tests that lasted throughout December—MRIs, CT scans, more CT scans, chest X-rays, cytopathology, antibody pathology, and single specimen pathology. They didn't find anything conclusive.

Late in the month, Scott had an aspiration, or a needle biopsy. This procedure hurt more than any of the others. The doctor inserted a long, large needle through the skin, between the ribs, and into the nine centimeter by four centimeter mass. He was hoping to score a hit and draw out tissue from the mass that would inform him as to its composition. Now, imagine spreading your hand wide open and poking a stick at it, but blindfolded. You're hoping to hit a finger with your stick, but you have just as much chance of hitting air. In Scott's case, the procedure hit empty space and didn't provide much information at all. The doctors considered doing it again, but Scott answered an emphatic "No!" It had hurt like crazy!

The pathologist and doctor thought that, according to the cancer markers from the extracted tissue, it might be a melanoma. Our family physician then thoroughly checked Scott for skin cancer. He removed a couple of suspicious moles and sent them to pathology, but none was cancerous. The doctor then said maybe it was an internal melanoma. What? We'd never heard of that. We could visualize treating an external skin cancer, but how do you combat a melanoma that you can't see?

After some of these tests, Scott called his mother, Mom B, in California to tell her that the doctor had found something on his liver. Because the doctors weren't saying much, he didn't have a lot to tell her. Nevertheless, she heard a tone in his voice that she had never heard before. His petite blond mother hopped on a plane the next day and came to Provo, Utah, to be with us.

"Mom, why did you do that?" he asked, but he felt so much better having her here. I was surprised she was so intuitive but pleased that she would come to support Scott. In addition, she had read the same natural healing material that we had, so that gave us an additional voice of information.

Of course, we told our children that Dad had a problem and that the doctors were trying to figure it out. The oldest two and their spouses—Sara and Allen, Ben and Lindsey—became as involved as they could be, asking often about the latest information, and generally cheering him on. Seventeen-year-old Katie handled it by staying busy at the high school, and Jacob, in California, was torn, wishing he could be in two places at once. But his wife, Jenise, was pregnant with their second baby, so he was exactly where he needed to be. The twenty-year-old twins, however, were on LDS missions at a facility just down the road, learning the Gospel of Christ in Romanian and Hungarian.[1] Their task was overwhelming enough, so I kept the emailed letters to them cheery but vague. After all, the doctors hadn't found anything definitive yet, so I didn't want to worry them.

At home, Scott immediately began making a binder to add to other health binders he'd created. By his own nature and from his training as a chemical engineer, Scott was careful, logical, and methodical. His folders already included:

- **Heart problems:** His grandma had a heart attack at sixty but survived and lived to age ninety-seven. His father had a heart attack at fifty-four that killed him by fifty-five.
- **BYU comprehensive wellness program:** My five-foot-eleven husband was in excellent shape at 155 pounds with about 5 percent body fat. He skied in the winter, played racquetball the rest of the year, and biked to work daily—even in the snow. He was a four-time champion of faculty tournaments at Brigham Young University (BYU), where he'd been an assistant professor in chemical engineering and now was an engineering consultant. (He played/trained with the college guys, and since their racquetball team was number one in the nation, it said a *lot* that he could keep up with them!)
- **Prostate:** His PSA was 3.0, well under the goal of 6.0.
- **Stomach cramps:** He had cramps about every other year—so severely that he would just lie on the cold bathroom floor for an hour.
- **Poison oak:** He and our oldest son didn't realize that poison oak grew on our vacant lot. The Weedwacked fluid sprayed everywhere, it became

---

[1] Aaron and Matt were among the ninety-eight thousand (as of 2020) proselytizing or service missionaries of the Church of Jesus Christ of Latter-day Saints. At a missionary training center (MTC), they would prepare to become messengers of the Lord as well as learning a new language; then they would serve for two years in the country of their language. They would teach people that life's greatest happiness comes from following the teachings of Jesus Christ, and they wouldn't be paid for their service. Refer to https://en.wikipedia.org/wiki/Missionaries_(LDS_Church).

a huge problem in their bodies that year, and the problem even resurfaced the next year!

- **Colonoscopy:** He'd had this procedure done two months earlier and was fine.
- **Thrombosis and factor V Leiden:** This disorder afflicts 5 percent of the population and causes blood to clot too quickly. So that's why he never bruised when a 140-mile-per-hour racquetball hit him!
- He labeled the new binder "**Liver.**"

~

The liver is an amazing organ! It performs more than five hundred functions daily, most of them vital. What a friend! It manufactures amino acids—the building blocks of proteins; it removes waste and toxins from the bloodstream; it's the organ that detoxifies environmental chemicals (yes, even the ones that are ten syllables long!); it helps turn food into fuel—called metabolizing—and can even function when only a quarter of it is healthy.[2]

There are more than a hundred known liver diseases. Toxins cause many of the diseases, and some have to do with alcohol.[3] Cirrhosis would not be an issue for Scott, as he did not drink alcohol or smoke, and he ate a balanced diet of vegetables, fruits, and grains with moderate amounts of meat. Cancer was another serious liver disease, but since it "usually starts elsewhere in the body and spreads to the liver," that seemed out too.[4] As far as tests showed, there had been no other cancer from which to metastasize.

Although we'd been told that the nine centimeter by four centimeter mass was not related to blood clotting, Scott wondered if it could be related to a very hard fall he'd taken in the spring while skiing with two of our sons. By December 9, though, Scott had been told the mass was a solid tumor, although

---

[2] "Medical Essay." Supplement, Mayo Clinic Health Letter (February 2003).

[3] "As the trappings of modern society expose us to more and more...toxins, our livers are becoming more and more overloaded. People use more than 6 percent of their livers [just] for storage of toxins." Ted Aloisio, Blood Never Lies (Florida: Llumina Press, 2004), 45.

[4] Mayo Clinic Newsletters, 1990.

the only way to find out if it was benign or malignant was to operate. The surgeons we chose were two men in our neighborhood who attended the same church that we did. We knew and trusted both. Dr. Richard was a well-established physician, and Dr. David had recently been hired as a liver specialist. They told us that an operation would be a two-in-one blow: find out what the mass was while hopefully removing it. Scott wrote in his journal, "They need to operate, which I will probably have him [Dr. David] do next week. Then we will find out what this is."

When Scott wrote that, however, he was forgetting that we were in charge of a Christmas concert the next week. We weren't just in charge—it was *our* concert! Our family was a musical family and a performing family. We played, we sang, and the youngest danced. Scott (primarily an instrumentalist) headed the Brewster Family Band, and I (primarily a singer) supported him.

Scott's dad's ukulele playing and his mom's beautiful soprano voice inspired his love of music. Scott taught himself guitar and actually earned the money for my wedding ring teaching lessons at a local music store. At my house, I had grown up singing "Whispering Hope" as a duet with my mother and hearing my father's clear voice sing alto in church on Sundays. At the time we married, Scott played banjo and rhythm guitar proficiently, having even performed in a band in Japan on national television, and I had sung in Europe and won major voice contests.[5] His banjo and my opera were unlikely bedfellows. Nevertheless, we performed at church events and for college crowds, often with his brother Quinn on lead guitar.

When our children came along, they learned piano, violin, or both. Scott had always wanted to play music together as a family, and when the older children had enough skill, we made his dream happen. Playing mostly bluegrass and Celtic music (that's "Celtic" with a *K* sound), we performed as a family of eight (nine including a son-in-law) for fifteen years. We toured all the western United States, Kansas, and Canada, finishing off our programs

---

[5] You can hear a twenty-three-year-old Elaine by Googling "Rachmaninoff PBS Special Mormon Youth Symphony and Chorus 1973" (video results). I sing at one hour, seven minutes.

with rousing audience pleasers like "The Devil Went Down to Georgia" and "Orange Blossom Special."[6] We played for an ice sculpture event at the 2002 Olympics and had become headliners at major venues. Just a couple of months earlier, as a matter of fact, we had given concerts at several city fairs and festivals, as well as our second concert at the beautiful outdoor red-rock O. C. Tanner Amphitheater just outside Zion National Park in southern Utah.

The Brewster Family Top: Sara, Jacob, Matt, Ben Seated: Aaron, Elaine, Katie, Scott

A decade earlier, it had been Scott's idea to give a free Celtic Christmas concert as a gift to the community. This was to be our tenth annual concert. In previous years, we'd performed in some beautiful places, such as the ornate Assembly Hall in Salt Lake City and the Victorian-era Tabernacle in Provo, both built in the 1880s and both having intricately carved wood with flower-designed stained-glass windows. This year our program would be held in another venerable building, the newly restored Academy Square, built originally in 1892. On its second floor was a large, graceful ballroom,

---

[6] "The Devil Went Down to Georgia" by Charlie Daniels; "Orange Blossom Special" by Ervin T. Rouse.

its cream-and-gold fluted columns stretching up two stories as if they could take one to Mount Olympus.

For this special concert, guest artists would perform on hammered dulcimer, violin, and mandolin, and a children's Irish troupe would dance. We had also been practicing with friends who would replace missing family members. Several of those friends would prove integral to Scott's journey of healing.

How the Spirit Works

Thought leader Clayton Christensen was one who was very sensitive to the Lord's Spirit. He tells us *how* to listen for that quiet voice.

"Here on Earth we speak to each other in physical ways, through vocal cords vibrating. A speaker's sound waves hit the eardrums, causing them to vibrate, which creates tiny electrical signals that transport those vibrating patterns to the listener's brain. Then neurons zip around the listener's brain, distilling the speaker's concept. Our wonderful ears, then, are converters; they transform mechanical vibrations into electronic signals.

"God's Spirit, however, can communicate with our spirit *directly* to our brain (through thoughts) or our heart (feelings). A lot of people get confused because they try to hear God's voice with their ears. Instead, we need to listen inside of ourselves—to a concept or a sentence that just emerges inside of our head, or as a peaceful, warm feeling inside the heart, as if the Spirit of God gave our spirit a warm hug to say, 'This is right.'"[7]

[7] Clayton Christensen, *The Power of Everyday Missionaries* (Salt Lake City: Deseret Book, 2012), 96. Clayton Christensen was #2 on Thinkers50, the world's most prestigious ranking of business management thought-leaders. (Used by permission).

Several Vital Functions Identified with the Liver

The liver is one of the most versatile organs in the human body. Most biological systems of the body (circulatory, skeletal, muscular, digestive, nervous, etc.) rely on one or more functions of the liver to carry out their intended roles.[8] The liver:

- Processes digested food, that is, carbohydrates, proteins, and lipids, from the digestive tract
- Controls levels of fats, amino acids, and glucose in the blood
- Combats infections in the body
- Clears the blood of particles and infections, including bacteria
- Detoxifies or degrades drugs and toxins
- Manufactures bile
- Produces cholesterol
- Produces clotting factors (chemicals needed to help blood clot)
- Stores iron, many vitamins, copper, glycogen, fats, and other essential chemicals
- Manufactures, breaks down, and regulates numerous hormones, including sex hormones

Makes enzymes and proteins that are responsible for most chemical reactions in the body, for example, those involved in blood clotting and repair of damage.

---

[8] "Mayo Clinic Medical Essay." Supplement, *Mayo Clinic Health Letter* (February 2003).

CHAPTER 2

TRUST IN THE LORD

DECEMBER

I
t's odd to think of the many normal life activities that one continues to do, even in a time of crisis. Maybe the normalcy helps us cope. Maybe we just don't know how to say no because we don't recognize the urgency of a situation thrust upon us. In any case, Scott and I continued to lead busy lives.

In December, in addition to all his medical testing, Scott was driving north to Ogden, Utah, to work every day to a company that produced 70 percent of the world's automotive airbags. They had needed someone with a Ph.D. in chemical engineering to head one of their units, and Scott was hired. He told me that every time an airbag goes off, it's like a tiny explosion—an explosion that needs to be reliable at 120°F down to minus 40°F or so (think Arizona to Alaska). As an engineer, Scott had worked on different fuels for combustion (mostly coal) his whole adult life, so he was perfect for the job. He liked the work, and he loved the people in the company, but he *hated* the commute—an hour and a quarter up, and two hours back because of traffic.

One thing he really liked, though, was the company's ties with Japan, because it gave him a chance to speak Japanese. He had learned the language while serving a mission for the Church of Jesus Christ of Latter-day Saints in Central Japan.[9] However, conversational and religious Japanese didn't equip him to know words that applied to automotive parts when his company dealt with manufacturers like Toyota, Mitsubishi, Nissan, and Honda. So, when he got home from work, he was involved in a class on technical Japanese. With the rest of his spare time, he practiced the hammered dulcimer, guitar, and banjo for our program.

Scott plays the hammered dulcimer with wooden hammers

Being a fabulous storyteller, he was also preparing *The Baker's Dozen* by Aaron Shepard[10] which he would memorize and tell at our December 10 performance.

---

[9] The Church of Jesus Christ of Latter-day Saints is often referred to as LDS or the Mormons.

[10] Aaron Shepard, *The Baker's Dozen* (New York: Atheneum Books, 1995).

On my end, I was tending our seven-month-old grandson, Davis, while Sara, our oldest, taught English and her husband, Allen, attended school. I was also arranging the entire upcoming concert—the advertising, the flyers, the extra musicians, the dancers—while occasionally doing some practicing of my own. In addition, I was involved with a home business in energy technologies and I taught singing lessons. And, of course, I was doing the things a mom does: driving our youngest daughter, Katie, to eleventh grade every day; having dinner with our oldest son, Ben, and his wife, Lindsey, who were finishing up at BYU; mailing things to our second son, Jacob, his wife, Jenise, and their fifteen-month-old baby, Courtney, who were in California. In addition, I had just finished preparations to send Aaron and Matt to live in Hungary and Romania for two years.

Despite all this craziness of life, on December 10, our family and friends presented a delightful evening of Celtic music and Christmas carols. If you had been there, you would not have known that the man in charge had a serious challenge that was underlying all his thoughts. What you would have seen was a group of people enjoying Christmas music together. What you would have heard would have been the ancient sounds of haunting music on dulcimer and harp that made you think of the starry night when Christ was born. You would have heard the buoyant sounds of violin and penny whistle that made you want to dance yourself to the manger. You would have heard angelic voices sing about the birds coming to see the Baby, and about his tender mother pondering her new role. Best of all, you would have smiled as all the little children in the audience came to sit at Scott's feet, looking up at him in rapt wonder as he told his tale with characteristic energy and intensity. He was a delight to see—his eyes sparkling like black gems and his dimpled smile full of wonder, becoming a child himself again as he told his tale.

After the program, Scott came home tired but pleased that his part had gone well. He was happy with the wonderful response from the audience—our family, friends, and community. A man of few words, he mentioned our special helpers and guests in his computer journal entry that night and then finished, "The program went very well. About 350 people were there. In fact, everything went very well. Elaine did all the work. I just had to show up and tune my instruments."

∾

Two musician friends who replaced our missionary sons were Chris and Rebekah. Scott and I loved these women—Chris with her ethereal harp, shimmering flute, and solicitous manner, and Rebekah with her silvery voice, tremendous faith, and unfailing cheerfulness. They loved us in return and were happy to fill in. Our rehearsal had gone well until it was almost over. Then Scott happened to mention that he'd gone to the emergency room recently and told them what the doctor had said. They quickly laid music aside and turned their attention to him—this man whom they both admired and respected. The news alarmed both women, but they sensed that this "something on his liver" might be a real blessing for Scott that would allow him to learn new life lessons. Interestingly, they both remarked that it would be through *love* that this thing would be excised and he could be made whole.

> This "something on his liver" might
> be a real blessing for Scott.

Rebekah and Chris knew very well that Scott liked to have a tight control over his surroundings. (As an example from his workplace, Scott rarely had the secretaries do work for him; he could type faster than they could and knew better what he wanted, so he'd do the work himself instead of delegating.) Our two friends kidded with him and then told him that joy and hope would come through "letting go," through ease, flow, and relaxation.

Allowing or letting go were concepts that didn't make complete sense to a man as competitive as Scott was. How could they help him be whole, let alone get rid of a nine centimeter by four centimeter mass in his body? Words like "flow" seemed to stand in direct opposition to one of his main strengths: diligence. The bastion of hard work had always served him well, from making top grades in school to obtaining a Ph.D., and from rebuilding car engines to learning all his musical instruments. It had continued to be his hallmark as a husband, a father, and an assistant professor in chemical engineering at BYU. Added to this industriousness were the autocratic male role models of his father and grandfather, so it was no wonder the concept of letting go baffled him. He *wanted* to believe Chris and Rebekah, but he couldn't really understand how changing the way he lived his life would help him to eliminate this thing inside him. The way he approached endeavors was with earnestness, diligence, and persistence. Those were good things, weren't they? It didn't make sense to him to change.

> Allowing or letting go were concepts that didn't make complete sense to a man as competitive and driven as Scott.

"Love," in connection with this hurt in his side, didn't make sense to him either. Rebekah said warmly, "Love this thing on your liver and ask it to leave your body. Tell it to go to the Savior who can find a good use for it, that it's out of place and doesn't have a use in your body." I could tell by looking at his eyes that he didn't understand her statements. Even though we had a home business that dealt with Eastern medicine, teachings and techniques from our Western culture were more ingrained. Western medicine advocates "attack" (just like our national troops that were starting to gather in Iraq), whereas Rebekah's ideas were gentle and benign, quite out of the norm.

By way of helping him understand the energy of love differently, Rebekah asked if he had seen Dr. Masaru Emoto's fascinating photographs of crystals found in frozen water. This was something new. Emoto's research had started as a way to discern earthquakes through changes in water sources in Japan. Over time, his work had evolved to display photos of well-formed, beautiful crystals in pure water, whereas there was no crystallization in municipal chlorinated systems or polluted water. His research showed that whatever was *in* the water created frequencies that truly changed the *nature* of the water. And since we are mostly water, whatever the water is composed of changes us.

Emoto's research had branched out to show that *other* frequencies—even positive words and music—affected changes in water to create beautiful crystals. Emoto's personal favorite was the crystal created by imbuing water with the words "Love and Gratitude."

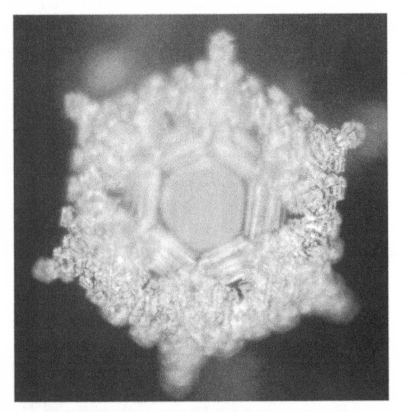

Water crystal "Love and Gratitude" taken by Masaru Emoto

This was wild research, but there were the photographs! Rebekah reiterated that because water is responsive, and because the human body is at least 70 percent water, our bodies actually "become" according to what the water in us is doing.[11] The bottom line is, we want to be filled with *love* so the higher energy—through the medium of water—percolates all through us.

---

[11] Masaru Emoto, *The Hidden Messages in Water* (Oregon: Beyond Words, 2004), 5.

Chris built on Rebekah's thoughts. Chris was one of our partners in our energy technology business. Chris was an advocate of integrative health in her own right, and she had compiled a book on wellness, summarizing topics such as rapid-eye therapy, alkaline water, essential oils, magnetic therapy, far infrared treatments, muscle testing, and mind/body connections. But preceding those health modalities was a beginning chapter on—of all things—love. She told us the beginning sentences of her book: "Do I love, accept, and nurture myself? Are my thought patterns positive in nature? Do I forgive myself and others?"

I could see Scott struggling to make sense of what Rebekah and Chris were telling him about loving and letting go. What *did* make sense during this conversation was his relationship with God. Scott and I, as well as Chris and Rebekah, had a deep, central, and unshaken belief in Christ as our Redeemer. Just like the Samaritan woman at the well, our belief was "This is indeed the Christ, the Savior of the world."[12] These beliefs or practices—the Gospel and music—were deep common bonds among the four of us.

Chris asked, "Do you have your scriptures handy? I just read something this morning."

I handed her a Bible from the end table. She opened and read from Proverbs:

> Trust in the Lord with all thine heart;
> and lean not unto thine own understanding.
> In all thy ways acknowledge him, and he
> shall direct thy paths.[13]

Rebekah nodded thoughtfully, and said, "I agree. Trusting the Lord is the best thing you can do, Scott, even though it's the hardest thing to do. Whatever happens on this journey of yours, the Lord will be with you."

---

[12] John 4:42, King James Version (KJV).

[13] Proverbs 3:5–6, KJV.

Scott and I agreed with them both. Our conviction was that both Heavenly Father and His Son, Jesus, knew us individually and cared for us deeply. We believed that their influence came through the Holy Spirit to guide and inspire, to teach and uphold us. Underlying even more than that, we knew that Christ had given his life to atone for our own sins and follies as well as those foisted upon us. The scriptures had shown us that it was Christ who made it possible for us to live again eternally. It was Christ who was the link—the mediator—between Heavenly Father and us.[14] Knowing all that, we felt that our Savior, Jesus Christ, was the one Being we could trust.

This statement from Elder Jeffrey R. Holland, a personal friend and an apostle in the Church of Jesus Christ of Latter-day Saints, conveys our thoughts and feelings about the Lord:

> God is always faithful; He never flees nor fails us. One of the great consolations is that because Jesus walked such a long, lonely path utterly alone, we do not have to do so. His solitary journey brought great company for our little version of that path—the merciful care of our Father in Heaven, the unfailing companionship of his Beloved Son, the consummate gift of the Holy Ghost, angels in heaven, family members on both sides of the veil, prophets and apostles, teachers, leaders, friends. All of these and more have been given as companions for our mortal journey because of the Atonement of Jesus Christ.[15]

Both women hugged Scott, their tears wetting his shoulders.

Chris said, "Scott, I'm sure the Savior knows what you're going through."

Scott told them, "I pray every day. I feel He's with me."

Rebekah added, "He *is* with you, and He loves you. You are a good man, Scott."

As they left, the feeling in our house was as peaceful as a church.

---

[14] The Apostle Paul stated, "There is ... *one* mediator between God and men—the man Christ Jesus." 1 Timothy 2:5, KJV.

[15] Jeffrey R. Holland, *Ensign*, May 2009, 88.

CHAPTER 3

ACIDITY VERSUS
ALKALINITY

DECEMBER

The technologies that Chris, Scott, his mom, and I worked with in our energy businesses were products created from the natural frequencies of the earth, air, and sun—using magnetism, negative ions, and far infrared (FIR) waves in the form of reflective ceramic fibers. These technologies had been researched primarily in Japan, China, Korea, and Germany, starting in about the 1950s. It was a Japanese physician, Dr. Tadashi Ishikawa, who created the first patent for far infrared healing (in 1965), and it was the Japanese who coined a phrase for the characteristics of chronic fatigue or fibromyalgia as "magnetic deficiency syndrome." It was the Far Infrared quilt that had attracted Chris to our energy company in the first place. She knew before most other people in America the astonishing importance of these wavelengths.

Natural energies, however, weren't designed to *destroy* cancer (or whatever was going on with Scott's body). They were designed to work *with* the body. (Perhaps the use of them even staved off his cancer for a good long while before he ever knew it was there.) But now Scott needed something stronger. Besides having all the tests and diagnostics that he was undergoing through Western methods, he wanted to know more extensively what natural treatment had to offer, and Chris's knowledge was greater than ours. He asked her to bring over her hefty blue binder of health information.

She brought the binder the next day and shared ways that Scott could make life easier for his liver, since doctors had at least identified that as a problem. She suggested treating the liver kindly by eating mostly vegetables and fruits—preferably organic so as not to contaminate the body with chemicals and pesticides—eating the right kinds of fats, and avoiding meats and processed foods. Since the liver is the main organ to break down substances, food in its natural state (as opposed to processed) would mean that the liver was not being overworked.

> *"Scott, your body will be able to better combat whatever is going on in there if you can make it more alkaline."*

In addition, she said, "Scott, your body will be able to better combat whatever is going on in there if you can make it more alkaline." She then introduced us to the classic book *Reverse Aging* and the importance of creating more alkalinity in the body to offset disease. The book's astounding premise is:

"The key point of health...is the management and disposal of waste products."[16]

The author also indicated a relationship between acidity, alkalinity, and disease:

---

[16] Sang Whang, *Reverse Aging* (New Jersey: Siloam Enterprise, 1994), 38.

I think that Japanese doctors are correct in assuming that any disease that is not caused by bacteria or viruses is caused by too much acid in the body. When doctors say they don't know the cause, chances are that it is acid. Somehow American doctors are not looking into the properties of acid and alkaline. In the Orient, people are always looking at the balance of yin and yang, minus and plus, and acid and alkaline.[17]

The term "pH" is used to explain how alkaline or acidic a substance is. The pH scale goes from 0 to 14, with 0 being extremely acidic, 7 being neutral, and 14 being alkaline.[18]

The pH Scale of Common Substances

1 = battery acid

2 = gastric acid

3 = grapefruit juice

4 = tomato juice

5 = black coffee

6 = urine

7 = pure water

8 = seawater

9 = baking soda

10 = Great Salt Lake

11 = ammonia

12 = soapy water

13 = bleach

14 = drain cleaner

---

[17] Ibid., 62.

[18] "Figure 1. The pH Scale of Common Substances," opentextbc.ca/anatomyandphysiolgoy.

Ted Aloisio, a microscopist who has taken thousands of pictures of live blood cells, has noticed the effect of pH on our bloodstream. He said that acidity, which leads to disease, is often the result of our diets.

> North Americans are the most acidic people on the planet. No wonder North America leads the world in degenerative disease... The typical North American diet is almost pure acid—pizza, beer, hamburgers, hot dogs, bread, French fries, deep-fried foods, processed and preserved foods, rancid oils, sugar, carbonated beverages, coffee, artificial sweeteners, additives, preservatives and so on.[19]

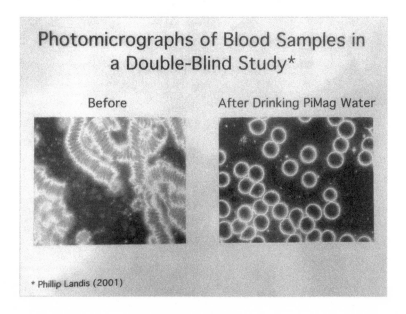

Photomicrographs of Blood Samples in a Double-Blind Study*

Before   After Drinking PiMag Water

* Phillip Landis (2001)

Mr. Aloisio even picked out four substances (notice he didn't call them foods) that are so pernicious, he calls them "the Four Horsemen of the Nutritional apocalypse."[20] They are sugar, trans fats, white flour, and carbonated beverages. Of the latter, the author of *Reverse Aging* also had strong thoughts:

---

[19] Aloisio, *Blood Never Lies*, 66–67.
[20] Ibid., 71.

Animals instinctively know what's good for them, while people eat or drink whatever the TV tells them to. All soft drinks are very acidic, especially colas. In order to neutralize a glass of cola, it takes about thirty-two glasses of high-pH alkaline water.[21]

The bloodstream has an extremely narrow limit as to how much acidity it can handle. If it becomes too acidic, the bloodstream is buffered by grabbing from the tissues. If it can't find the right nutrients, the body is forced to pull calcium from the bones. Of course, this can result in osteopenia and then osteoporosis. In our home, we saw firsthand the effects of the lack of calcium. That experience is the story of Nicodemus.

∽

Nicodemus was the iguana of Aaron, one of our twins.

About a foot long, he was the most beautiful sea green color you can imagine! Aaron and the other kids played with him all the time. They carried him

---

[21] Whang, *Reverse Aging*, 22, 46,

around on their shoulders, played "dinosaur" with him, and even managed to put a little plastic football helmet on his head. We all looked forward to the time he'd get huge and climb all over the place.

Aaron had had Nicodemus for more than a year when he noticed that Nicodemus wasn't standing up on his front legs. He supported himself weirdly, just squatting on his belly with his feet splayed out to the sides. Utterly distressed, Aaron shelled out fifty dollars and we took Nicodemus to a veterinarian.

The vet asked, "What's he been eating?"

"Vegetables," Aaron answered. "Mostly head lettuce."

"Ah, Green Death," said the vet.

Alarmed, I asked, "Why do you call it that?"

He answered, "Although lettuce can be part of his diet, there is not enough calcium in head lettuce. His body has been leaching calcium from his bones in order to live."

Aaron and I were both dismayed. *That's* why he couldn't prop himself up on his forelegs like iguanas are supposed to do. His bones were dissolving!

The veterinarian gave Nicodemus a prescription, but warned sadly, "When they're to this point, they usually don't make it. But maybe he will; otherwise, he's pretty healthy."

Before Aaron got home from school the next day, Nicodemus was dead. I felt horrible and still do. Here was a creature in our care, in our responsibility, and we failed him. However, we are to learn from the events of life, and I learned from Nicodemus. I changed our eating habits to include things like dark lettuces and spinach—leafy greens that contain more calcium. I think of Nicodemus daily, because what could happen to a little creature could happen to us.[22]

---

[22] Although acidity wouldn't cause complete disintegration of bones in humans, the conditions of osteopenia and osteoporosis *are* extremely prevalent in society.

I felt horrible and still do. Here was a creature
in our care, and we failed him.

~

Alkalinity, then, was truly a great starting point in creating a better internal environment for Scott. Chris led us to a lady in our neighborhood who was about my age, and she was on an alkaline diet. The lady, Maren, was using her alkaline diet to help combat a chronic disease she had, with a side benefit: her weight had dropped to her high school weight![23] Maren *loved* what she was learning from this diet: "Forget [counting] cholesterol and carbohydrates. Forget calories and fat grams. It turns out that the single measurement most important to your health is the pH of your blood and tissues—how acidic or alkaline it is."[24] Well, we'd learned that with Nicodemus: bloodstream is more important than bones.

Maren invited Mom B and me to a lunch. Her kitchen was certainly set up differently than mine—instead of canisters of basics like flour, sugar, and pasta noodles on the counter, she had rows of avocados, seeds, and fruits. Lunch was a luscious salad made of many ingredients, topped with seeds and a bit of nonacidic dressing. For our beverage, Maren served us alkaline water. We told her that was something we also had in our home. After investigating two Japanese-based companies that created alkaline water, Kangen and Nikken, we had bought the Nikken PiMag water system.[25] The system declustered water into its optimal hexagonal molecular structure as well as filtered, created alkalinity, and gave energy through the Pi elements. (Water deserves its own chapter, but suffice it to say that *all* chemical reactions in the body do so in a fluid medium. Clean water that is energized with a certain degree of alkalinity goes a *long* way in allowing the body to work the best it can.)

---

[23] "Weight will reduce as tissue acid wastes are eliminated." Dr. Theodore A. Baroody, *Alkalize or Die* (North Carolina: Holographic Health Press, 1991), 121. Baroody also lists many alkaline foods as well as recipes.

[24] Robert O. Young and Shelley Redford Young, *The pH Miracle: Balance Your Diet, Reclaim Your Health* (New York: Wellness Central, 2002), 5. Shelley gives many recipes.

[25] Refer to www.nikken.com/ca/uniqueTech.

Back home, Scott said simply, "You've been gone a long time."

I felt guilty, since we'd been gone longer than expected, and he needed his own lunch. But it had seemed impossible to leave until Maren had finished everything she wanted to say, because she was trying so hard to help us. This alkaline world was different than the world I lived in, but her low weight and energy (after bearing eight children) confirmed that it was a desirable way to eat!

Now we heard more fascinating information as we listened to Chris, who had come over again, read Mr. Aloisio's statement: "Anything that affects the delicate balance in our biochemistry affects our cells, affects our organs, and affects the entire electromagnetic processes of our bodies. Excess acid in our bodies creates a biochemical breakdown."[26]

Chris looked up from reading that and smiled. "Scott," she said, "you are experiencing a biochemical breakdown! We don't know yet what this is inside you, but we do know some things that will help."

> *"Scott, you are experiencing a biochemical breakdown! We don't know yet what this is inside you, but we do know some things that will help."*

Scott laughed a little and agreed absolutely to cut out the toxic "Four Horsemen of the Nutritional apocalypse." He said he would try to sleep at least eight hours a day and drink lots of alkaline water. Mom B and I said we would buy organic vegetables and fix even healthier food than he'd had before, steaming the veggies for three minutes only. And Chris put him on a high-nutrient shake from a private company that had gotten rid of cancer in a lady that she let us talk with. The shake had six times the daily requirements but no sugar, so it would substantially increase his energy and nutrition.

In addition, Scott adopted a practice that had saved his Japanese friend,

---

[26] Aloisio, *Blood Never Lies*, 66.

Takuji, who had been flying a gyroplane when it crashed to the earth. Unconscious, Takuji was so broken, doctors didn't expect him to live. He did live, and one of the health measures he had used was to drink pure pressed potato juice morning and evening, and his body had restored itself. Scott pounced on his new Chris-and-Takuji eating regimen with characteristic resolve.

Scott was easily the most persistent person I knew, who had remarkable determination and stamina. For instance, his Lake Powell story of 1978 was legendary. We had boated a long way from the marina, and we needed to get back. His father had asked, "Does someone want to ski back?" No one else wanted the beating that the choppy water of late afternoon would give their legs, so Scott volunteered. He skied an entire hour. Sometimes, for a break, he held the line in the crook of his elbow, and sometimes he'd shift the line from hand to hand, but he skied behind the boat the whole bumpy sixty minutes. The man was truly made of steel!

With that same steely resolve, he turned down sweets, fats, and meat all through December, which was not easy to do at his workplace! The entire month, his coworkers brought to work the most delectable, the most unique, and the most tantalizing Christmas treats, canapés, and appetizers they could devise. He would come home and tell me what delicacies they had brought that day, but he didn't sample any of them. Not one. I was constantly amazed at and proud of his willpower to resist such wonders. He really wanted to get well!

One night, instead of just hearing about it, I got to see him in action at a company Christmas party. After a snowy hayride through standing herds of elk (not reindeer, but close!), we went back to his boss's big, warm house. Scott picked out strawberries, celery with spiced hummus, and asparagus wraps, but didn't touch the crab croissants, buttery artichoke dip, or chocolate-raspberry mousse!

~

The True Cause of Cancer

If the condition of our extracellular fluids, especially the blood, becomes acidic, our physical condition will first manifest tiredness, proneness to catching colds, and so on. When these fluids become more acidic, our condition then manifests pain and suffering, such as headaches, chest pains, and stomachaches. According to Keiichi Morishita, M.D. in his *Hidden Truth of Cancer*, if the blood develops a more acidic condition, then our body inevitably deposits these excess acidic substances in some area of the body so that blood will be able to maintain an alkaline condition.

As this tendency continues, such areas increase in acidity, and some cells die; then these dead cells themselves turn into acids. However, some other cells may adapt in that environment. In other words, instead of dying—as normal cells do in an acid environment—some cells survive by becoming abnormal cells. These abnormal cells are called malignant cells. Malignant cells do not correspond with brain function nor with our own DNA memory code. Therefore, malignant cells grow indefinitely and without order. This is cancer.[27]

---

[27] Herman Aihara, *Acid & Alkaline* (Oroville, CA: George Ohsawa Macrobiotic Foundation, 1986), quoted in Whang, *Reverse Aging*, 50.

CHAPTER 4

EASTERN MEDICINE, WESTERN MEDICINE

DECEMBER

Scott was a do-it-yourselfer. He was like my dad; he could fix anything! It's one of the reasons I married him. Scott planted, pruned, and maintained the yard. He installed the sprinkler system; he made repairs on the house and cars. He was a self-taught musician, having learned both rhythm and fingerpicking guitar styles, banjo, hammered dulcimer, bodhran, ukulele, and Hawaiian steel guitar. As a missionary in Japan, he had learned both katakana and hiragana writing systems (which have forty-five and forty-six characters, compared with English's twenty-six letters), and he even tackled the hardest—Kanji—which has fifty thousand symbols. When he was in Air Force basic training, he finished a self-paced program for radio school in half the time because he disliked being there and wanted to get home. And when he conducted engineering research at BYU year after year, he spent his time in a small, windowless office by himself. In the coming months, he would need all those skills of focused concentration and self-motivation.

One of Scott's do-it-yourselfer-isms was a dream to be an independent business owner. He envied the men he'd seen in Japan who cooked food in their small, busy diners at street level and were able to just walk upstairs to their living quarters and families at the end of the day. The men's businesses were small, but they were *theirs*, and they were proud of what they did! Well, opening a restaurant wasn't something he would do, but he imagined forming a business with his three brothers—one a mechanical engineer, one an electrical engineer, and one in automotives.

As the years went on, that became more and more unlikely. So, five years previous, when his job at BYU had been in question, we had diversified our income by starting a home-based business in healthcare—a smart move, since healthcare was one of the largest sectors of the global economy. The Japanese-based research and development company that we represented focused on *wellness*, not illness. Think of the difference: ancient Japanese physicians were not paid unless the emperor stayed healthy, whereas in North America, we don't even see a physician until we are sick!

Being involved with a wellness company brought us into contact with ideas from Eastern cultures for the first time. Their ideas, their focus, their whole outlook is different from the concepts that Scott and I had been raised with in America. These new ideas, though, allowed us to step closer to the concepts about healing and healers that Chris presented.

One of the healers Chris helped us learn about was master herbalist Dr. John R. Christopher. Dr. Christopher was known to say, "There are no incurable diseases"—a phenomenal statement from a man whose youthful body was weak from rheumatoid arthritis. His mother once asked him how he could want to be a doctor when he couldn't stand the sight of blood and couldn't even bear to see chickens killed for an evening meal.

With foresight, he said, "Mother, I will be able to heal people without cutting them up. There will be natural ways of doing it."[28]

Born in 1909, Dr. Christopher grew up in a time when pioneers in the West were still using old remedies from their European ancestors. He became the only practicing herbalist in the United States Army during World War II. Soldiers came to him to cure impetigo, jungle rot, scrofula, eczema, ringworm, shingles, and chronic boils—things that no other doctor in the Army was helping with.[29] He healed himself and his fellow soldiers using nature's remedies. Later, he helped thousands of others by creating the School of Natural Healing.

One student who followed in Dr. Christopher's naturopathic footsteps was Dr. Richard Schulze. We got to "meet" him via his videos. Schulze was the man who would teach us about cleansing and natural healing. Bald, bearded, and dressed in dark, collared shirts, his motto was "We have a natural healing filter inside us." His smiling "everyman" persona was approachable, positive, and energetic, albeit a bit brusque. Schulze opened the first of his Natural Healing Clinics in America in the 1970s, and along with the European clinics he managed, he'd personally treated thousands of patients. Through his videos he was reaching out to share his life's mission: to educate people on how to heal themselves naturally, without doctors, drugs, or hospitals. Chris left the videos with us, and Mom, Scott, and I watched them. They had intriguing titles: *Create Your Own Healing Miracle* and *There Are No Incurable Diseases*.

Schulze narrated his story with passion. It began at age eleven with his fifty-five-year-old father dying in his arms from a massive heart attack. Three years later, when he was fourteen, his mother also died of a heart attack. Two years after that, a rather obese Schulze with a cholesterol level at 300 was diagnosed with a genetic heart deformity.

He said, "I was basically pumping 'mud' through my veins and arteries. I was told unless I underwent gruesome open-heart surgery, I would be dead

---

[28] John R. Christopher, *School of Natural Healing* (Utah: Christopher Publications, 1976), ii.

[29] Ibid., vii.

before twenty." He continued: "Sawing and cracking my rib cage wide open, yanking my heart out, and stabbing it with scalpels sounded frightening, horrific, and insane. I knew there must be another way."

His heart was dying; he was an orphan; he had nothing to lose. So, remembering how his grandmother had used herbs, he started making his own tonics. He used the purest, strongest herbs he could obtain, and within days he felt like a new person. He kept it up, and, amazingly, within three years, his heart was healed. His doctor checked his before and after X-rays repeatedly to make sure they were of the same person!

Doctors said that what he did couldn't be done, and they were right in a way: based on what *they* had been taught, it couldn't be done. Dr. Schulze was showing the public with his own story that there are natural ways to heal that aren't necessarily taught in medical schools. He said,

> Maybe it was watching my mom and dad butchered, poisoned, and killed by medical doctors when I was a child…but my soul is driven to…make damn sure that I have offered every American the Choice, the Freedom, the Opportunity, the Truth, and the Education to heal themselves and maintain their health, naturally.[30]

> *Doctors said that what he did couldn't be done, and they were right: based on what they had been taught, it couldn't be done.*

≈

Schulze's concepts marked a significant demarcation in Scott's treatment. Prior to viewing these videos, Scott planned on doing, by default, pretty much everything that physicians said he should do: imaging, testing, surgery, and so on. After watching the videos and animatedly discussing what we heard, he, his mom, and I came to a new appreciation of the body and its inherent ability to heal itself. Scott had to decide whether to treat the body as a passive

---

[30] Dr. Richard Schulze, *Herbal Product Catalog* (California: American Botanical Pharmacy, 2002), 2.

object that needed external input to succeed, or to treat it as an entity that was designed internally to heal itself.

> *Scott had to decide whether to treat the body as a passive object that needed external input, or to treat it as an entity that was designed internally to heal itself.*

In addition, we found that ancient cultures like the Chinese, with their venerable healing traditions, would rather do anything first than cut into the body. Surgery weakens the body, which needs to be strong to fight whatever is going on. It also cuts across nerves, muscles, and energy meridians, thus making it harder for the body to heal. Scott now wanted to thoroughly investigate natural healing and Eastern modalities. At the same time, he wanted to cover his bases by thoroughly exploring Western medical offerings.

~

East, West. When I was younger and someone mentioned Eastern medicine or complementary healing, such as acupuncture, my response was "acupuncture, schmacupuncture." In my "great" wisdom, I tossed it off as being of no consequence. Now, after five years of studying via our natural wellness business, I had begun to see the sense of prevention and of balance as practiced in the Eastern part of the world. It occurred to me that the civilizations that utilize these principles have amassed their knowledge over thousands of years, whereas the United States has been a country and gathering knowledge for only around four hundred years. Next, our focuses were different. Here in the West, our focus is on symptoms and locales, such as a migraine in the head, a cancer of the liver, or a bone spur on the heel. The East focuses on the body as a whole unit. They believe, for instance, that if a throat exhibits tonsillitis, the entire person has tonsillitis—the throat is simply where this problem is manifesting. Finally, the West waits until something is broken before attempting to fix it; the East prevents it. For instance, long flights to Japan include arm- and neck-stretching exercises between movies. Led by the flight attendants, everyone on the plane does them. No American airline ever does that, and, true, it does look a bit comical. But the Japanese apparently don't care how it looks; they care about preventing problems!

I had a singing student once who was a nurse. She told me, "The body is designed to heal. Think about what happens when you get cut." What a wonderful concept—healing is inherent! But the body must have the proper internal environment to do it. A natural healer named Maggie Sale said that with natural or complementary healing, "the body is doing what it does best: cleansing and healing itself." Natural modalities simply urge that process along. She summarized the differences between Eastern and Western medicine by comparing them this way:

> In natural healthcare, i.e., holistic healing, we focus on the body as an energetic system that is an integrated whole—no part can be adequately addressed in isolation from the body as a whole. The beauty of thinking holistically is that you don't have to know anything about the condition you are attempting to resolve —all you need to know is that everything and anything will improve if the body is placed in an optimal environment.[31]

Everything and anything will improve if the body is placed in an optimal environment.

I have come to believe that the only way our Western medical system can become more viable is through prevention. And that doesn't mean the quasi-prevention of diagnoses, but the prevention at the root of individual self-care—taking responsibility for what we put in and on our bodies.

Dr. Schulze recommended that everyone start with the basics— detoxifying and cleansing.[32] His memories of the basics were significant but

---

[31] *Team Diamond* Magazine, August 2000, 14–15.

[32] "When Dr. Bernard Jensen, a chiropractor, coined the phrase 'Death begins in the colon,' his medical contemporaries laughed. 'With the advancement of medical science, drugs and surgery, why be overly concerned about just another organ?' they mused. Dr. Jensen didn't die until nearly 100 healthy years of age." Aloisio, *Blood Never Lies*, 45.

not pleasant. He remembers his dad (who died quite young, remember) taking his reading material into the bathroom once a week for an intense hour-long session. Much later Schulze would preach that the body wants to eliminate waste about an hour after every meal, which would be several times a day.[33]

Words in the Western and Eastern Health Systems

Words associated in the Western and Eastern health systems vary acutely:

WESTERN MEDICINE	EASTERN MEDICINE
Fix	Prevent
Locale-oriented	Systemic
Surgery as a first measure	Surgery as a last resort
Testing, diagnosis, symptoms	Balance, whole, holistic
Traditional, conventional, standard	Complementary, alternative, natural
Allopathic	Holistic, integrative, functional
Drugs, prescriptions, chemicals	Energy, meridians, chakra, Chi
Side effects	Cleansing
Medical science	Science, quantum physics
Scientific method	Physical evidence
Randomized trials and studies	Observation over millennia

The nerves of the colon are designed to signal us when it's time to eliminate waste, if we haven't restricted the peristaltic action (and some say, stretched out the nerves) by waiting too long. It's funny how we work so hard to get toddlers to recognize their urges as we potty train them, only to tell the same

---

[33] "The average American has only two or three bowel movements a week. This makes Americans 70,000 bowel movements short in their lifetime!" Richard Schulze, *The American Botanical Pharmacy* (California: American Botanical Pharmacy, 2011), 28.

children later at school that they must wait until recess. Then, by the time we're older and in the workforce, the cultural thinking has somehow shifted so that the longer we hold back our urges, the cooler we are. The truth is that the coolest of us pays attention to our body. Dr. Schulze said,

> When you do any detox program, the whole idea is to start juice fasting, [use] saunas, exercise, whatever, that will dissolve and purge accumulated waste, poisons and toxins out of your skin, fat, muscles [and] every cell of the body. All this waste that is removed, *all of it*, is deposited into your colon for final removal. If your colon is sluggish, constipated, or blocked, then all of this dumped toxic waste will just sit there. It can even be reabsorbed back into your body.[34]

Of course, there was much more—all of it quite fascinating—that made good sense and boiled down to taking responsibility for your own health. I've wondered, is that one of the legacies given to us by our beautiful, sterile hospitals —that many of us would rather have a costly procedure done by others instead of doing something cheap and simple ourselves? Physiologist Dr. Gary Lindner encourages, "Be healthy by choice, not by chance."[35] In other words, taking measures ourselves to ensure our own health. (And that's exactly what I see people doing more and more nowadays—researching, discussing, and doing what they feel is best for them.)

Dr. Schulze put it this way: "Getting well is easy! Just stop what you did that made you sick and start new programs that will make you healthy."[36]

That's precisely what Scott was now attempting—to figure out what had made him become diseased and to change it!

The very next day, Mom B and I went to the natural food store. She laughed for the first time since she'd come to Utah as we chose colorful organic veggies. At last we were *doing* something instead of waiting fretfully for the next

---

[34] Schulze, *American Botanical Pharmacy*, 1.

[35] Gary Lindner, www.SelfCareHub.com.

[36] Schulze, *American Botanical Pharmacy*, 18. As of 2020, he'd helped more than twenty thousand patients.

inconclusive medical test! Scott's cleanse began with herbal tinctures, supplement capsules, fresh garlic, vegetable juices, and potassium soup to both flush him out and build him up.[37]

There was one more Dr. Christopher–inspired technique that came through Dr. Schulze. That was the hot/cold shower. Scott showered in water as hot as he could stand and let it spray directly onto his hurting right side. When it became too hot, he'd abruptly change the water to cold. Hot and cold, hot and cold. This was designed to dramatically increase life-giving circulation and break up stagnant energy. At first, he hooted and shouted! Finally, he just gritted his teeth and counted to fifteen in breathless seconds until he jumped out. But he kept it up every morning. I personally could not do this; if I were told that I would die unless I did this, I'd say, "Pack me off; I'll see you later!" I am a total wimp when it comes to temperature. But Scott wanted to get well, believed he could get well, and had the willpower to tackle this fight.

Schulze himself had admitted it might not be easy. Of opening his own clinic, he said, "I had to kick some butt and do some convincing to get my patients to understand."

His admonition became our new creed: "Suck it up, get tough, and get well."

Dr. Schulze on Natural Healing

I read something in a newsletter from Dr. Schulze in 2004 that has stayed with me ever since. He said, "The human body was way too complex for me or any other doctor to really understand and figure out."

He went on to explain that often the ego gets in the way. Medical doctors believe they know the answer, which leads them down dangerous paths. What Dr. Schulze knows to be true, and what he said that made me trust him even more, was that faith

---

[37] See Appendix A for potassium broth recipe.

was the foundation of healing. Faith in God, nature, and the ability of the human body is what we need to help the body heal itself. I couldn't agree more.[38]

---

[38] Richard Schulze, *Natural Healing Newsletter*, July 2004, 19.

CHAPTER 5

POWERFUL ALLIES

DECEMBER

E ven though Scott had wanted his own business, it took the advice of a physicist from Baltimore, Neal, to get him to consider the Japanese-based wellness company we became involved with. Scott needed to trust in someone like Neal—someone who also had a Ph.D., someone who worked meticulously and methodically—because the energy technologies that the company offered seemed a far cry from the complex combustion programs with which he dealt. One of the things Scott researched was the effect of coal dust blown into refineries. Even though coal dust is as fine as face powder (warning: don't get any in your pores or it will stay there for a week!), the residue that is not combusted builds up in the corners until it can pull the roof down, closing the refinery for years.

To prevent that eventuality, Scott worked on programs that were so massive that he had to keep them running all weekend. Several times on

Saturdays and Sundays, he would drive over to the university just to make sure the programs were still going. Even if they were, the programs would only yield a tiny bit of data by Monday. Neal had given Scott a reading list, and Scott was surprised to find that what he was reading concerning these energy technologies was similar to what he had studied for his engineering degree: things like heat transfer, conductivity, and electromagnetism![39] Neal's reading list convinced Scott that the products created by the company were both viable and effective.

Now, five years later, Neal had prostate cancer. He had not chosen chemotherapy as a treatment. That was of interest because he could have gone anywhere in the world or chosen anything he wanted for treatment. The therapy he chose came right from his home state of Maryland. Neal's wife supported his choice by saying, "I knew Neal. I had faith in his judgment and in his intelligence. I knew he would never take an unnecessary chance with his life and his family's future on a mere whim."[40]

Scott respected Neal's opinion so much that he wanted me to find out what he was using. The main product that Scott was curious about was called elemental cesium high pH therapy, a substance that would counteract acidity. It was available through the lab of Neal's friend, Allen Hoffman, who was a radiologist. It would make Scott's body more alkaline, which was one of our focuses in December.

I remembered that Neal's name was in that folder marked "Cancer" that I had made for my sister. After quite a bit of searching, I found the folder! Neal's name was there but not his phone number. For some reason, Allen's lab number was, though. I wondered why. Finally I remembered. My sister had ordered some supplements from the lab when her cancer had resurfaced. So I called, hoping the number might still work and could lead me to Neal.

I half expected to talk directly with Allen, perhaps because he's the one

---

[39] See Dr. Neal Deoul's Reading List on Vibrational/Energy Healing Methods, Appendix E.
[40] Kathleen Deoul, *Cancer Cover-Up* (Baltimore, MD: Cassandra Books, 2001), 57.

I had talked with previously when I had ordered my sister's supplements. Therefore, I was mildly surprised when I heard a woman's voice on the other end of the line, but I was taken aback by the way she answered. Her voice was almost a whisper, careful and cautious, as if she were standing behind a post looking both ways, hoping no one would see her. She questioned me professionally, but also defensively: What was my name? Where had I gotten the lab telephone number? Why was I calling?

When I explained that I was the physicist's friend, had used Allen's products before, and had talked with the man himself, she grew easier and talked more normally. The woman, who was a nurse named Lorna, said, "You'll need to ask Allen directly about elemental cesium. I have taken over his lab, but you could call this other number and probably reach him."

I thanked her and called the number she gave me.

Strangely, it was another cautious woman who answered, this one even more quiet and restrained than the first. She sounded Hispanic and very humble. She even sounded so subservient that I wondered in passing if she might be at the bottom of the chain of authority at the lab. In a whispery voice so soft I could barely hear her, she said, "This is Rosa." It dawned on me who she was. With astonishment I asked, "You're Allen's wife, aren't you?"

"Yes," she confessed, and I was surprised that she started opening up to me. Maybe it was because I knew who she was. Perhaps she just needed a sympathetic ear. As I continued talking with her, I realized that what I had first taken as meekness was, in fact, fright. She sounded like a scared rabbit, her statements begging for succor.

"They have him up for criminal proceedings." Her voice was breathless, almost pleading now. "No, you can't talk to Allen; they won't let him talk to anyone! They've taken away our lab, and now they are taking away our house. We don't know where to go!"

My heart broke for her. The pain, confusion, and bewilderment in her voice were palpable. I had never talked to another individual in such dire circumstances!

Having no other recourse, I called Nurse Lorna back. She had bought Allen's lab after an FDA SWAT team (yes, you read that right) "dressed in flak jackets and carrying weapons had raided his offices."[41] They said he had a substance on his shelves that he, in fact, did not have. Even though the charges were spurious, they stripped the shelves and confiscated all his products, computers, and files. And now Rosa had indicated that they were after their home too. I didn't realize my heart was racing until Lorna answered the phone.

"It sounds awful," I said.

"Yes," she admitted. "It has been really hard for them."

Since she was the new owner, I got down to business with her.

She methodically asked many questions, took a medical history, and listened to the techniques we were currently using. I was surprised how long and thorough the history was but was happy that she approved of the alkaline diet and the cleansing that we were doing with Scott. She mentioned the ultra-nutritional shake, though: "If he has cancer, improved nutrition alone will probably not get rid of the cancer. Good nutrition won't kill." Nevertheless, it was pleasant to talk to her because it felt proactive, not just waiting like sitting ducks for the medical world to tell us what to do or being told we didn't know anything because we didn't have a medical degree.

I told her that I was calling to find out about the elemental cesium high pH therapy.

Straightaway she said, "Your husband can't use it unless we know he has cancer."

My heart dropped and I sighed in disappointment. I reminded her that, at that time, we didn't know if he had cancer.

Responding to the frustration in my voice, she offered, "There are other things he can use. You really do want some 'allies' that can cause strong results in the body, stronger than everyday supplements you might have previously bought. They are so powerful I hesitate to call them supplements. One of their

---

[41] Deoul, *Cancer Cover-Up*, 100. See also Appendix E.

purposes is to raise the immune level and to start the killer T cells working more efficiently. The more you support the immune system, that's your best shot."

Her words were consonant with what we had learned in our wellness business as well as what we were doing for Scott with alkalinity and cleansing. It seemed that, really, that's what natural healing was attempting—to get the body back into a healthy enough state that the immune system could work its magic. The immune system—that amazing system underlying all of health, but that people in our society didn't understand and didn't talk about.

> *That's what natural healing was attempting—*
> *to get the body back into a healthy enough state that*
> *the immune system could work its magic.*

The author of *Reverse Aging* had strong thoughts concerning the immune system: "A study of the God-engineered immune system and enhancing the power of that immune system are *much better* than developing drugs to cure diseases after the illnesses develop."[42]

Research was Lorna's forte, and her studies were exhaustive. "I research every one of these supplements to make sure the quality is the highest, because I give them to my aging father, who has cancer. I just wish I knew which one I give to my dad is keeping him alive! Earlier he had chemo and radiation until his lung was burned up, and then he went to cesium. I give him other substances too." She went on with pride, "I've spent well over $2,000, but I've kept him alive three years longer than what the doctors predicted."

As an R.N., she had the background to understand the effects of different substances; as a researcher, she was competent and meticulous; and as a daughter and friend, she was full of love and empathy. Her sole desire was to help others. When we ordered supplements, for instance, she charged wholesale; she didn't even want a profit. Lorna was easy to trust.

---

[42] Deoul, *Cancer Cover-Up*, 40.

The downside of this relationship was the length of the conversations. She had a tremendous need to be both thorough and medically correct. Let me explain the medically correct game: people who do not have medical degrees, which consists of almost the entire alternative health world, are not allowed to say things that could be construed as diagnoses. They have to substitute words. Instead of saying "diabetes," they say, "blood sugar disorder." Instead of saying "fibromyalgia," they describe the symptoms, such as "feeling achy and hurting all over," and instead of saying "pain," they talk about "discomfort." They can say "excruciating agony" or "dreadful hurt" but not "pain," since "pain" is evidently a medical term.

After talking with Rosa and hearing of Allen's lab being taken away, I could understand Lorna's desire for cautiousness. I didn't think she needed to be so cautious with me, however, and it lengthened our phone conversations by three times. She had such a hard time just saying something straight out that often the only way I got an answer was by asking her everything else, having her say no to all those things, so that the yes was the only unmentioned item left! It was as cumbersome as trying to speak a language you don't know well.

Lorna recommended two particular immune builders, or modulators, that Scott could use right now. The first was colostrum, that substance that is expressed just before breast milk comes in. It contains antibodies to protect newborns against disease. "Colostrum is a magical substance," Nurse Lorna gushed. "After all, God made women! We all need the antibodies in it. Allen himself took one bottle a day. And there is no toxicity" (meaning there were no side effects).

The second was a special aloe, and she was partial to it. "Aloe soothes inflammation while it boosts T lymphocytes. In other words, it stimulates killer cells in the immune system. There are quite a few aloes out there, but Allen's aloe product is the best. It's filtered, concentrated, and cold-pressed. With aloe from stores, 51 percent is undigested and just goes to waste."

After listening to her extensive list and the reasons behind each product,

I ordered what she and I felt would help Scott the most—Graviola, Artemix, N-Tense, and C-Buff. She went back over what I had ordered and told me the protocol for each one—when to take it and how often. I was going to need to be organized for this!

CHAPTER 6

GREEN TEA

DECEMBER

In a very short time—within the first two weeks of December—Scott's regimen included cleansing, hot/cold showers, high-nutrient shakes, potassium broth, potato juice, colostrum, aloe, and other potent supplements, while avoiding the "Apocalyptic Four." All this was in addition to driving about an hour and a half each way to work (and still hating the commute), studying technical Japanese, and rehearsing for our Celtic Christmas program.

Our friend Chris now introduced us to another treatment that was proving to be of benefit: green tea. It was one of many treatments that we would learn about that cured people's cancers. In the case of every treatment or therapy we investigated, we would personally talk to someone whose cancer had been eliminated via that treatment, in addition to reading all we could about it.

Once you hear about something new, it seems to be everywhere! After Chris told us about green tea, we saw it on Dr. Mercola's site,[43] the *Herb News,*

---

[43] See information about osteopathic physician Dr. Joseph Mercola at www.mercola.com.

and the *Journal of the National Cancer Institute* (*JNCI*), just to name three. It is interesting that something that might help one's life just "emerges" and makes itself evident on several different fronts. We are not tea drinkers in our house, but for medicinal purposes, it was certainly worth a look.

The literature said a compound in green tea "prevents cells from getting large enough to divide. Consequently, they simply die off by a process known as apoptosis or programmed cell death. This process literally stops cancer before it starts."[44] It appeared that green tea would create such a healthy internal environment that even a large tumor, if that's what Scott had, would stop growing and even start shrinking.

> *It appeared that green tea would create such a healthy internal environment that even a large tumor would stop growing.*

Chris knew of some people who could verify the efficacy of green tea. Because of our health business, we were already used to talking to and relying on individuals all across North America for health information. Calling someone for verification of a product or to quiz them about their business was not foreign to us. I am a strong proponent of the scientific method, but I also like hearing people's personal experiences. They, in essence, become their own live study.

First off, we called Aidra in Arizona. She'd had liver cancer and three heart attacks during the previous ten years. Recently she'd been spending about twenty-three hours a day in bed because of her lupus and fibromyalgia. She started a green tea regimen and found that her energy was greatly increased after just three days. After two weeks, her hurting body was feeling much better. And just this last August, her doctor had declared her cancer-free.[45]

Next, we called Albert and Marie Bowen from Idaho, both in their seventies. Albert had been using green tea for four years. They sounded happy

---

[44] Dr. Varro Tyler, former dean of the School of Pharmacy and Pharmaceutical Sciences at Purdue University.
[45] Author's notes do not indicate how long she was on green tea before this declaration.

and kind and were absolutely ecstatic to share their good news, even with complete strangers.[46]

Marie talked first. She'd had three spots on her liver, but after recently taking green tea, the spots were down to one. She said that Albert had had terminal cancer of the bladder, with three months to live. "We heard about green tea through Paul Harvey and decided to give it a try. We took it just the way it's supposed to be taken, and in one month Albert's cancer left! Here. Here's Albert." She handed the phone to her husband.

He sounded so jolly that I pictured a Santa Claus dressed in khakis and polo shirt, holding a cup in his hand! In a cheerful, husky voice, he said, "Green tea has a substance in it that destroys a protein in the blood cells that have cancer, but it makes the healthy cells right next to it more healthy!" He chortled. "Now, how many things do that?" He went on to say that his prostate had been removed but had grown back. "My doctor said, 'If I weren't the one who removed it, I'd have never believed this!'"

Being the breadwinner in their family, Albert was excited about another aspect of green tea. "Would you know, green tea only costs eight dollars a pound? And you only need about two pounds a month!" He chuckled deeply, clearly considering that a coup.

Then he turned all businesslike as he told us how to take it. "Steep two teaspoons of leaves in two quarts of boiling water; turn the heat off and let it sit. Do it before bed and let it sit all night and then strain it in the morning. Drink it at room temperature or cold, but never hot," he warned. "Drink twelve to fifteen cups a day! And eat lots of deep greens, and no meat except once or twice a month."

He ended, "Give it about a month. I'll mail you a book if you'll promise to read it." We promised. As we ended the conversation, we were full of hope. Scott was doing so many wonderful things for his body. Something was bound to work, wasn't it?

---

[46] At the time of writing, Albert Bowen was in his eighties, healthy, and still happily spreading the word about green tea.

We ordered the tea and obtained information over the internet (which was still somewhat of a new phenomenon) while we waited for the book and additional research that Scott had found through NIH (National Institutes of Health). When the book came, we learned that green tea did *all* kinds of good things: boosted the immune system, reduced body fat, lowered blood pressure, and helped regulate cholesterol levels. One writer said, "Population studies demonstrate that green tea consumption may actually be one of the major reasons why the cancer rate is lower in Japan. When Japanese men leave their homeland and come to America, they become twenty times more likely to develop prostate cancer than if they'd stayed home."[47]

In all ways, green tea seemed like a wonderful treatment choice! There was only one glitch, and for us, it was a big one. A major one, actually. As part of our LDS religion, we don't drink black or green tea. This brought up a religious dilemma, so Scott decided to ask what our local church leaders, like the bishop of our ward, thought.[48] The LDS Church is based on priesthood authority, believing that now—as in Jesus' time—a person had to be "called of God, by prophecy, and by the laying on of hands by those who [were] in authority."[49] LDS officials don't seek leadership positions, nor are they voted on or elected. They are called of God and are highly respected. Scott knew that church leaders who care for their congregations could receive inspiration on their behalf. As a free agent, he was certainly *not* required to ask their permission, but Scott figured he needed all the help he could get! As for myself, I didn't think it was necessary for him to ask, but if it made him feel better, then that was fine. I really hoped they would agree that green tea was a great treatment for him.

---

[47] Michael T. Murray, *Encyclopedia of Natural Medicine* (Rocklin, CA: Prima Publishing, 1991); Nadine Taylor, *Green Tea* (New York: Kensington Books, 1998), 41.

[48] A "ward" is named after a nineteenth-century jurisdictional term; it's a local community of about three hundred people (like a parish). A grouping of five to nine wards is called a "stake" (like a diocese). Its name comes from Isaiah's command to Zion to "strengthen her stakes." The leader of a ward is a bishop, and the leader of a stake is a stake president.

[49] Articles of Faith 5, Doctrine and Covenants. (The Apostle Paul is an example when he says he is "ordained a preacher and an apostle.")

While we waited for his priesthood leaders to decide, we continued to learn about green tea. It seemed like such a fine plan!

~

Meanwhile, life moved on, as it does. Christmas Day was a subdued but happy occasion. Scott's mom had flown back to her husband, Lorin, in California. Here at home, we opened presents. We had food. We had Santa. Ben and Lindsey came over for gifts, dinner, and games, and Jacob, Jenise, and little Courtney even came from California! Sara had decided that our house was the place to be, so their little family had slept over on Christmas Eve. The presence of so much family made Katie happy because she was missing her twin brothers, who were down the road at the missionary training center. Since the facility was only for missionaries, we hadn't seen them since they had entered in October and November. She wasn't the only one who missed them; the whole family missed them and were thrilled when they telephoned us from the MTC. So, other than the twins' being gone and the persistent, awful hurt in Scott's side (and someone turning off the oven, so we had soup instead of turkey!), it was a pretty fun and normal Christmas.

~

The day after Christmas, though, I saw how far away from "normal" it was. Scott had me make an appointment with our family physician for that very afternoon. This was a radical departure for us; usually I was gleefully shopping with the girls on the twenty-sixth, and Scott might be skiing with the boys. It shows where I was mentally with this situation that I was honestly amazed that he couldn't wait one day before going to the doctor. But I made the appointment, and we went.

Our primary care physician was a great guy. He advocated a balanced life-style and practiced what he preached. (At that time, he rode his horse almost every afternoon after office visits, and as a result of that horseback riding, he could do the adductor machine, which works the inner thigh muscles, at its max of two hundred pounds! Normally, it's pretty amazing if someone can do the abductor machine, working the outer muscles, at that weight!) He was lean and trim—something like 3 percent body fat. He always swept into the little examination room with a big smile and a "How are you today?" He let you talk, and he actually listened. Previously, we had talked to him about some of the innovative health technologies we had encountered. Today, Scott asked him about green tea.

"Green tea!" he enthused. "That's interesting that you would ask! I am part of a group of LDS physicians that meets every summer to talk about the moral and religious aspects of healthcare products and techniques. We met this summer on just this topic!" Scott knew that he would understand the dilemma that green tea presented. "The conclusion of our summer conference was that as an antioxidant it is unsurpassed, and that it certainly can be used medicinally."

Scott told him that he was asking some church leaders what their opinion was.

"Good. Meanwhile, I'll tell you what," said the doc. Then he picked up his pad with a flourish and wrote a "prescription" for green tea, to show his stamp of approval. Smiling, we left his office.

Soon after, each of the three priesthood officials responded to Scott individually. We were excited to hear what they would say, especially after such a positive doctor's visit. Two of the three, though, said they "didn't think it was in Scott's best interest to use it." We were stunned. Disappointed. That wasn't the answer Scott wanted or had expected! Green tea seemed so perfect: potent, available, inexpensive, and even doctor approved. Scott and I discussed their responses. He had not asked any of his leaders why they felt that way, so he didn't know if their decision came as a result of prayer or merely from hearsay. And if it was from hearsay, surely we had read more than they had, and we had more information than they did, especially after talking with our physician, with Aidra, and with the Bowens. Had our leaders said that because society *expected* chemotherapy or radiation? I journaled a thought: "It's funny how we say no to something with identifiable, researched goodness, and readily say yes to chemotherapy, which poisons the whole body, merely because of societal conventions."

> *"It's funny how we say no to something with identifiable, researched goodness, and readily say yes to chemotherapy, which kills the whole body, merely because of societal conventions."*

If Scott had wanted to, having autonomy for his own life and knowing that this was for medicinal purposes, he could have overridden their decision and taken the green tea of his own accord. But he reasoned, with a slightly pleading voice, "If I obey my leaders, even if their information is wrong, the Lord has to bless me anyway, doesn't He?" I had to agree with him. So, with faith in his priesthood leaders, and with overarching faith in Christ, we put away the green tea with its hoped-for miracle.

CHAPTER 7

WHAT HAPPENED AT AGE THIRTEEN?

DECEMBER

Worry was Scott's constant companion. The future that had been so sure and hopeful when he took his new job in Ogden now seemed as transient as dirt brushed off a worker's hands. More than that was this ever-present hurt that doctors couldn't identify without surgery, and he was now viewing surgery as a last resort. As noted, surgery not only cuts through skin, muscle, and veins, it cuts through nerves and even energy circuits—in short, it completely severs pathways that the body needs to send healing communication, nutrition, and new growth.

Chris continued to talk with us to see how Scott was faring. She sensed how frustrated he was. She had a friend, Reginald, who owned a large biofeedback machine that analyzed numerous locations in the body. She asked Scott if he would like to be checked by Reg on his machine. The purpose would be for Reg to provide additional information during this period of time when the doctors weren't able to tell what the mass in his side was. Reg's machine would pick up information in the form of vibrations emanating from the body—from nerves, from vessels, and from all the organs of the body. Instead of bringing information from one locale, like a stethoscope might, the biofeedback machine provided information from well over one thousand locations in the body.[50]

Reg was an energy practitioner, as was his father. His dad had been awarded the Discovery of the Year Award by the American Naturopathic Medical Association. Reg, following his father's integrative health outlook, was committed to helping people have a better life, and as of this printing, he has certified in and practiced seventeen different modalities. I was curious to see how Scott would respond to Reg's biofeedback. If he considered it a soft science rather than a hard science, he might not be amenable to Reg's suggestions. Chemistry and physics, for instance, are considered hard sciences—fields that can be tested in controlled experiments with quantifiable data. On the other hand, sociology and psychology are considered soft sciences because they are more theoretical. Biology is somewhere in between. I, however, had previously had two amazing experiences in fields definitely outside of the hard sciences that convinced me of unusual possibilities. On separate occasions, a reflexologist and an iridologist had told me I had no thyroid. They determined this just through feeling the sole of my foot or looking at my eye. Neither looked at the scar on my throat or knew about my 1973 thyroidectomy![51]

Still, Scott had hope, and he came. He walked slowly into Reg's building, bent like a tree hanging over a fence. He was fatigued from pain and from his recent visit to the doctor. He and I barely fit into the small space, which was more like a science lab than a healthcare professional's office. Tall, rugged Reg

---

[50] There is now a microcurrent medical device by Healy Company that gives instantaneous biofeedback in many more areas than Reg's old machine. It is cleared by the FDA and can be found at www.healyworld.net.

[51] Reflexology provides an aid to health through putting pressure on areas in the sole of the foot. Iridology helps to determine information about a patient's body by looking at the iris of the eye.

settled himself down next to his massive machine; there wasn't even room for Chris, who now stood in the doorway.

Reg used several wires to hook Scott up to his machine and then asked him to hold still while he turned on the scanner. Scott sat patiently but with a quizzical expression. While the machine silently did its work, Reg said he had studies that he could put in our doctor's hands if we wanted.

He also commented, "Through biofeedback we can shrink a tumor from golf ball–size to tiny BB–size in thirty days."

That statement lifted our hearts: look what was possible!

Reg went on: "We go to a doctor and get hooked up to a machine that takes our blood pressure. This is just a machine that takes in more information than that."

Scott nodded his tired head in vague understanding.

While he was being scanned, I told them that while I was earning my master's degree in music, one of my professors, Dr. Rosalie Pratt, had used something similar in her research with boys who had ADD and ADHD. These boys had surface electrodes attached to their heads and wires that went from those attachments to an image on the wall, like a thermometer or ducks in a pond like you'd find in a shooting gallery. The boys were told to "Raise the mercury" or "Shoot the ducks" just by thinking about the task. When their thinking became focused, their energy intensified until the wires picked up the greater emissions and the deed was done. The mercury rose or the ducks got shot, giving the boys great satisfaction! Not only was it fun, but they could boast to their fellow students of the cool stuff they had done—just by *thinking* it![52]

Harking back to our school days, most of us were taught how certain body systems function. For instance, when I taught elementary education, I

---

[52] Rosalie Rebollo Pratt, "Art, Dance, and Music Therapy," *Physical Medicine and Rehabilitation Clinics of North America* 15, no. 4 (2004). On a side note, even though Rosalie's research was arts-based, she worked with all kinds of situations and people in hospitals. At one time, she stated, "I wish they would abolish football. The boys are cheered wildly when they're on the field, but as soon as one takes a hit to the head that permanently debilitates them, no one goes to see them in the hospital. Believe me, no one sees what they look like then."

taught the muscular, skeletal, and circulatory systems. I didn't teach other systems like the lymphatic, immune, and endocrine systems. And the energy system? The body as an electrical system? Never mentioned at all! Studying the energy system—or Chi (also spelled qi)—in America is still rather new. Luckily, it is happening more and more!

All of us recognize attributes of energy: lots of energy = alive; zero energy = dead. We are beings of energy. A holistic chiropractor said, "Scientists now realize that the human body is nothing more than a very highly complex energy field."[53] What makes us uncomfortable is that we don't really know *what* energy is or *where* to locate it.

The "what" of energy can be viewed as an electrical system in living beings, and it *can* be measured and improved. Dr. Norman Schwartz, a specialist in environmental medicine, considers the flowing of electrons to be "the classical energy currency of all biological life-forms."[54] According to classical Chinese philosophy, qi is the force that makes up and binds together all things in the universe.

The "where" of energy is along channels or meridians with chakra points— that is, focused points or knots of energy that have been observed for millennia in ancient Eastern lands, such as China and India.

> The "where" of energy is along channels or meridians with chakra points—that is, focused points or knots of energy that have been observed for millennia in ancient Eastern lands.

Chris had mentioned right before we went into Reg's tiny office, "He'll measure you, Scott, but he won't tell you if it's cancer, even if he thinks it is. He's a technician, not a doctor, so it's not ethical for him to make disclosures. But I think we'll be able to tell from what he says."[55]

---

[53] Bradley Nelson, "5 Secrets to Losing Stubborn Fat," http://www.Healers Library.com/news/articles/5-secrets-losing-stubborn-fat/.

[54] Candace B. Pert, *Molecules of Emotion* (New York: Simon & Schuster, 1997), 281.

[55] Reg later sold this large machine to a woman who *did* make medical claims for a couple years. She was shut down by the FDA, and the machine was taken away from her.

Reg did not, in fact, diagnose anything, but when the scanning process finished, there were a lot of other things that he picked up from his data printout.

"This indicates that your liver is in stress."

That was an interesting first comment, since we had told him nothing about Scott's condition before we went in. He also indicated that Scott's oxygen was not adequate, and that other organs were stressed. Reg suggested liquid oxygen drops—O2Go, taken three to four times a day—to oxygenate the blood, as well as a couple of other supplements.

He continued looking at the printout. "Also in stress is the right side of your body."

That's where Scott's tumor was. Reg was batting a thousand just by looking at the data! He also mentioned extreme tension near his right shoulder, and, finally, as he looked up at Scott, he saw Scott's right shoulder spasm then and there. As he watched, it twitched again. A concerned line creased his forehead. "How long has that been going on?" he asked.

"Oh, this?" Scott glanced at his shoulder unconcernedly, as if he were casually tossing salt over his shoulder. "For a while."

"Twenty-eight years, actually," I corrected, with raised eyebrows.

Reg waited patiently, so Scott reluctantly told him his story. "I got this in graduate school. I felt like they had put me in a box and told me to come out three years later with my Ph.D. My professor was so busy he didn't have time to help me, and I didn't know what I was doing. Besides that, I hated my topic! Every lunchtime, I used to walk around the parking lot—sometimes two or three times, all the way around it—just to try to keep going. Now I realize that it was depression, but we didn't know that then. You know the ironic thing? I had a calculus teacher in high school with a muscle twitch. We used to make fun of him. We'd throw spit wads on his desk, or in his briefcase, or at the light above him just to bug him, and *we* were the good kids, the smartest kids in the school. This is the one thing I never, ever wanted to have."

The rest of Scott's shoulder story is that the twitch fired off approximately every six seconds all day long, and had for the greater part of our married life.

That's an awful strain on an ongoing basis for something that should not be happening at all! All day long his shoulder twitched. All day, every day. I think it was responsible for Scott's not receiving a couple of jobs or promotions. It's a condition that makes a person look nervous or unreliable, even though he or she is brilliant and doesn't personally feel or act that way.

The only thing Scott had found in the Western world of medicine to help his shoulder were muscle relaxants, but then that was dangerous for driving and impossible for the quick reaction needed in sports. There was one thing that *did* work, and that was a pair of rolling magnetic balls called MagBoys from the company Nikken.[56] (They were one of the reasons we became involved with energy technologies.) After these MagBoys had been rubbed on his shoulder for about a minute or a minute and a half, the spasms ceased—for twenty-four hours: a *vast* improvement!

To make a permanent change, Scott would have needed to use them several times daily for several months. But he had become inured to the condition and then ignored it altogether. He never looked at himself in a mirror to see what was happening, so he never bothered to stop the problem. The spasms continued day after day, year after year, until they became a habit, stopping only when he went to sleep. Even then, as he was relaxing into slumber, his body would shoot off one last enormous jerk, bouncing our bed like a bucking bronco!

Reg looked thoughtful. It seemed like he had something he wanted to say, but he only said, "It would be good to get that stopped, Scott."

Reg then tilted his head as he looked again at his data and asked a strange question. "Scott, what happened to you at about age thirteen?"

"What do you mean?"

"With most people, there are two, three, or even four events that were so traumatic or extreme that the body remembers it. When a cell dies, the vibrations are duplicated in the new cell. In your body, Scott, there is only

---

[56] The 2020 iteration of the two handheld rolling balls from the company Nikken is called MagDuo.

one event. And it's at about age thirteen."

Scott thought for a moment and then shook his head. Nothing of importance came to mind.

"Well, work on it. It will be good if you can remember and then let that thing go."

There was that idea again of letting go, just as Chris and Rebekah had mentioned. But he couldn't let it go because he couldn't even think of what it might be. As we talked about it on the way home, I was proud of Scott that he wanted to figure this out and didn't just shoo it under the rug. He remembered silly, rash things that had happened at that tender age of puberty, but none of those experiences felt right. None of them spoke with authenticity to his soul that would indicate it was the experience his body had kept locked up for almost forty years. Nevertheless, he let thoughts percolate in the back of his mind, realizing it was important to pull this age thirteen event out of those forgotten vaults rather than keeping it hidden away there forever.

~

The beautiful, busy Christmas season ended a few days later when Jacob's family left to return to California. Before leaving, Jacob and Ben gave their dad a priesthood blessing. A priesthood blessing is a prayer that calls upon the powers of Heaven for the benefit of the person being blessed.[57] Their sincere prayer indicated that the Lord was pleased with Scott and that God would be with him. I especially remember they asked for a blessing of healing, if it were the Lord's will. That word—"healing"—brought a sudden, comforting balm to my soul. What a glorious word: healing.

On New Year's Eve our family performed at "First Night" in Salt Lake City, a late-night citywide celebration to welcome in the New Year. Katie consented to perform at the last minute because a guy named Aidan had

---

[57] "Priesthood Blessings," The Church of Jesus Christ of Latter-Day-Saints, churchofjesuschrist.org/study/manual/gospel-topics/priesthood-blessing.

asked her out for New Year's Eve in Salt Lake and he wanted to see us, well, *her*, perform. What was she supposed to do when a cool guy said he wanted to see her dance? We performed our Celtic repertoire that night—from the haunting "Winnifred's Strathspey" to the enchantingly happy "Butterfly slip jig."[58] When we finished, the audience jumped to their feet and burst into applause. There couldn't have been a better way to end the year!

---

[58] "Winnifred's Strathspey" composed by Mark Jardine for his mother; "The Butterfly (Slip Jig)," traditional Irish.

CHAPTER 8

YOU'VE GOT YOUR HUSBAND BACK!

JANUARY

T he New Year started. The older kids went on with their lives, Katie went back to school, Mom B was back to California, and Scott and I took out the Christmas tree. How commonplace that last phrase sounds, but this was a new occurrence. Usually, there was a power struggle over when to take the tree down, which door to take it out, and even where to hold the trunk as we carted the sappy thing out. We usually couldn't agree who would vacuum and who would sweep, and the needles would stay on the floor for days, a prickly symbol of discontent.

But this year we took out the tree *together*! He vacuumed and I swept; we picked up the pieces of Christmas *together*. In fact, we were doing everything together—from going to medical appointments to talking about alternative choices together. To me, it finally felt like a partnership, a collaboration of respect and equality. Scott was in a new place in his life, and despite his constant pain, there was a greater tranquility in our home.

His inner calm came from a perspective of gratitude that he wrote of in his journal: "I see every day now as a gift, one more day given to me." Recently, he had stood in the kitchen, eyes shining as bright as two dark gems, and beamed, "You've got your husband back! This is the real man you married."

I was thrilled! I smiled gratefully at him as my heart soared. But I wondered: if I had him back, where had he been? It seems that for his whole adult life he'd been living in a place of desire for perfection and control. I remember twenty-eight years earlier, when we were newly engaged, he had leaned over as he was talking and had plucked a piece of lint off the carpet. I thought how lucky I was to have someone who cared so much! It quickly became apparent that his perfectionistic expectations extended to everyone around him, and as a wise therapist said, "Being a perfectionist is a hard way of living—both for the individual and for those around him or her."[59]

> *Being a perfectionist is a hard way of living.*

I, too, came into marriage as a perfectionist, but, luckily, six children drummed that out of me! Scott was at work; he wasn't home as often with them, and nothing ever drilled it out of him. His expectations were high, and he was full of "shoulds"—for himself, for me, and for the children. On seeing tomato juice encrusted on the pointed blade of the can opener, he once declared, "You should clean this off every time you use it." Oh, if I did every one of his "shoulds," I wouldn't have been able to do anything else! No reading stories to the children, no working on geography or spelling bees, no helping them with household chores, no sewing pajamas or dresses, no singing or teaching lessons, no taking them to lessons, and no checking on

---

[59] Bill Marshall (therapist) in discussion with the author, November 14, 2002.

their practicing or who they were playing with. Cleaning is all I would have done, and that still wouldn't have been enough.

Early in our marriage, I found that I couldn't really talk to him about our differences. His logic and language were better than mine, and he had an inexplicably competitive paradigm that made him have to win.[60] Plus, he really didn't enjoy talking about emotions or about changes that I thought needed to be made. (It may be stereotyping, but this seems to be the typical male model of yesteryear.)

One of the natural changes that was occurring in our lives made him nervous: our children were growing older. As they became more independent, he felt his influence waning, and that scared him. It made him feel like he had to hold on tooth and nail, especially in the matter of money. On the one hand, he paid them generously for the performing they did, but on the other, he rationalized and manipulated payment for extra household chores so he didn't have to pay as much. It was strange. We certainly weren't rich, but we had never starved. We'd never had the one-can-of-beans-until-payday meal, yet he couldn't let go of money without a fight. Maybe that came from having to give back his boyhood allowance when his father discovered that his mom was paying him twenty-five cents a week.

The only one who could call him on his behavior was our oldest daughter. "You're doing it again, Dad; you're manipulating." Brought up short, he would duck his head sheepishly, saying, "Am I?" Until she pointed it out to him, he couldn't *see* what he was doing. People won't change if they don't see a need to.

People won't change if they don't see a need to.

Early in our twenty-eight-year marriage, Scott called me daily from his office just to say hello. He opened the car door and politely helped me out, and

---

[60] It turns out that his competitive nature was innate. I recently found a coming-of-age letter his grandmother wrote to him when he turned twelve. After telling him what an honest, clever, and handsome boy he was, she wrote, "Consider others. They too want to always win and be first in things." Edna L. Karren Brewster.

he gave me cute little notes and cards from time to time. Now the amenities of marriage had gone out like dry leaves blown in the wind. I thought of the evening after I had sung as soprano soloist for my first *Messiah* production at Christmas. My arms laden with flowers, music, and makeup bag, I tried to jostle open the passenger car door while he opened his driver's side. He was silent and dour, which was frustrating because performers really like to talk about their performances afterward. Finally, I couldn't stand the silence, and I asked him, over the top of the cold car roof, how he thought I had done. (People inside the hall had responded positively, but he hadn't said anything.) Looking dutiful, he replied that I had done well. I asked, "Why didn't you say anything?" He shrugged. "I expected you to do well." Well, that's nice in a way, but it seemed contrived. Too little, too late.

Situations like that happened a lot when I performed. I finally decided that perhaps he was jealous of the attention I received as a singer, but was I supposed to hide my light under a bushel? And if the reason he felt eclipsed on occasion was because it allowed one of his bad memories to crop up—that of not getting tenure from the university—well, there was nothing I could do about that. That was his issue.

So, was it my fault—not appreciating him enough? Was it his fault—tired of being polite? Him or me—I can't answer that, but all kinds of crazy things were happening at this time. Now, instead of opening the car door for me, he walked silently into the house, leaving me sitting in the garage until the overhead light went off. (That's when I figured he wasn't coming back.) There was no more conversing with me in the car, although he would converse with male friends in the car. There was no more talking with me during an entire four-hour football game—not one word. There was no more walking home with me from the games (he consistently walked six feet in front of me, talking with his friends). In the past, whenever he'd thought up clever inventions or new dreams for the future, I had stopped everything to listen,[61] yet whenever

---

[61] One of the things Scott invented in his mind was the ability of cars to automatically slow freeway speeds if another car came too close, an invention that is used in cars today.

I talked, he'd back slowly out of the room. (One time I realized that I was in the middle of a sentence, and no one was there but me!)

But it wasn't just me; he was blaming the children for normal child-growing issues, saying things to them that a parent *just doesn't say* to a child.[62] I have a long list (don't we all?). I'm sure he had a list, too, of things about me that bugged him.

But the worst time was when I felt kidnapped in the car. We were driving from our house near the foothills toward the freeway, and I needed to stop at a friend's house to buy some makeup from her. She lives in the most awkward location in our town. I still can't tell you her address; I only know how to get there. He kept asking for an address, and I kept saying I didn't know it. He'd retort, "Well, I can't take you if you don't know." To which I'd say, "I *do* know; I'll show you when we get closer." But he was a man of logic, and he wanted words, not gestures. To my utter dismay, he gunned past the turnoff, hands tight on the wheel and anger pouring out of his eyes onto the road in front of us. I felt utterly helpless. More than anything I wanted to open the door and roll out of the car just to get away, but we were going too fast.

As an aside, it was around this time that I began stuttering. T-t-t-true s-s-s-stuttering because I felt absolutely worthless. I do enough dumb things in my life, however; I wasn't going to include stuttering to my lexicon of idiocy. During the next three weeks I worked very hard at pausing and thinking before I said anything, and I was able to get rid of that habit. (Just don't ask me for too much at one time!)

~

At some point I realized that I had tried to change tactics in our marriage about every five years. I had come into marriage doing what my mother and his mom did in the fifties and sixties—the *Leave It to Beaver* moms whose sole purpose was in making the husband's life smoother. For about the first five

---

[62] Not to excuse bad behavior but to understand it, we later found out that Scott's muscle twitch was a form of Tourette's syndrome; people with Tourette's are known for saying all manner of untoward things.

years, I bent over backward making amazing sack lunches (sandwiches that had *three* slices of bread like a Korean colleague's wife made for her husband), getting dinner on time and cleaning up (even though I was working too), and letting him buy the tools he wanted for the house and auto maintenance. Finally, I looked around and thought, "I'm not getting the things *I* need, like a blender or a sewing machine." I felt like the bending-over-backward tactic wasn't working too well.

The next five years, I unconsciously shifted to a more aggressive stance, as per women's lib, which was rampant in the seventies and eighties. I tried to *make* (that means force) things happen. That strategy didn't work either. I wasn't getting his attention or his praise. I didn't realize it at the time, but, of course, it made things worse.

During the next five years (again unconsciously), I'm afraid that my tactic was bitterness. I was beyond making things happen. I was downright mean. My soul was cankered, grasping, and spiteful. All I could see was what *he* was doing wrong, and of course I was right. When someone can only see one point of view, they are always right.

> *When someone can only see one point of view, they are always right.*

A friend who knew I was struggling suggested that I read a book manuscript, *Bonds of Anguish, Bonds of Love*,[63] which was written by C. Terry Warner. I was sitting on my bed reading one day when I came to the chapter on "collusion," a word I had never heard before. This is my retelling of one of the stories in the manuscript:

> A sock is dropped on the floor. The wife asks her husband to put it in the hamper. He forgets. He doesn't mean anything by it; it's just not a habit for him yet. Now she perceives the sock on the ground as a gauntlet, and when he comes home that night, his wife has taken a stance. He can't figure out why she's mad, and he

---

[63] The book was published under the title *Bonds That Make Us Free* (Utah: Shadow Mountain, 2001).

takes a reactive stance. She sees his stance (not realizing at all that it is reactive) and reacts against that! Of course, he does the same, on and on, until each is standing in and defending their own corner. And neither sees how his or her part contributed to the whole.

When I read that, I was stunned as sharply as a bullet is shot. I had only seen the things my husband did to which I objected. I had never noticed how *I* played into his responses! When the realization came that *I was just as responsible for our unrest as he was*, something literally broke in me. I felt a fracturing sensation deep within my chest, and I heard a cracking sound, like a dry branch breaking. It was not audible, but a sound transferred within the bones. I felt a cool rush inside me that was followed by a flowing warmth. I cried and cried, and then cried some more.[64]

Warner's book (the title changed to *Bonds That Make Us Free*) is one of the finest, most honest books in print. It would be a good "must-read" prior to marriage or parenthood. He uses many poignant stories to help readers relate to his subtitle: *Coming to Ourselves*. He writes, "I call the violation of that sense (sensing others' needs and feelings), self-betrayal. We may or may not betray someone else when we do wrong by others, but we always betray the most sensitive and humane part of ourselves."[65]

> *"We may or may not betray someone else when we do wrong by others, but we always betray the most sensitive and humane part of ourselves."*

After that moment, I was never bitter again. I saw that it was incredibly damaging and didn't serve to change anyone. I was still frustrated, and life wasn't perfect, but I wasn't bitter.

∽

---

[64] Feelings are chemical and can kill or cure. Bernie Siegel, *Peace, Love and Healing* (New York: Harper, 1989), 16.

[65] C. Terry Warner, *Bonds That Make Us Free*, 21.

At least once a year in the summer, when we vacationed, Scott was happily able to "come to himself." He'd check the oil and tires on our '72 Winnebago (the one we'd bought from his grandma) and empty the holding tank while the kids and I loaded the RV with food, clothes, and sleeping bags. Then, strapping on our seat belts and saying a family prayer, we backed out of the driveway for an adventure. As soon as we were on the road, we turned on the Oak Ridge Boys. Only and ever the Oak Ridge Boys.[66] The adventure of "Leaving Louisiana in the Broad Daylight," the energy of "Elvira" (even though no one in the RV was a bass), and the exuberance of "American Made." There was something about the amazing blend of their voices and their lyrics of traveling and going far away that eased us to an August place, which January through June didn't allow. "Dream On."[67] Their music let us dream again. Like Halloween costumes that let people put on a different persona, their music let us be different people than who we were the rest of the year. When the Oak Ridge Boys were on, work and worries, trouble and time were left behind!

Scott loved traveling and seeing new places. He would drive great distances just to see a waterfall or a petrified tree. We stopped at so many historical markers that the kids started dubbing them "hysterical markers." He could round corners in the Winnebago like it was five feet long instead of twenty-one feet long, and he relished driving on incredibly narrow mountain passes where the passenger seat (my side) overlooked a thousand-foot drop. He was always the first to spot a pronghorn, an elk, or a moose, and he made up great driving games guessing distances, with M&Ms as the reward.

His favorite thing, though, was making a campfire with his children (his fellow pyros) where he'd sit and play his guitar or banjo, singing inane songs like "Boa Constrictor."[68] and "M.T.A."[69] When it got darker, he'd tell stories by the orange flames, like the scary "Taily Bone" (made famous by David Holt)

---

[66] Oak Ridge Boys, *The Best of Oak Ridge Boys: Millennium Collection*, MCA Nashville, 2000.

[67] Ibid.

[68] The Brothers Four, "Boa Constrictor," *Cross-Country Concert*, Columbia Records, 1963.

[69] The Kingston Trio, "M.T.A.," *The Kingston Trio at Large*, Capitol, 1959.

or the silly bear stories he collected. (A true one from Mathias Nash in 1901 told how Nash decided that the four bears on the trail ahead of him would make great rugs. He killed one, and the others ran—except they ran right at him! He ditched his rifle and climbed a tree. When it looked like they'd be there all night, he "unloosed a vocabulary enriched by long association with expert mule drivers." Amazingly, his swearing made them leave, and he concluded that one rug was just fine).[70] If Scott had had his way, the fire, music, and stories would have lasted all night. Maybe all year.

~

A couple of times, I had dragged Scott to a marriage counselor. He not only felt totally out of place in the office, but again, he didn't really trust the "soft science" of psychology. On our first visit, he sat with arms folded tightly, legs rigidly together, and a scowl on his face. The young counselor, a graduate student, pointed out Scott's closed body language to him. But what did that do? It just made Scott feel more insecure, stupid, and wrong. It is no surprise that with that counselor, nothing of consequence occurred.

Another counseling office seemed more interested in bringing in money rather than helping us. They didn't last either.

As of the last several months, though, we had been seeing a master therapist who was finally making a difference. Dr. Bill was approachable, real, and fair. He didn't put Scott down as if he were some kind of lower animal, that is, the bad guy who was always in the wrong. He was able to show Scott that the ways he was acting weren't beneficial for himself, our partnership, or his children. Dr. Bill had plenty to say to me, too, particularly asking me not to be the victim.

Scott and I both worked on the things Dr. Bill suggested, and slowly, ever so slowly, change was occurring. We enjoyed our sessions with him (individual and combined sessions) and talked with one another after every visit.

---

[70] Jeanette Prodgers, *The Only Good Bear Is a Dead Bear* (Montana: Falcon Publishing, 1986), 29.

Because of these sessions, I was highly encouraged for the future. Now, with this new danger of Scott's, we weren't seeing Dr. Bill anymore, but we were still making improvements. For the first time ever, Scott and I were working as a team, as Mr. Competition gave way to a partnership. The guy who had to be the best, the fastest, the wittiest, and the cleverest with his work, his children, his marriage—his everything—was starting to back off, to give way to others' ideas, and to calm down. A new reality had set in because of this "thing" on his liver, and it brought Scott and our marriage back to life as nothing else had!

Standing in the kitchen, he had sheepishly asked, "May I call you sweetheart?" Of course the answer was "Yes!" but I wondered, "Why had those words not flowed out easily in previous years?"

There in the kitchen, thinking also of some of his own personal demons, he added, "I've been out of integrity with the Lord." He promised in our prayer together that night to "live with more exactness" and committed to the Lord to "give up past sins and pride." I ended the day feeling more hopeful than I had in a long time. Conversation had been exchanged, help given, and love expressed. It is amazing that in the midst of the turmoil created by his health, my journal entry contentedly stated, "I am filled with happiness. Thank you, Heavenly Father!"

My journal entry contentedly stated,
"I am filled with happiness."

CHAPTER 9

EFFORTS FOR A NEW YEAR

JANUARY

The first week of January brought another CT scan, a new MRI, and more blood tests. No results; we still didn't know precisely what the mass in his right side was. Doctors were still not using the C word, and they were still pressing him for surgery. He was half wishing he'd had the surgery in December, because the hurt was still there and our methods hadn't made this thing go away yet. We continued to do good things for his body, though, to encourage greater alkalinity, to provide better nutrition, and to detoxify and cleanse.

> *Doctors still were not using the C word.*

This was his schedule:

6:00 a.m.—hot/cold shower; oxygen spray; potato juice and garlic plus twelve supplements

8:00 a.m.—an extra-nutrient shake; supplements; larch (a supplement to support immune function and promote growth of probiotic bacteria in the GI tract) in water

10:00 a.m.—an extra-nutrient shake; supplements; larch in water

11:30 a.m.—one ounce of wheatgrass juice (swallowed by itself so it could be absorbed more completely)

12:00 p.m.—an extra-nutrient shake; oxygen spray; three supplements

1:00 p.m.—larch in water

2:00 p.m.—an extra-nutrient shake and supplements

3:00 p.m.—larch in water

4:00 p.m.—an extra-nutrient shake and supplements

6:00 p.m.—a potato; oxygen spray; four supplements

7:00 p.m.—an extra-nutrient shake; potassium broth; juice vegetable; supplements

8:30 p.m.—Chi machine; hot/cold shower

9:00 p.m.—bed

That schedule looks like a full-time job, yet Scott continued to drive through the snow on his long, miserable commute because he was so committed to his family.

"I have twins on missions, and I'm supposed to go to Japan again. I've got to keep up."

(I realize that people back east and in California have long commutes, but in Utah, it is very unusual. When people heard he worked in Ogden, they always raised their eyebrows in amazement.) And January is never a great month to drive around the "Point of the Mountain," that fog- and accident-filled finger of foothills that separates Utah Valley from Salt Lake Valley.

Once, when he complained about the drive, I said pragmatically, "Rent a room during the week and just come home on weekends. They're paying you enough to do that."

Sulkily he said, "What would I do up there with all that time in the evening?"

"The same things you do here: practice your hammered dulcimer and study Japanese."

He shook his head and answered, "No, I need to be with my family."

So, Katie and I, who were the ones at home, listened good naturedly to his daily grumbling. The only thing he fussed over more than the drive was his side; it still hurt a great deal, no matter what we did.

Now that the craziness of December's performances and most of the medical testing were over, Scott said we needed to get cracking on a treatment choice. Last month we had hoped it was green tea or elemental cesium high pH therapy, but the tea he'd put aside, and the cesium was on hold until it was determined if he had cancer. He needed to find something else. For the Western medicine portion of his investigation. he would be seeing two chemotherapists and a radiologist this month. I was to come up with the best choices I could find in the natural healthcare sector. I approached my research the same as I had when we were building our house: I narrowed down every decision to two or three possibilities and let Scott choose one. (During house building, by the way, he invariably chose the same door or brick or color that I would have chosen, but I never influenced his decisions.)

On January 1, the fridge was full of fresh fruits and vegetables. On January 2, we obtained a Chi machine that aided his lymph system in removing impurities and was good for the spine. (Lying on the floor, one puts their heels on the machine, which then swishes the body back and forth like a fish swimming upstream.) On January 3, he had me buy a recliner with a matching footstool so he could rest without having to lie flat on a bed. Flat was getting very hard to do. On January 4, he had his first chiropractic appointment ever. Later, he had several enemas. My journal indicated, "Natural health concepts make so much sense to him." Our doctor said that enemas to clean the colon had not been clinically proven, yet it seemed obvious to Scott, after watching Schulze's

DVD, that a clean colon was common sense.[71] Still, he felt sick, and his side still hurt. On January 6, I read about three different kinds of poultices or packs: castor oil, garlic, and one called black salve.

Of course, there are some practices from olden days that are simply old wives' tales, but others are efficacious today. I thought that castor oil might be the former because of my mom's reaction. When she was little, castor oil was commonly given to children every night before bed, and she hated the taste! She actually relegated a yellow rose bush to the farthest corner of our yard because she said the roses smelled like castor oil. And poultice? I didn't even know what that was! I asked Chris, and to my surprise she said a castor oil pack or poultice *was* efficacious. "The castor oil will promote circulation, improve liver function, help the liver to detox, and relieve pain."[72] Well, he needed all of that!

Dr. Schulze said the castor oil pack was to be used if a tumor wasn't showing. There was no tumor showing, so after Scott came home from work, I placed a castor oil pack on his hurting right side, with a hot-water bottle over the top to heat the pack. The pack was made from a couple pieces of flannel soaked in castor oil, folded together like a sandwich, and covered with plastic wrap.

"How long do I stay here?" he called, lying uncomfortably on his left side.

"Until the water bottle starts growing cold," I hollered from the kitchen, where I was juicing some of those wonderful veggies from the fridge.

The castor oil pack seemed to soothe him, and he relaxed under its warmth—that is, until it cooled. Then it was not relaxing. Also, I had apparently wrapped the oil "sandwich" inefficiently, and it dripped all over the bed and ruined the mattress. We were trying, but we really didn't know what we

---

[71] Iridologist Nancy Coones indicates that a colonic can flush *good flora*, so she advises only one or two total, except in the case of cancer, when one has multiple colonics for a short time in the beginning. Nancy Coones, presentation, May 5, 2015.

[72] Of a castor oil pack, "The Basic Cleanse" by Walter Last indicates, "This greatly increases the blood supply to these areas [gastrointestinal tract, liver, and gall bladder] and stimulates liver and bowel activities." The entire regimen is found at https://www.health-science-spirit.com/Healing_the_Body/The-Basic-Cleanse.html.

were doing. We only used it for two days.

The relaxing nature of a pack could not be said for the second kind we tried a couple of days later. This pack was suffused with garlic. The literature said, "Garlic has strong antibacterial, antiviral, and antifungal properties …and there are no known side effects." I beg to differ. Topically there *was* a side effect: he went through the roof! We found that if you leave a garlic poultice on longer than ninety seconds, it can actually burn!

Meanwhile, the castor oil pack seemed to have its own side effect: it pulled Scott's tumor out his side. One day, he just noticed that he could no longer put his right arm straight down; there was a bump in the way. He looked in a mirror and called me to come quickly.

"What is that?" he asked in alarm, holding his right arm up out of the way. There was a grotesque protrusion sticking out past his rib cage. Originally a bump the size of half a golf ball, it later grew to the size of half a large grapefruit.

The third pack was called black salve. This is one of those things that jumped off the page when I read it. (You've probably had things that show up in "neon lights" when they are or will become important to your life. One of those for me was the first moment I saw Scott. When I walked into a girl-friend's wedding reception to sing, he was the only person who was sharply defined and in focus in the wedding line. All the other members of the wedding line were slightly fuzzy, as if taken by a soft camera filter that blurs edges.)

I had never heard of black salve before, but it intrigued me. Schulze's magazine said that it was extremely potent and that this remedy was used if a tumor was already showing. *Potent* is what Scott needed! Schulze gave the ingredients, but no recipe—ingredients like burdock, bloodroot, slippery elm, comfrey, activated charcoal, and rhubarb root. I bought the ingredients for sixty dollars at a natural foods store and mixed them together, but it was a twiggy, woody mess, and I could tell that it could not be applied the way I had put it together. The timing didn't seem right, either, so I threw out the batch I'd made and tucked the idea into the back of my mind.

In the evening, Scott forcefully blurted out, "Why doesn't He heal me? How can God expect me to drive?" I saw such ambivalence in him. On the one hand, he was grateful for every new day, but on the other, he was deeply conflicted that his faith and his hopes weren't being rewarded with a lessening of pain and this "thing" going away.

Later I used a portable TENS unit (electrical stimulation) to dispel some of that torment in his side.[73] No matter what we did, though, it just kept hurting.

~

On Thursday, January 9, Scott mostly slept. He had given up driving to work for now. He'd been up three times the night before, having me TENS him each time. We had gone to the emergency room again and had gotten another pain prescription and another CT scan.

The next day, a blood test was scheduled for 9:00 a.m. and radiology at 11:00 a.m. He slowly, achingly got into the car and let me drive—a new phenomenon for him. We had barely left our street when I saw something that was worth a short detour.

"We might be a minute late," I warned. "Hold on."

U-turning the car, I pulled into a large church parking lot. A group of missionaries from the nearby missionary training center were walking through the lot, and one of them looked familiar. I looked hard—yes! It was Elder Matt! (All the male missionaries are titled "Elder.") We hadn't seen him since November 30! I pulled silently up behind him, rolled down my window, smiled broadly, and waited. All the missionaries facing my direction started

---

[73] TENS stands for transcutaneous electrical nerve stimulation. The TENS unit we used allowed an electrical current to go to a local site before pain, which ran on the same pathway, could arrive. This is how it stopped pain.

smiling too. Elder Matt was the last one to turn around and see what they were grinning at.

"Mom! You're not supposed to be here!" he exclaimed.

"Too good to pass up!" I laughed. "We love you!"

Scott leaned across the seat to look at him. "I love you," he said, smiling weakly up at his son. We drove away triumphant and let the missionaries go about their business.

On Saturday, Scott slept in till almost 10:00 a.m. and felt a little better when he got up. Later in the day, though, he hurt so much he groaned, "I can't *do* this!"

As I read my journal now through the benefit of hindsight, some of the comments floor me. Mostly statements like "He still hurts." *Still?* As if a little oil pack or a little organic food would take that thing out of his side. As if sleep would make everything better. As if not driving to work would make him feel all right. It's crazy how we humans think sometimes! All the efforts, all the strange and new things he was doing to better his health, all the crazy, unusual additions to his life that he was so willing to try—everything we did for him was "kindergarten," and he should have been spending that first month getting a "graduate degree"! It turns out that potent treatment would not come for a while.

What were we thinking? What were we really thinking? That's easy to ask now. At the time we didn't know it was cancer. And at the time we were doing everything we could for him. The doctors weren't saying anything; they were only testing him, week after week after week. Until they came up with something more definitive, we figured that creating a healthier internal environment in his body was all for the good.

> What were we thinking?
> What were we really thinking?
> At the time we didn't know it was cancer and
> we were doing everything we could for him.

CHAPTER 10

A BLESSING FROM THE TWINS

JANUARY

S cott was not only hurting; now he was having a hard time breathing. He could breathe better by bending over, but that only helped so much. It seemed that the surgery he had tried to put off was now necessary. He scheduled an operation for the following Friday, January 17, under Dr. David, the only local liver surgeon. Meanwhile, Scott had our assets put into a trust. He felt very strongly about this and was committed to completing the trust before his surgery.

On Sunday, January 12, Scott went to church. I didn't think he'd be able to, but he *really* wanted to go. Bent over uncomfortably, he walked the short distance slowly and could only stay an hour. (The LDS Sunday worship meetings were at that time a combined three hours long.) He could hardly breathe, and he was scared. Out of all the people in the congregation, he happened to sit right in front of one of the surgeons, Dr. Richard. I knew Scott wanted to talk to him, but I didn't think he would ask. That's part of being a do-it-yourselfer; you don't ask.

A good example of Scott's not asking or communicating was when he was newly hired as an assistant professor in chemical engineering at BYU. He needed to become involved in some sort of research to obtain tenure. He definitely didn't want to continue the research he'd done to obtain his Ph.D., but he couldn't decide what to do. He saw a small group of faculty members working on combustion and thought, "That looks interesting. I'd sure like to join them! But no, I should be contributing something new to the department, and they probably don't need another person working on that." He talked himself out of even saying a word to them. Meanwhile (as I found out later), the professors in the small combustion group were saying to each other, "We sure could use one more person on our team, and you know who would be great—Brewster. But we don't want to influence him, so we won't say anything." And they didn't. Neither talked to the other, and that became a contributing factor in my husband's lack of continuing status. He decided too late on a research topic and was denied tenure. What started as a brilliant career became mostly drudgery, a feeling of unacceptance, and the underlying idea that he couldn't control his circumstances.

During the sacrament meeting, I silently prayed that Scott might say something or that the surgeon might notice him. To my delight, Dr. Richard leaned forward as the service closed. He patted Scott's shoulder and asked with real concern, "How are you doing?" The surgeon was alarmed to see how hard breathing was for him, so he left the church with Scott, walked slowly with him to our house, and talked with him for a long time. Later, Dr. David came and talked with him for about an hour and a half. Scott appreciated their support and caring tremendously. The result was that the surgery was rescheduled for two days earlier.

~

That evening, Scott and I had the rare privilege of going to the missionary training center to be with Elder Aaron and Elder Matt. As I mentioned before, the MTC was only for missionaries; families were not allowed. The twins had been just down the street this whole time, but except for one "sighting" each, we hadn't seen them for two months. The MTC was a large complex of buildings for housing and teaching missionaries. Up to fifty languages were taught, each in its own small classroom. If you asked the Elders and Sisters what their favorite place was on the campus, I think they would have replied, "The cafeteria." The real focal point, though, seemed to be a huge map of the world. Every missionary would stand in front of it and proudly point to where she or he was going and have someone take a picture of it.

Aaron was going to Hungary and Matt to Romania. Aaron and Matt didn't room with each other but with other Elders who were learning their specific languages. Still, they managed to see each other fairly often. They were not look-alike twins who could trade places as a joke, but they did manage to trade name tags once, which got them into a bit of good-natured trouble.

A teacher asked, "Elder Brewster, why is your name tag different from everyone else's in this class?"

Sheepishly my son replied, "Because it's actually my brother's."

"Well, get yours back!" the teacher had barked.

Now, as the four of us sat down in a small room together, the boys could tell it was serious. Just the fact that we were *there* made it serious. They knew their dad had a health challenge, but they didn't know how serious it apparently was. They had not been home for any of the testing, doctors' visits, evaluations, or conversations. Instead, they'd been receiving letters from home for two and a half months that sounded concerned but still hopeful and cheery.

The little room was very still as Scott began, "We're meeting with you now because I might not be here when you get back."

Tears sprang to their eyes, and I could see they were trying to hold themselves together. This was worlds away from anything our letters had indicated. Sitting by his side, like a supporting role in a movie, my face flashed surprise and distress. Was this something he truly felt the Spirit was telling him, or was it his super worrywart-self speaking? I looked on with both sadness and confusion—sadness because this was so hard and sudden for our boys, and confusion because Scott had told me he wanted to live and had assigned me to research possibilities. After all, I'd had that statement from the Spirit:

"Scott will make a choice; once chosen, it will be irrevocable."

And Scott had told me he *wanted* to live. That sounded like he'd chosen to move along a path that would lead toward healing. So where was this coming from? This was the first time he had voiced this possibility that sounded so final, so defeatist. Nevertheless, all of us felt that what he said couldn't be true, mustn't be true, and I was just left to wonder.

Nonplussed by anyone's reaction, Scott went on: "But it won't matter whether I'm here or not, because *that's* what you'll be preaching about. You'll be proclaiming eternal life through the Atonement of Jesus Christ. I know that I'll live again, and you'll tell them that through our Savior *all* mankind will live again. And through temple covenants, *we* will still be a family forever, even if I'm not here anymore."[74]

> *It won't matter whether I'm here or not, because that's what you'll be preaching about. You'll be proclaiming eternal life through the Atonement of Jesus Christ.*

More tears. Words of love and comfort. Affirmations that they wanted him here when they got home.

"You can do it, Dad!"

Tight, tight hugging all around. Then his twenty-year-old missionary sons, who had the authority of the ancient Melchizedek Priesthood, laid their hands

---

[74] Covenants made in LDS temples (with the ability to eternally bind or seal families together) are made through the same power that "Jesus Christ gave to His disciples when he said, 'And I will give unto thee the keys of the kingdom of heaven: and whatsoever thou shalt bind on earth shall be bound in heaven.'" Matthew 16:19, KJV. Mormon.org/faq/topic/temples.

on his head and gave him a priesthood blessing as if they were the father and he the child. Elder Aaron anointed him with consecrated oil, as the apostles did under Jesus' direction, and then Elder Matt gave him a blessing.[75] It was a beautiful, mature blessing of comfort and of healing. Healing: there was that beautiful, *blessed* word again. I especially remember the comfort and reassurance that word gave me. Afterward they each hugged their dad fiercely, and we felt love flowing and filling the room.

The experience in that little room in the MTC was serene and holy, wrenching and heartbreaking. The next day, Aaron would go to Hungary, the day after that, Matt would go to Romania, and the day after that, their dad would have surgery. Who knew what would happen to any of them? Regardless, through the grace of Jesus Christ and the sealing power in temples, our family would still be together!

---

[75] Mark 6:13, KJV.

CHAPTER 11

MY LAST DAY
ON EARTH

JANUARY

On Monday morning, Aaron left for Hungary; on Tuesday morning, Matthew left for Romania, and by late Tuesday afternoon, our lawyer had amazingly whipped up an estate trust two days earlier than planned and had it ready to sign. Wednesday would be Scott's surgery. Dr. Dave would perform a biopsy and whatever surgery he felt would be beneficial after that.

> *"I am treating today as my last day on Earth."*

On the day before his surgery, Scott told me, "I assume I am going to make it; nevertheless, I am treating today as my last day on Earth." I was piling up some of his papers, but my hands and body stopped dead, stunned to hear that. I immediately thought of what my dying dad had told me when I'd asked if he'd like me to wash his hair with a powder so he wouldn't have to get his head wet. Sitting on his favorite chair in his living room, he shook his head slightly, and said pragmatically, "No, I won't wash my hair anymore." Never wash your hair again in this life! What a statement.

And now I heard much the same thing from my husband. But *I* felt that his surgery would go well, so I didn't let myself dwell on it. Besides, I didn't have time to think about it much because he kept me busy all day. He showed me how he did budgeting (not a great thing to speed-learn!), and he gave me two four-by-six cards with several combinations of computer passwords that he said were important. (I didn't realize how useful those were until later! Then I was very grateful for them.)

Physically Scott was now bent almost double, but there was one more thing he desperately wanted to do this day, one more special place he wanted to go. Humbly he said, "If I die tomorrow, I want Christ to know the last thing I did." So, even though he could barely breathe, we went to the temple.

LDS churches and temples have different purposes. A church is a place where you go to worship, learn, and renew your baptismal covenants through the sacrament (communion). A temple is a place where you go to worship and learn and make solemn promises to our Heavenly Father and the Savior that you'll live the way they would have you live. Any person is welcome at church; adults who are willing to commit are allowed into temples. An LDS temple is peaceful, beautiful, and sublime inside and out—the most sacred and special place on Earth. It is, literally, God's house.[76]

After we returned, two men from our ward came over to give Scott another blessing. It never hurts to invoke the Lord's aid multiple times and let Him know you really want His blessing! One of the men was our bishop and the other was our "home teacher," which is a church member assigned to visit us monthly. Their presence was extremely comforting to Scott. The bishop pronounced the blessing—one final calm assurance before the next day. His prayer was remarkably like both the blessings from the twins and their older

---

[76] "Temples," Church of Jesus Christ of Latter-day Saints, https://www.lds.org/topics/temples?.

brothers: the Lord loved him; the Lord knew he lived a good life; the Lord was aware of his needs; and a promise to be healed if it was the Lord's will. I smiled through closed eyes as I heard again that wonderful word "healing." The statement the Spirit had given me flitted through my mind:

"Scott will make a choice; once chosen, it will be irrevocable."

I pictured "healing" as the course his choice would take that would bring him back to full health. He was already doing so much!

After they left, Scott did two more things on this "last day" of his. First, he wrote down his desire that his grandchildren learn music like their parents had. Next, he wrote out his belief in Jesus Christ and in His saving power through the Atonement, which is the "reconciliation of man to God."[77] He also wrote of his love for me, his children, his grandchildren, and the grand-children who would come.

> I have a testimony that Heavenly Father lives. Jesus Christ is his son. I have a testimony of the Atonement, and that it covers each and every one of us. I never dreamed that this would be happening. I was in good health, I thought, and had no complaints. It just goes to show how important it is to live the Gospel each and every day of our lives. The Gospel provides the iron rod, which, if we cling to it, we will always be prepared. I love my wife and children. There's no other family in the world I would rather have for my own.

~

In the morning, I drove him to the hospital. He was prepped and laid on a hospital gurney. This man who had once cleverly signed a Mother's Day card to me "From your handsome, intelligent, industrious, multitalented, humble husband" was now the one in need. He reached up to grab hold of my hand, looking up at me beseechingly with his beautiful brown eyes. Over and over

---

[77] "Bible Dictionary," in *The Holy Bible* (Salt Lake City: Church of Jesus Christ of Latter-day Saints, 1979), 617.

and over he mouthed, "I love you, I love you, I love you." My heart soared. For so many years he hadn't looked at me that way, and I had been longing for genuine affection and sweetness like when he'd courted me. You see, I'd been the ingénue—the heroine—in all the musicals and operas I'd been in. I was Guenevere to *Camelot*'s Lancelot, Zerlina to *Don Giovanni*'s Don, Celia to *Promised Valley*'s Jed, and Abigail to *The Crucible*'s John Proctor. I had grown used to my leading man capturing me in his arms and looking deeply into my eyes. I *liked* being "worshiped and adored" and looked at lovingly, but that look hadn't happened for many years. Now, finally, here it was, with no teasing, criticizing, or even mundaneness. I told him I loved him and smiled at him encouragingly, soaking up my real leading man's deep brown eyes shining with love, until the elevator doors closed. I wouldn't see him for two to six hours.

I said a fervent prayer as I sat down in the waiting room. I later found out from the surgeon's wife that Dr. Dave had spent a large part of his Tuesday night on his knees in mighty prayer, praying that this surgery would be the thing to make Scott well. When I was called on the hospital intercom to come to a consultation room to meet with the doctor after only two hours, I knew it was a bad sign.

Sure enough, Dr. Dave said somberly, "I'm afraid I don't have good news." While he was doing the biopsy, he had been able to scrape out about a cup of the mass. I listened to a death sentence as he continued, "I think this tumor started in the liver: it's invaded the liver, the diaphragm, the chest wall, the back, behind the ribs, and maybe even bone."

I pictured microscopic tendrils invading tissues and organs like minuscule worms digging into earth and thought in passing how crude and large even the most finely made surgical tools must be in comparison to invading cells. He showed me a picture that he had taken of the mass. I looked at it in fascinated horror—that moisty, fleshy, bubbly red bloody mass was the enemy. That was the thing that was causing all the pain, all the uproar, all the furor. I wish I had that picture; it certainly made visualizing this horrific opponent more real. What the surgeon did by surgery was to buy us some time. Now that Scott could at least breathe, we could figure out how to proceed next.

～

Scott's postsurgical experience boded well for his recovery. When his eyes opened in the recovery room, he was almost surprised! Even though he said he thought he'd make it, deep down inside he thought he wouldn't. He looked at me again with those beautiful brown eyes shining with genuine love and appreciation. He whispered several times, "I love you," each time looking deeply at me, which was so fulfilling. My journal simply exulted, "Wonderful!"

Then he looked toward the foot of his bed. His mother, who had gone back to California after Christmas, had now returned just two weeks later. She walked in right as his gurney was rolled into his room. His little mother's tearful appearance at his bedside was more than he could have asked for. For her part, she stood wordless, drinking in the sight of him, just grateful to see him alive.

After giving him a gentle kiss, she leaned over to me and said softly, "Remember, Neal got to use the elemental cesium high pH therapy after he had a diagnosis."

Ah! That brought hope. I thought, "When pathology gives us their report, we'll probably have a label of 'cancer.' *Then* he can start elemental cesium high pH therapy. And if cesium doesn't work, there are other choices!"

～

Scott woke from a nap and sat up with wide eyes and new energy. Speaking like a true assistant professor, he declared, "I think I signed up for this!" Maybe he had. Some people believe that we are allowed to choose our own set of difficulties in a prelife before we are born. Three times during his cancer journey he said this, always with wide eyes as if he were just realizing something, and always just on awaking.

Our children called and came. Ben and Lindsey came by, sharing concern and love. Jacob and Jenise shared news of their little Courtney over the phone, as well as how things were progressing in Jenise's pregnancy. Sara and Allen brought Katie and little sleeping Davis. The whole brood brought comfort and energy; they also brought normalcy and gooniness.

Scott was in compression socks that were hooked up to a machine to aid circulation.

Allen said, "That machine would feel good to my dad's legs. He has diphtheria."

We stared at him in puzzled astonishment.

Katie grinned. "He doesn't have diphtheria; he has diabetes."

"That's what I meant." He shrugged, and we all laughed.

With a twinkle in his eye, Ben mused, "Compression socks might have been cool when I was growing up. They really might have helped when I had cramping and restless leg syndrome."

Allen had just come back to the conversation after tending to Davis and asked, "What did you say about useless leg syndrome?"

We burst out laughing again. They were off and running now.

Sara said dryly, "Yes, I'll tell my children someday that William Brewster brought compression socks with him on the *Mayflower*, but then they were confiscated in the witch hunts in Salem, and that's why there weren't any when you were a little boy!"

Scott shook his head, grinning, and we all laughed again. (William Brewster, a Pilgrim on the *Mayflower*, *is* Scott's thirteenth great-grandfather, but the rest of that is so bogus!)

When tiny Davis woke up, he added to the fun, looking curiously at his grandpa, then standing up on the bed in his little blue sleeper by holding on to Katie's fingers. Scott happened to sneeze, and Davis imitated, "Achoo!" Then Grandpa Scott sneezed for fun, just to hear Davis giggle and laugh to the "Achoos!"

Katie finally told us she'd received her ACT score. "Come on, Katie; what is it?" her brothers and sisters coaxed. She'd gotten a twenty-nine—good for a junior taking it for the first time.[78]

"Whoa, Katie, I got into BYU on way less than that," said her sister.

Scott smiled contentedly at his mom, "I have *great* kids, don't I?"

I smiled, savoring the moment. This was such a turnabout from the perfectionist who, years earlier, had declared vehemently over some small transgression, "I have terrible children." Now here he was, sitting back and reveling in them! Instead of being irritated by small indiscretions, his surgery and the danger in his side had helped him gain a new perspective for his family. I sat back and reveled silently, "Good for you, Scott; good for you!"

> *Instead of being irritated by small indiscretions, the danger in his side and his surgery had helped him gain a new perspective for his family.*

During the eight and a half days he was in the hospital, church neighbors, family, and coworkers visited, writing their good wishes to Scott in a journal I had provided: "You're an example that I can always rely on." "Your happiness is contagious enough to spread to others." "My little world is and always will be such a positive place because of your influence." Some brought flowers, and some brought funny cards, like "People who think laughter is the best medicine apparently have never had morphine," and some brought cards with thoughtful sentiments, like "Suffering is a time to reeducate our hopes, our savoring reflexes. It offers us an elevated spot above the landscape, a rare view, a chance at real wisdom."[79] His workplace sent flowers, and when I got home late at night after that first day, there were forty-one calls on my answering machine! Their wonderful comments were manna to this man who'd spent twelve years working solitarily in an enclosed basement office, to this do-it-yourselfer who never asked anyone for help. Their support and

---

[78] Thirty-six is the highest possible score.

[79] Wayne E. Brickey, *Making Sense of Suffering* (Salt Lake City: Deseret Book, 2001), 60.

love for him surprised and delighted him. He said with an amazed grin, "Who would know such blessings would come from this?"

"Who would know such blessings would come from this?"

Such Blessings from This

Scott's epiphany that blessings could come through cancer was also noted by Tony Snow, former White House spokesman, who wrote an article for *Christianity Today* entitled "Unexpected Blessings." Snow said, "I don't know why I have cancer, and I don't much care. It is what it is... But despite this—because of it—God offers the possibility of salvation and grace. We don't know how the narrative of our lives will end, but we get to choose how to use the interval between now and the moment we meet our Creator face-to-face.

"To regain footing, remember that we were born not into death, but into life—and that the journey continues after we have finished our days on this earth... Most of us have watched friends as they drifted toward God's arms not with resignation, but with peace and hope. In so doing, they have taught us not how to die, but how to live... Even though God doesn't promise us tomorrow, he does promise us eternity."[80]

It was wonderful to hear his voice be softer and to see his eyes shine with genuine admiration for those around him. Where before there had been judgment, there was now appreciation; where there had been criticism, there was love. As George MacDonald wisely said:

There are two doorkeepers to the house of prayer, and Sorrow is more on the alert to open than her grandson Joy.[81]

---

[80] Tony Snow, https://www.christianitytoday.com/ct/2007/july/25.30.html.

[81] George MacDonald, *The Hope of the Gospel* (London: Ward, Lock, Bowden and Co., 1892), 98.

In the past, Scott had been so critical of his kids and never taken the time to stop and "smell the roses"—maybe because he thought good fathers were just supposed to plow through and keep going. Now he was forced to sit back. I sat to the side, watching him lying peacefully on his bed as he soaked in the presence and the goodness of everyone around him. Scott's brothers and sister came with their families, bringing more love and happiness. He said warmly, "I feel so supported." To me, being in the middle of this love felt like being in the middle of a spectacular masterpiece that was being painted on canvas right before my eyes! It felt as if someone had picked all the biggest, most vivid, colorful blossoms and had put them all together in one huge crystal vase! The images surrounding me evoked color and life, and I wanted this exhilarating feeling to stay forever. My journal recorded, "I hope Scott will keep the sweet, gentle spirit of Wednesday when he was just lying back on his bed, pretty much only able to look around and appreciate and enjoy everyone else. I hope I can find gentle ways to foster and encourage that."

> *I hope Scott will keep the sweet,*
> *gentle spirit of Wednesday.*

Scott's sister's husband, Kurt, asked if he would like another blessing. Scott said, "Yes." Kurt had not been present for any of Scott's other blessings, yet his prayer, coming through Heavenly Father's Spirit, was phrased almost exactly as the prayers from Scott's four sons and from his priesthood leaders. I found that remarkable. All the blessings strongly mentioned the word "healing," which my spirit soared to hear! All the blessings thanked Scott for his good life —a life spent in helping others, doing good things, and loving his Lord. All thanked Heavenly Father and asked for His help in this challenge. And they all mentioned, as Jesus is quoted in Luke 22:4, "Not my will, but *thine* be done."[82]

Then Kurt's blessing took a turn that none of the others had. It was appropriate that it came from a family member. With inspiration from Heaven

---

[82] KJV.

flowing through him, Kurt stated, "Your father is aware of your circumstances, and he is here with you now."

All of us were stunned. Scott's dad, Blair, had divorced Mom B when Blair was forty-four. He'd had a heart attack at age fifty-four and died at fifty-five. This had been when now-seventeen-year-old Katie was six months old. Kurt said afterward of the experience, "I wasn't planning on saying that. I wasn't even thinking about that. The Spirit just led me to say that!" His disclosure echoed what I stated earlier from Elder Jeffrey R. Holland—that "family members on *both* sides of the veil... have been given as companions for our mortal journey."[83] How comforting and gratifying for Scott to think that his deceased father was there—knowing what Scott was going through and caring about him.

The Separation Called Death

Elder Boyd K. Packer gave to children a clear description of the separation called death: "Pretend, my little friends, that my hand represents your spirit. It is alive. It can move by itself. Suppose that this glove represents your mortal body. It cannot move. When the spirit enters into your mortal body, *then* it can move and act and live... Someday, the spirit and the body will be separated. We then say a person has died. Death is a separation... When I separate them, the glove (which represents your body) is taken away from your spirit (your hand); it cannot move anymore. It just falls down and is dead. But your spirit is still alive."

Part of our belief in Jesus as our Savior is His resurrection and the conviction that we will continue to live beyond the grave. What a tremendous consolation that is—to know that because Christ was resurrected, we will continue to live! The following "frequently asked questions" help to clarify.

---

[83] Jeffrey R. Holland, *Ensign*, May 2009, 88.

Death is not the end. Death is really a beginning—another step forward in Heavenly Father's plan for His children. Someday, like everyone else's, your physical body will die. But your spirit does not die. It goes to the Spirit World, where you will continue to learn and progress and may be with loved ones who have passed on. Our existence in the Spirit World also promises a reunion between our bodies and souls that can never again be broken. It's an amazing gift given to us by the death and resurrection of Jesus Christ.

~

Scott's main job now was to get well enough to get out of the hospital. Doctors gave him about three weeks to get feeling better, so we knew that we had just three weeks to find something else before we would start feeling the pressure from them to do chemotherapy or radiation. The very next day, Scott started his hospital stay with a bang! He called me from his bed at 6:30 a.m., bright and energetic, wondering if we could have prayer together on the phone. I was delighted but mildly surprised. He'd never prayed with me on the phone before! Later, he had his mom and me push him down the hall in a wheelchair.

The second day after surgery, he started walking while pushing his own wheelchair. He looked like a mama duck leading a parade, his open-backed hospital gown flapping behind like a white-and-blue tail as he marched sure-footedly while Mom B and I hustled in tow with his IV tower.

The following day, he was determined to do what the staff wanted so he could get out of there. He walked so briskly that I had a hard time keeping up. This time he was on his own—the wheelchair was nowhere near! He also tried to get off the epidural drip with only Percocet to help. But the pain that had started at a level five out of ten finally grew to eleven! After a lot of evening visitors, he was so tuckered out that he drifted off to sleep in spite of his hurting.

That night, Mom B wanted someone to sleep in his room to keep an eye on him. She asked me if I wanted to. It seemed superfluous, and I replied,

"I thought that's what the hospital staff was for." I couldn't imagine that I'd be much help. She felt strongly about it, though, and Scott was amenable, so she stayed two nights on a cot next to his bed. It reminded me of a children's book she had given him on Mother's Day in 1989. *Love You Forever* was treasured so much by her that she recorded it on a cassette tape, the only book she ever recorded for him.[84] It tells how a baby is loved by his mother all during his growing up years, even into adulthood, and how he gives that love back to her in her old age. The sentiment of the book showed the deep love she had for Scott and that she would do anything for him.

∼

After such a glorious beginning, Scott got stuck in the "hospital cycle" like a car spinning its wheels in the mud. He was stuck in this cycle for days on end. The cycle went something like this:

Take a pill for your pain.

If the medication nauseates you, take a pill for that.

Still a problem? Try a liquid diet. Still feeling pain? Take a pill.

Can't take the pill because you're nauseated? Well, here's...

You get the picture. It seemed to be a "Catch-22," and it was maddening. Add to that my general dislike of prescriptions because of their side effects and because our culture has encouraged people to rely almost solely on drugs as solutions to health issues. Truthfully, the most maddening part was the picture in the back of my mind of all the pills my mother had to take for her numerous medical challenges. She was sick my whole life, had at least one major surgery every year for the last sixteen years of her life, and had

---

[84] Robert Munsch, *Love You Forever* (Richmond Hill, Canada: Firefly Books, 1986).

migraines that were off the charts. She would take her week's worth of pills the first half of the week, then live in hell for the last, and that was with the strongest doses that the doctors would give. Alternative choices hadn't really been introduced into the country at that time, so she didn't have much of a choice beyond what doctors prescribed. I wouldn't want anyone to have to go through what she did, but neither do I want anyone to take more medication than they need!

Scott had been doing so well and had been so energetic. Now he acted like a zombie, and it was awful. He was loony, and he wasn't himself. It was so different from those first few days! They said they were "leveling out his pain medication to get his pain under control," but it took so long. It seemed as if they were causing the very thing they were trying to fix!

At his lucid, non-zombie times, he, his mom, and I would talk about health options. One request he had was that I get hold of Neal, the physicist, to ask him about how cesium had affected his prostate cancer. I said I would but reminded him that Nurse Lorna had said Scott couldn't use it unless it was proven that he had cancer. We were still waiting for pathology to give their report.

On Friday, they started him on OxyContin for the pain. That same day, the pathology report came in. That bloody, bubbly mass had a name. It was called leiomyosarcoma (ly-o-myo-sarcoma). This sarcoma is a rare kind that started somewhere in smooth muscle—*leio* is Latin for smooth and *myo* is Latin for muscle. Since the surgery showed it was just now invading the liver, they thought it had started in the diaphragm. The surgeon said it was treated with chemotherapy and radiation.

Being new to these terms, I still didn't understand if sarcoma or malignant meant the same thing as cancer. I needed to know straight out. The next time I saw Dr. Richard in the hall, I cornered him and asked him point-blank, "Is this cancer?"

He looked down at me with profound sadness. "Yes, it is."

He probably thought I was out of my mind, totally delirious, from some planet that he'd never imagined, because I replied with determination, "Good." "Cancer" was the one word that would let Scott start elemental cesium high pH therapy.

CHAPTER 12

RADIATION APPOINTMENT

JANUARY

Scott's appointment with the radiation oncologist, Dr. Hayes, was the day after he was released from the hospital. He was still very weak, and now he was affected by pain from the surgery as well as from the tumor. Mom B and I supported him on each side as we shuffled slowly into the appointment. We were ushered into a small, dark anteroom to wait.

Scott leaned his head back wearily against the wall and mumbled to me, "I can't talk. You'll have to do the talking for me."

I agreed, and we sat back to wait.

This appointment and I did not agree well. Perhaps it was from the pressure that I expected them to put on us to start radiation. (About half of all cancer patients receive some type of radiation therapy.)[85] Perhaps it was from

---

[85] "Radiation Therapy to Treat Cancer," National Cancer Institute, www.cancer.gov/cancertopics/factsheet/Therapy/radiation.

information we had previously read on radiation—that it could cause the very malady it was treating.[86] Perhaps it was because I was protecting my weary husband, barely home from the hospital, so weak he shut his eyes through the entire appointment.

My aversion may have come, however, from the way the oncology team presented itself. After a wait of nearly forty-five minutes (that was so hard on Scott), Dr. Hayes and his team finally strode across the sunlit parking lot, his white coat waving behind him like a triumphant banner and his smiling assistants prancing in his wake like an agreeable all-girl backup band. When he entered, he looked down on the three of us in our shadowy darkness at the edge of the room; meanwhile, he, with folded arms, was illuminated in the sparkling brilliance of the overhead light. When he finally sat on a tall stool, he extended his legs at full length with ankles easily crossed while Mom B and I sat on low folding chairs supporting Scott, the three of us looking for all the world like small, huddled potato bugs in a corner. Basically, everything in this appointment made them seem like celebrities and us a mere paltry audience. They exuded confidence; we exuded timidity. They exuded knowledge; we exuded apprehension. It seemed that to them we were no more than cardboard cutouts, objects to be acted upon. Sitting there, the three of us in a row in semidarkness, I felt as though we may as well have been posing for mug shots, horizontal lines drawn on the wall behind us!

> *Everything in this appointment*
> *made them seem like celebrities and us*
> *a mere paltry audience.*

After some preliminaries, the doctor told us what would happen with radiation, and my eyes widened in horror. Scott would come into the office five times a week for two months while the oncologists would burn the area in the attempt to kill the sarcoma. Everything around it would be burned

---

[86] Some people who have had radiation therapy can also be more likely to develop a second cancer later in life. "Radiation Therapy," KidsHealth, kidshealth.org/teen/diseases_conditions/cancer/radiation.html.

as well, but he noted that normal cells are more likely to recover from the effects of radiation.[87] He did not discuss the words "more likely"—there was no guarantee that normal cells would revive and no guarantee that their DNA would not be permanently damaged. He went on to say that the oncology team would attempt not to burn the nearby lung and surrounding tissue. "Attempt"—another word that was bypassed quickly. At the end of two months, the team would assess and probably do more radiation after that.

I managed to show Dr. Hayes the scientific reports about elemental cesium high pH therapy from Dr. Brewer to see what he thought about that.

He glanced briefly at the papers, then dismissed them out of hand, saying, "I haven't seen those publications." (To be fair, our dermatologist once commented that over two dozen methodologies crossed his desk per week! "There may be something viable there, Elaine, we just don't have time to read it all.")[88] As Dr. Hayes thrust the articles back at me, it brought to reality a hierarchy noted by a scientist: "In the medical establishment, contrary to public perception, scientists are second-class citizens."[89]

Scott had told Dr. Hayes that I would be his voice because he was so weak, and as I mentioned, Scott leaned back with his eyes closed the whole two hours. Dr. Hayes followed Scott's wish and focused all his comments on me. As his eyes bored into me for over an hour, I felt myself sinking lower and lower. By the end, even though my outside body looked normal, my inside self had melted down to a puddle, my volition and capability just a tiny, indiscernible point of light. I felt inferior, small, and subservient next to his expansiveness, his surety, and his power.

As we left, they handed us their official patient information brochure that explained about coping with fatigue and skin care during radiation therapy. Apparently, it was assumed that those areas were of more concern to patients than learning about the dangers of radiation therapy and how it worked. The

---

[87] Ibid.

[88] Dr. Richard Moss in discussion with the author.

[89] Ralph W. Moss,Ph.D, *Questioning Chemotherapy* (New York: Equinox Press, 1995), 33.

message was "Don't worry; we'll take care of the big stuff, and you just worry about the little things."

When the appointment was through, it was all I could do to wait for the door to be opened before I darted out of the darkened room and into the sunshine. I tossed my head in the blaring, beautiful sunlight with a crazy urge to run all the way to the nearest mountain, and believe me, it's not that close! I wanted to sing or shout or yell or scream to get rid of the awful tension that had built up inside me. "How can he *do* this for a living?" I thought with revulsion. "Sit there so placidly in his white coat and tell me how he's going to burn into my husband!" But instead of running away, I eagerly drank in the sunlight, gulping great, sweeping draughts of air. And I helped Mom B escort a beleaguered Scott to our waiting car.

On the way home from the appointment, I had to turn on a CD to calm myself. (Normally, when I'm with people in a car, I leave music or sound off.) As for Scott, he was simply happy to be going back to his new recliner after almost two dreadful hours of sitting on a hard folding chair in that room. He told me quietly that I had done a good job talking to the doctor and thanked me for doing that.

The doctor had said that next week he would take Scott's case to a tumor conference, where a panel of doctors would determine if radiation was appropriate for him. There was no point in worrying further about it for right now. And what was coming tomorrow would be far more pleasant!

CHAPTER 13

VIBRATIONS ARE UNSEEN ENERGY

JANUARY

S aturday morning, January 26, started with Scott showering, putting on a T-shirt, and refusing pain medication for the first time in a week—wonderful improvements! After Ben and Lindsey had visited, Scott, Mom B, and I discussed several treatment choices we had discovered. My journal noted, "We feel fortunate to have so many options." I ran out after lunch to buy beets for more of Dr. Schulze's potassium soup, happy to know right where I was going, since I tend to get lost. I wanted to be home in time to welcome our visitor, Holly.

I had been drawn to Holly from the first time I'd seen her. There was something special about her. A slight, brown-haired pixie, she exuded an energy that pulled you in and made you want to be with her. We'd met at a meeting that was about energy technologies, and I had asked for a moment of her time. I told her about Scott—his surgery, his supplements, and his three-week reprieve before they pressed him for traditional treatments. She had sensed immediately that she had something to offer.

"I'll come over," she volunteered. "I'll test his supplements and do some other things. Did you know I do energy healing also?"

I didn't, but I was thrilled! She was a Jane-of-all-trades: she did massage, worked with magnets and far infrared, muscle tested people, and did energy work. I had, indeed, been led to the right person!

Holly's interaction with Scott was as tender as that of a nursemaid. She took a seat on the footstool that complemented the recliner, looking up at him as if he were wisdom and she a small child. She listened to all we had done via the Schulze method so far—the potassium soup, hot/cold showers, no sugar, no processed food, and so on. She concurred with all of it. It was encouraging to have a second opinion from another advocate of natural healing.

She kept me in the room with Scott during his session because she felt that I was a stabilizing force for him, but she kindly asked Mom B to go upstairs. She pointed out that parents often take on the emotions—either through compassion or through guilt—that their child is trying to release. Then she shielded me from unwanted negative energy that might be released. (Shielding more than one person would also make the session too complicated.)

Perceiving how weak Scott was, Holly asked him if she had his permission to muscle test for him. She reminded us that muscle testing, that is, applied kinesiology, is a way to obtain responses from the body rather than from the intellect. It's based on the innate wisdom the body possesses at a cellular level.

> *Applied kinesiology is a way to obtain*
> *responses from the body rather than from the intellect.*
> *It is based on the innate wisdom the body*
> *possesses at a cellular level.*

(An interesting experiment on applied kinesiology was conducted by Jeff Bell and his dad. They placed ten different substances in ten paper bags: three substances were harmful to health, two were neutral, and five were beneficial.

They marked what they were on the inside of the bags, but nothing was written on the outside. Volunteers held each bag in turn and were tested, and in every case, the volunteers tested "strong" for the beneficial substances and "weak" for the harmful ones.)[90]

Scott and I were already familiar with muscle testing because we used this technique in our wellness business to check people's responses to increased energy. It never failed that when someone stood on magnetic insoles or drank better water—thus increasing the "flow" in the whole body—the person was stronger and often more flexible.[91]

The way we were taught muscle testing was for the client to hold an arm straight out and resist the pressure of the tester, who was pressing down gently on the person's wrist while asking a yes or no question. If the answer was true, the client's arm would remain strong. If false, the arm would weaken and go down, sometimes quite a bit.[92] The crazy thing is, it wouldn't matter whether the person consciously knew the answer or not; the body would. How? Insightful author Deepak Chopra says that "Every cell is a little sentient being."[93] What a grand image! All the cells in the body have memory, and unless that memory is changed, the cells resonate the same as when the event first occurred After all, the body was there when the event happened.

Dr. Bradley Nelson, author of *The Emotion Code* and creator of the Body Code, an energy healing system, uses applied kinesiology or muscle testing in his chiropractic work, as do many other chiropractors. Holly brought up his name and was delighted when we said we knew of him and had even attended a workshop he had given. Telling Holly of that workshop, we quoted Dr. Nelson: "There are six general categories of potential imbalance that can be tested and identified in the body. They are:

---

[90] Jeff Bell's experiment: https://myhealthoptimizer.com/another-look-at-muscle-testing-for-health/.

[91] Dr. Michael Weintraub's double-blind study: www.youtube.com/watch?v=Mf9BviBrRPA.

[92] Try this experiment: Put your arm straight out to the side, say your name, and have someone gently push down on your wrist. Now try it saying a name that is not yours. Which way do you think your body will test stronger?

[93] Deepak Chopra, *Quantum Healing* (New York: Bantam Books, 1989), 137.

> *Unless that memory is changed, the cells resonate*
> *the same as when the event first occurred.*

1. "Energetic imbalances, which include 'trapped emotions' and other types of energies
2. "Circuits and systems
3. "Toxins
4. "Pathogens
5. "Structural misalignments
6. "Nutrition and lifestyle

"When any of these six areas becomes an issue through imbalance, the imbalances can lead to disease processes in the body. When those underlying imbalances are corrected, the body is free of them and is often able to heal."[94]

Dr. Nelson coined a term to describe the effect in the body due to the body's holding on to a response of a long-ago event. It's a very telling term: "trapped emotions." He explained that the unconscious brain knows where stress, parasites, or toxins reside. Muscle testing accesses this innate knowledge in the body, and the person being muscle tested does not have to actively remember anything that is asked. The remarkable twentieth-century healer Agnes Sanford put it this way: "Neither patient nor doctor may know the exact condition of the patient. But that inner control center, the subconscious mind, is in possession of the facts."[95]

> *Trapped emotions have a lingering effect in the body*
> *due to a response to a long-ago event.*

Dr. Nelson also said that the person being muscle tested doesn't need to share out loud the experience that they went through. The body will still respond, even if spoken words are not used.

---

[94] Personal communication with Bradley Nelson, used with permission; "*The Emotion Code*" and "*The Body Code*," Discover Healing, discoverhealing.com.

[95] Agnes Sanford, *The Healing Light* (St. Paul, MN: Macalester Park Publishing, 1947), 115–116.

Dr. Nelson demonstrated this work right before our eyes at the workshop Scott and I had attended. At the front of the room, he asked questions of a well-dressed, blond, forty-two-year-old lady who had volunteered to be muscle tested. She didn't answer his questions verbally; he let her arm "answer" the questions in how resistant to his touch her arm stayed.

He started by asking questions about which one of the six areas needed the most work right then. "Is it toxins?" he pressed down gently on her arm. No. "Is it parasites?" No. He continued asking until he got to "trapped emotions." Zing! Her body's response was obvious to all of us—her arm held up solidly against his gently pressing fingers.

Next, Dr. Brad began asking about decades. "Did this problem that needs resolution occur between ages zero and ten?" No. "Ages eleven and twenty?" No. "Twenty-one and thirty?" No. "Thirty-one and forty?" Bingo. Then he asked the body for an age in years, pressing quickly, until he got to age thirty-seven. At that point, he looked at her eyes. "Did something happen at age thirty-seven?" he asked kindly.

Tearing a little, and somewhat amazed, she answered, "Yes, that's when I got divorced."

"Do you think that's kind of important that the body would remember it?"

"Yes," she agreed, and added, "My dad died that same year."

"Wow, a double dose. That's hard."

All of the attendees sent our tender feelings and heartfelt love toward her.

~

Bringing people back to wholeness is Dr. Nelson's purpose. He has allowed me to share some significant illustrations from his website. They symbolize the groundbreaking work on biological stress done by Hungarian Nobel nominee Hans Selye (1907–1982). These images—showing imbalances leading to disease—are burned into my memory. Whenever I realize that I've moved one picture to the right, I work to move back to tall, straight, and healthy on the left! I desperately wanted Scott to move back to tall, straight, and healthy again!

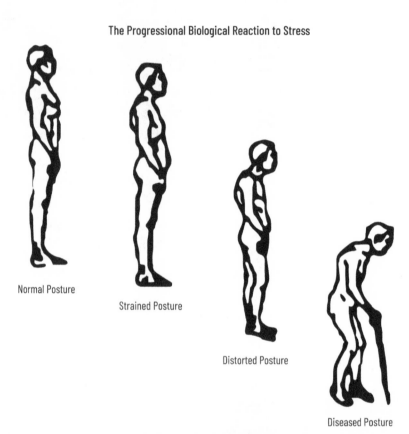

The Progressional Biological Reaction to Stress

Normal Posture

Strained Posture

Distorted Posture

Diseased Posture

Used by permission of Dr. Bradley Nelson

∼

Holly asked Scott if it would be all right if she muscle tested his supplements. He agreed, and she went to it. She checked all of them, saying "Yes" to this, "Wait" to that, "Decrease" or "Increase" to others. I was so happy to have someone close at hand do this. The supplements Nurse Lorna had recommended were powerful and of great efficacy, but I wasn't sure that she, while in Maryland, could tell Scott what his body needed right at this moment.

Testing supplements was why I had initially requested Holly to come, but that was just the start for her. Next, she stood and pressed her hand gently on his spasming right shoulder, the one that fired off every six seconds.[96] It was a credit to her gentleness that he allowed her to touch him. She asked him about it, and unlike his vague response two weeks earlier to Reg, he told her exactly how long he'd had it and how persistent it was. I was proud of him for opening up with her. She continued massaging it gently and told him he needed to get rid of it.

"Yeah," he smiled wryly, "I've heard that."

The third technique Holly used was moving her hand down his right arm to sense what vibrations emanated from him. But her hand was two inches away from his body—that is, not even touching him! *This* was Scott's initiation into what I simply call "energy work"—the work that people with special abilities do that creates or allows internal change at a cellular level.

> *"Energy work" is the work that people with special abilities do that creates or allows internal change at a cellular level.*

Western civilization is just coming around to studying the body's energy system, but even a toddler looking at a squashed bug knows that *something* that previously existed in the bug is now gone. In China, life energy is called Chi, spelled qi, and in India, it's called prana or "the breath." (As a singer, I like that.) As examples of energy, who would you rather be around: The girl who just got engaged or the woman who is very sick? The guy who just batted his first home run or the man whose retirement was lost in a scam? Life is full of events that get us "up" and full of challenges that get us "down." *What* gets up or down? Our energy, that's what. It's energy that lets a guardian know immediately that the day wasn't okay for a schoolchild, even when the kid says it was. It's energy that makes everybody at a party flock to a particular

---

[96] See Chapter 9.

person or that causes people to look up at the door when someone enters. It's energy that causes some people to be drawn to one person and not to another. It's energy that lets you sense that someone is standing behind you, even if you can't see the person.

Energy is real. It's just generally not seen, and it's sensed rather than felt. A singing teacher taught me to *see* energy in the form of auras, but I didn't know that this day with Holly I would *feel* energy. When Holly got to his right side where the mass lurked—that hideous intruder wreaking unwonted damage—she became disturbed as she felt a great deal of interference.

"Oh, there's a lot going on here." She placed her open hand near his side. Every now and then, she shook it off to the edge of the room.

After a while she said, "Come feel this, Elaine."

I was surprised. I didn't know how to feel energy at this time. I was happy that Holly included me in her work for Scott, but I kind of rolled my eyes because I didn't know what to expect.

"Put your palm here and be patient. You'll feel energy coming out."

I did as she directed, holding my palm facing toward Scott's tumor, which bulged from his ribs, but not touching it. After a bit, I could feel a barrage of tiny pellets shooting into my hand from his side.

"Shake those off!" Holly advised. "You don't want to keep that stuff in *your* body!"

I did as she said and shook my hand off to the side like shaking off water droplets. Scott was not bothered by anything Holly did; he seemed to like it. Besides, he was lying back on his new recliner, so he was relatively comfortable —as comfortable as a postsurgical man with a horrible, persistent pain in his side can be.

Auras

My singing teacher read a great deal about the unseen vibrations that singers and listeners call sound, but those vibrations do more than create sound; they can heal. "Of all the physical modalities, music most activates the life energy and uplifts the soul. Only pure love can do more."[97]

My teacher was telling me about auras one day, and I eagerly said, "Oh, I hope I can see those in the next life after I die!" She laughed merrily and said, "You don't have to wait till then! I can teach you how to see them now."[98]

The way my teacher taught me was this: look at the empty space between someone's neck and shoulders; stare as if you were looking at a 3D picture, and as the eyes readjust, you will start noticing a fuzzy light around the person's head and upper body. This is more than the narrow half-inch strip of light refraction that the eye can normally sense around objects. This fuzzy light will usually extend out from the person about three inches for starters. As you keep focusing on the light, it may become a brighter haze, and it may reach farther out than three or four inches, particularly when the person seen is giving service or feels good about himself or herself. My teacher quoted a nurse who said she'd seen an aura arc all the way from the stage to the back of the hall when a person was speaking.

The most energetic aura I ever saw was at a national convention of singing teachers (NATS) in Las Vegas.[99] I had just taught a fellow teacher how to see auras when we became separated in the huge warehouse that served as the performance hall. Featured that evening was a friend of mine who had won the national NATS contest. There he was, performing in front of the voice teachers of America—what an intimidating crowd! As I listened to his glorious, bell-like tenor voice, my eyes shifted, and I started seeing his aura. I allowed his dark hair and dark tuxedo to juxtapose the light that emanated

---

[97] John Diamond, M.D. *The Life Energy in Music, vol. 1* (Archaeus Press, 1981), 5.

[98] An aura is life energy that exudes or escapes outside the physical body. (I believe that the light emanating from Jesus Christ was so bright that people could readily see it. That light became represented in art as a halo.)

[99] The name of the organization is National Association of Teachers of Singing (NATS).

from him. Soon I could see bursts of light shooting out from his body like the rays of a star! It was glorious. After the concert, my friend ran across the back of the warehouse and found me. "Did you *see* him?" she exulted. "He was on *fire!*" I knew then that she had seen what I had seen.[100]

~

Always directing her questions to him, Holly asked gently, "Do you understand about vibrations and healing, Scott?"

"A little," he responded.

"Everything around us vibrates." Sheepishly she amended, "Well, you're a chemical engineer; I don't have to tell *you* that!"

He chuckled feebly and said, "Yes, pressure gradients, vectors, velocity. It's all over the place."

She accepted his string of words and continued. "And, of course, we both work with Japanese wellness products, so we've seen changes happening to people as the result of better energy, which is higher vibrations. When people vibrate at a higher frequency, they are healthier."

> *"When people vibrate at a higher frequency, they are healthier."*

I then volunteered that Scott and I were musicians, so we also dealt daily with vibrations that are unseen. She was delighted. In addition to everything else, she was also a musician!

Now she moved into new territory. She asked, with some trepidation, "Scott, did you know that healing the body also requires healing the mind and the emotions?"

"It makes sense," he replied pragmatically.

---

[100] On another occasion I saw a man's aura, and it was lavender. I kept shaking my head to make it go away, wishing it to be white. Later, I read that a lavender aura is the color of someone who is extremely loving and giving, which is what he was. I am told that plants have lavender auras, too, but I've never bothered to look.

Then she said something curious. "Scott, there is something from about age eleven to age thirteen that is holding you back."

Scott and I looked at each other. There was that mystery again, the same one that Reg had mentioned. And, like Reg, she didn't mention any other age. She saw us looking at each other and waited.

Scott said, "I was told that a couple of weeks ago by a guy who does biofeedback. I've thought about a lot of things, but none of them seems right."

"Well, keep thinking. When it's right, you'll know. It's important that you figure out what it is, so you can let it go."

There was that concept *again*—letting go.

After she left, Scott groused, "Why does everyone want me to let things go? Why can't they just help me get well?"

The chemical engineer guy wanted things that were streamlined, efficient, and quantifiable. The idea that changing his outlook would have anything to do with his physical health seemed far removed from his technical training.

Holly finished by doing some real massage that melted him into his recliner like a puppy dog settling into a lap. She promised she'd come back in three or four days.

"Why not sooner?" I asked hopefully.

Holly smiled. "We've done a lot of work today. It takes a while to process through the body and leave. We don't want to overwhelm the body."

This time I smiled reluctantly and said, "It makes sense." I invited her back in three days.

~

That evening, while Katie and Aidan took a long walk around the nearby temple, Mom B, Scott, and I enjoyed watching Sandra Bullock fall in love with the wrong guy in *While You Were Sleeping*. It was fun to watch and fun to talk about how important it is to be forthright instead of going on assumptions. Mostly it was a relief, after Scott's eventful day, just to sit together. Afterward, Scott wanted to sleep right there on his new recliner. He asked me to sleep next to him on the couch, so I brought blankets and pillows down from our bedroom. It felt like a sleepover!

Energy and Energy Healing

Everything is made of energy. "Every living thing has a frequency or a constant measurable rate of electrical energy (or vibration)."[101] Music is energy. Thought is energy. Emotion is energy. Living takes energy. Bruce Tainio built the first frequency monitor in the world in 1992. He determined that a healthy body's frequency is in the range of 62 to 72 hertz (Hz). Susceptibility to colds and flu starts at 58 Hz, and a person with a serious disease (such as cancer or AIDS) is at 42 Hz. Canned foods, by the way, have a frequency of zero.[102]

"Human beings are energetic beings, and when we are exposed to inharmonious frequencies, it creates a state of inner imbalance and dis-ease (which becomes disease). It causes our physical matter to begin to break down."[103]

"Energy medicine is 'vibrational' medicine that cannot be seen, but we know it works because its results can be measured." Energy healing is a branch of complementary or alternative medicine that includes methods such as PACE, Brain Gym, biofeedback, BodyTalk, acupuncture, reflexology, iridology, Ayurveda, Alexander Relaxation Technique, Resonance Repatterning, Quantum-Touch, craniosacral, Jin Shin Jyutsu, therapeutic massage, chiropractic, magnetic therapy, and other modalities too numerous to name. "A healer is able to channel healing energy into the person seeking help by different methods: hands-on, hands-off, and distant."[104] but "all require some mental effort to create change. The faith and intention of both the healer and the one being healed are very much at play with energy healing."[105]

---

[101] Connie Boucher, *Super Simple Wellness* (Utah: Aroma Tools, 2009), 21.

[102] Ibid., 24.

[103] Private conversation with biofeedback engineer, Deepak Chari.

[104] "Energy Healing," Wikipedia.

[105] Bradley Nelson in discussion with the author, 2018.

CHAPTER 14

ELEMENTAL CESIUM HIGH PH THERAPY

JANUARY

Scott, Mom B, and I developed a routine. Together Mom B and I would help Scott with his first supplements and food of the day, which he generally accepted with enthusiasm and a solid stomach. Scott invited one of us to pray, and then we recited a scripture that he had chosen:

> Search diligently, pray always, and be believing, and all things shall work together for your good.[106]

Scott genuinely felt that if he believed, all things would work together for his good. What he prayed for was to be healed. What he wanted was a miracle.

---

[106] Doctrine and Covenants 90:24.

Scott genuinely felt that if he believed, all things would work together for his good. What he prayed for was to be healed. What he wanted was a miracle.

Scott and I did our best to follow the promptings of the Spirit of the Lord. Day by day, whatever we felt guided to do, that's what we did. We truly believed "the Holy Ghost...shall teach you all things."[107] and we truly felt that whoever or whatever came into our path and gave us a secure, peaceful feeling, that person or concept was brought to us by God.

After organizing for the day, I would go upstairs to research treatment choices on the computer and phone, and Mom B would stay on the main floor with Scott to read to him, walk with him, and try to get those potent supplements down him!

It was typical for Scott to wake cheery and energetic, ready to plow into another day. But then the nausea—the constant nausea—would cut into his cheer. Every day he threw up, or felt like he would, so every day his supplement schedule was different. Mom B couldn't give him the 11:00 a.m. supplements because he was working to keep down the 10:00 a.m. ones. Pretty soon it was noon or 1:00 or 2:00, and we had to move on. We couldn't backtrack and pile up everything he needed! Every day we just did the best we could, and every day Scott endured.

Scott was not only the most persistent person I knew; he was also the most prepared. We never had a tree catch fire at Christmas because he always checked the wires. Our children never burned themselves with pots on the stove because he always made sure the handles didn't stick out over the edge. Our cars rarely had flat tires, or oil or transmission problems, because he kept them maintained. Now that the doctor had confirmed Scott had cancer, Scott wanted to immediately start elemental cesium high pH therapy.[108] However,

---

[107] John 14:26, KJV.

[108] I consider cesium chloride to be *very* dangerous for normal-health individuals. If it were still in my house, it would be under lock and key.

being the prepared and methodical person he was, he also wanted to be reminded as to *why* he wanted to use it before we spent a large amount of money to purchase it. "Mr. Preparedness" asked me to explain what the elemental cesium was supposed to do, as well as to continue researching additional therapies and/or facilities for treatment in the world of natural healing.

I still could not find Neal's phone number or anyone who had it, but Neal had given us articles by the noted physicist Dr. A. Keith Brewer,[109] as well as a dozen smaller articles by other researchers. (Some were the papers I had tried showing to Dr. Hayes.)[110] Praying that I could somewhat understand the physics presented in the papers, I reread them and grasped what I could from them. The next morning, I bounded downstairs to make my presentation, complete with stick figures and diagrams on a piece of large brown cardboard.

Here's the gist: When the large cesium element is taken into a cell through its membrane, it can't get out. Since the cesium is alkaline, the cell becomes too alkaline, and so the cell dies. The only cells cesium enters (because of cell membrane behavior) are cancer cells, and you *want* them to die. Thus, "Elemental Cesium High pH Therapy alkalizes cancer cells to die from the inside out" and that is why cesium therapy was desirable.[111]

An impressive example of Dr. Brewer's testing was of a woman whose tumor was about the size of Scott's:

> One woman with two hard tumor masses eight to ten centimeters in diameter was given three to six months to live. She had discontinued chemotherapy because it weakened her. She was given a fifty-gram bottle of Cesium Chloride and was told to take four grams per day. Being very frightened she took the entire fifty grams in one week. At the end of that time the tumor masses were very soft, so she obtained another fifty grams of Cesium Chloride and took it in another week.

---

[109] A. Keith Brewer, "The High-pH Therapy for Cancer," cancertutor.com/cesium-chloride.

[110] H. E. Sartori and Dr. Lawrence Plaskett.

[111] Tanya Harter Pierce, *Outsmart Your Cancer—Alternative Non-Toxic Treatments That Work* (Nevada: Thoughtworks Publishing, 2009), 256–257.

By the end of that time she could not find the tumors, and two years later there was no sign of their return.[112]

I listed a series of U.S. clinical trials of elemental cesium high pH therapy that were initiated in 1981, with the results published in the *Journal of Pharmacological Biochemistry and Behavior*: "Tests have been carried out on more than thirty humans. In each case the tumor masses disappeared. Also, all pains and effects associated with cancer disappeared within twelve to thirty-six hours; the more chemotherapy and morphine the patient had taken, the longer the withdrawal period."[113]

Scott agreed that, from what we had read, chemotherapy retarded other therapies. Since he hadn't had chemo, he could move ahead more actively with a therapy of his choice. He and Mom B resonated to Brewer's remarkable success with his U.S. human trial in 1981. The rate of survival was 50 percent—much higher than most chemotherapies offer—and the pain went down markedly (that idea made Scott very happy). In many cases, there was "a complete disappearance of the cancer."[114] One woman, considered a terminal case, was even brought in comatose, but was able to walk out after five days of treatment![115]

> *I cannot emphasize too strongly, these (subjects) were all patients who were supposed to die. They had exhausted every other alternative. Some were even comatose. They had no hope, no chance for survival. But, despite the dire prognosis, half of them did in fact survive!*

---

[112] A. Keith Brewer, "The High pH Therapy for Cancer; Tests on Mice and Humans"—article from Pharmacology Biochemistry & Behavior, Vol 21, suppl. I. pages 1-5, 1984.

[113] Ibid.

[114] H.E. Sartori, article: "Cesium Therapy in Cancer Patients from Pharmacology Biochemistry & Behavior," Vol. 21, Suppl., 1 page 2, 1984.

[115] Ibid.

Brewer added, "I cannot emphasize too strongly, these (subjects) were all patients who were supposed to die. They had exhausted every other alternative. Some were even comatose. They had no hope, no chance for survival. But, despite the dire prognosis, half of them did in fact survive."[116]

Corroborative evidence of cultures that have hardly any cancer was also impressive to Scott and Mom B. Examples were the Hunza of North Pakistan, Hopi and Pueblo Indians of Arizona, and Indians in Peru and Ecuador. All these groups lived in areas rich in potassium, rubidium, and cesium, so, of course, their *diets* contained what the *soil and water* contained.[117] Microscopist Ted Aloisio supports this concept:

> If minerals are not in the soil, they are not in the plant. [For instance], if broccoli is grown in selenium-deficient soils, it has no nutritional selenium. It doesn't matter what the dietician says. It doesn't matter what the four food groups say. It doesn't matter what the vegetarian says. If there is no selenium in the soils, there is no selenium in the crops grown in that soil. Period.[118]

If minerals are not in the soil, they are not in the plant.

When I finished my presentation, Scott had a better feel for why he had wanted the cesium in the first place and what he could expect it to do for him. Cesium chloride, or elemental cesium, could lessen the pain, soften the tumor, and potentially eliminate the tumor. He suddenly became energized, took charge, and gave me the go-ahead to order it. Combined with the other vitamins and minerals that were needed to make the cesium absorb into malignant cells, the check came to $1,000. If it did what the research indicated, it would be well worth it!

---

[116] Deoul, *Cancer Cover-Up*, 37.

[117] Keith Brewer, "The High-pH Therapy for Cancer; Tests on Mice and Humans," *Pharmacology Biochemistry and Behavior* 21, no. S1 (1984): 1–5.

[118] In 1955 the U.S. Bureau of Indian Affairs donated surplus food to the Hopis. Unfortunately, the food had not nearly the high mineral content of their native diet, and within one generation the cancer rate among Hopis had reached 60 percent of the overall U.S. rate and was continuing to rise. Aloisio, *Blood Never Lies*, 56.

Elaine's Simplistic Summary
of Elemental Cesium High pH Therapy

According to Dr. Brewer's theory, elemental cesium high pH therapy is made possible because of the transport in and out of cell membranes. When cancer cells form, the membrane is inflamed, and the outer walls of cells become hardened. This makes it difficult for oxygen to enter the cells, and the cells start fermenting glucose for energy. The fermentation results in increased lactic acid in the cells. The acidic pH, under 6.5, overwhelms the cell's DNA capacity to control cell growth. At that point, mitosis ceases and uncontrolled growth of cancerous cells occurs.

Cesium chloride is one of a very few molecules that can penetrate cancer cells, and its high alkalinity changes the cancerous cells' pH to 8.0 or higher. (Normal cells [pH of 7] do not take in cesium chloride.) Brewer noted, "Transport differs markedly whether double bonds are in the ground state or an excited state. In the ground or static state, the strength of the transport is only strong enough to accept Cesium, Rubidium and Potassium." Once one of the three is accepted into the cell, the cell becomes more alkaline (ten times more alkaline than normal). Thus the term "high pH." Later, dead alkaline cells are readily absorbed by the system and eliminated in the urine.[119]

---

[119] Brewer, "High-pH Therapy."

Differences between Two Powerful Treatments:
Protocel and Elemental Cesium High pH Therapy

Another powerful substance for healing is a liquid called Protocel. Marketed as a supplement, it is a powerful antioxidant. (Similar formulas were previously labeled as Entelev or Cancell.) Protocel interferes with the cell respiration of cancer cells (or any anaerobic cells) by blocking their production of adenosine triphosphate (ATP). Protocel kills cells by shifting down their energy to a point below the minimum that cancer cells need to remain intact, so they cannot hold themselves together anymore and they simply fall apart. Elemental cesium, on the other hand, raises the pH within the cancer cells to such a high alkalinity that the cancer cells can no longer function, and they die off as a result. So, cesium high pH therapy alkalinizes cancer cells from the inside out, whereas Protocel alkalinizes from the outside in.[120]

---

[120] Tanya Harter Pierce, M.A., MFCC, *Outsmart Your Cancer—Alternative Non-Toxic Treatments That Work* (Nevada: Thoughtworks Publishing, 2009), 124, 256..

CHAPTER 15

RAW FOODS

JANUARY

That word "cancer" single-handedly changed our household. We gave up all pretense of a normal life before the *C* word: Scott stayed home from work; I didn't tend Davis, teach singing lessons, or go to students' recitals anymore; Katie went by herself to a meeting that was supposed to be with parents—poor kid; and Mom B came every morning to our house from Scott's sister's, forty-five minutes away. Our energies were concentrated on getting rid of Scott's cancer.

On one of my runs to a natural health food store to obtain supplements and vegetables, I saw a flyer advertising a class on raw foods. A lady named Becky would tell how she reversed her cancer. Several years prior I had heard Michio Kushi in person talk about getting rid of his cancer, so I knew about the macrobiotic diet that he espoused.[121] But I wasn't sure how uncooked or

---

[121] Michio Kushi advocated grains, vegetables, beans, some sea veggies like nori or kombu and fruit, seeds, nuts, and white fish as well as exercise. He avoided sugar, dairy, meat, poultry, and EMFs—electromagnetic radiation. Author's notes from a lecture by Mr. Kushi.

raw foods could help with cancer. Scott thought Mom B and I should go, so we did.

When we walked in, the presenter, Becky, was gliding around the room like a tall lily, greeting people with effortless ease, radiating warmth and compassion for every person there. She had a light around her that took my breath away. The light she radiated was second only to one other person I'd ever met—and that is saying a lot, considering that my vocations as a singing teacher and wellness coach constantly involve active, vibrant, healthy people! Becky let the small audience know how happy she was to have them there. I was completely charmed by her calm manner, and I settled right in to listen.

She started off by telling about the cancer she had had several years prior. "I gave it to myself," she said brightly of her cancer, "so I decided *I* would be the one to take it away."

> *Suppressed negative feelings [that are]*
> *not resolved as they occur…remain very much alive*
> *in your physical energy field (body) and these*
> *feelings affect each day of your life…*
> *Negative feelings will be realized.*

Before continuing, it needs to be pointed out that we don't *consciously* give ourselves any illness or malady. Nevertheless, there *is* a link between our body and our thoughts. Holly had asked us to buy Karol Truman's classic book *Feelings Buried Alive Never Die*. The introduction states, "Unresolved, repressed and suppressed negative feelings [that are] not resolved as they occur…remain very much alive in your physical energy field (body) and these feelings affect each day of your life…Negative feelings *will* be realized [i.e., manifest]."[122] Another energy worker simply stated, "Time moves on, but strong emotions don't. Things in the subconscious have no time frame; to the subconscious, the event just occurred. Strong emotions stay locked at

---

[122] Karol K. Truman, *Feelings Buried Alive Never Die* (Utah: Olympus Distributing, 1991), 2.

the time they occurred until you can change the energy and remove them."[123]

One of Dr. Bernie Siegel's patients explained this concept very understandably:

> Most of the time illness is not a premeditated act; all of the time there is some relationship between an illness and our thoughts. Nothing happens onto us; we are the happeners. The mind and body work together, with the body being the screen where the movie is shown.[124]

Becky painted a bleak picture of herself starting to bleed to death, with a fibrous tumor in her uterus the size of a soccer ball. She was scared and delirious with a high fever, and for three days her husband sat by her bed crying. She was also anemic with a blood hematocrit (the proportion of the blood that consists of packed red blood cells) of sixteen—most people with a level of sixteen die. She said twelve ounces of wheatgrass juice a day was like a blood transfusion, and within a week her hematocrit level was twenty-two. The following week it was up to thirty-four. She continued, "I went to the writings of the people who are known for getting rid of cancer: Norman W. Walker, Dr. Max Gerson, Dr. Bernard Jensen, Dr. Christopher, and Dr. Richard Schulze among others." (Later, she could have added Dr. Lorraine Day.) "On big pieces of butcher paper, I wrote down every step in each person's program, and then compared the steps. I found that every regimen was essentially the same. Each program started with cleansing." (Which is also what we had started with, so that made me happy.) "I found, though, that those who used cooked foods (such as Schulze with his potassium soup) required an extra step or two. Thus, it made sense to me to eat a diet of uncooked foods, mainly fruits and vegetables. This is called a raw foods diet."

Dr. Gabriel Cousens said, "Once food is cut off from its life force source in the earth, it begins to lose its energy. Raw food is filled with more life-force

---

[123] Deepak Chari in discussion with the author, January 8, 2021.

[124] Evy McDonald, quoted in Siegel, *Peace, Love and Healing*, 83.

energy than *any* cooked food."[125] When enzymes are processed out via cooking (i.e., high temperatures), they have to be added back in.

Becky happily reasoned, "Why not *not* take them out in the first place?"

She lovingly picked up an apple, almost caressing it as she twinkled, "Look! The perfect fast food, and it even comes with its own packaging!" She advocated eating pretty much what God created, in the way He created it—not messing around with it. She said that many people start with 80 percent raw and 20 percent cooked, but when she went to 100 percent, she felt enormous energy!

> *Holding up an apple, she said,*
> *"Look! The perfect fast food, and it even comes*
> *with its own packaging!"*

She also said that cooking over 110°F destroyed the enzymes in food, so "the body is starving for nutrients." To be safe, she stopped at 105°F. Another raw food advocate agreed:

> Enzymes are the key to life. No enzymes, no life. We destroy all the digestive enzymes in our food by cooking and baking, and thus the body has to draw the necessary enzymes to digest this dead food from the body organs, which...become unbalanced. Fortunately eating raw food and/or taking enzyme supplements can help to restore our health.[126]

Becky said that an interesting experiment would be to plant a raw seed and a roasted seed. She quipped, "I guarantee only one of these seeds will grow!" She then talked about "dead" food. It sounded horrible! As she talked, I thought of the hated canned peas, or even worse, slimy canned asparagus that my mother served our family long ago when canned foods were all the rage.

---

[125] Gabriel Cousens, foreword to *Living in the Raw* by Rose Lee Calabro (California: Rose Publishing, 1998).
[126] Ibid.

The stuff looked and tasted like khaki green snake innards. Ugh! Compare that with the vibrant colors and tastes of the same vegetables—raw or steamed; obviously there would be a difference in nutritional value just as there was in the look and taste!

Someone asked her how she managed to dine out. Brightly, Becky answered, "There's almost always *something* on the buffet that you can eat, so I choose that! If I know there won't be, I just bring along a little something for myself."

"Wow," I thought, "raw foods, even though a pure diet, seem really labor intensive."

She went on with a serious face. "I never impose my way of eating on another person. They must choose it for themselves and because they want a change for themselves." She smiled cheerily again. "I invite them, though!" The invitation of her literal *being*, so complete and serene, was almost enough to make one want to join the bandwagon! She said that she always wanted people to embark on the raw foods journey happily, never with a grudge or a hint of "I can't have this; I can't have that."

She told how her youngest child was given a diet of only raw foods and said with a wistful sort of triumph, "She is four years old and processed food has never passed through her lips. Not even crackers. That's *got* to make a difference in her health, doesn't it?"

I agreed; it seemed it would!

Becky took seriously whatever she put into her mouth. She passed around small chocolate candies to everyone. With each of us holding a few in our hand, she pointed out that if we ate them, the body had to figure out what to do with them. "The body has to figure out what to do with *everything* we put into it."

Looking at those little pieces in my hand, I thought about how the stomach had to digest them, then how the liver had to further pull them apart and decide where to send the different parts—some directly to waste, some through the bloodstream, and so on. I thought about how the extra sugar in these tiny little chocolate pieces would raise the acidity level in my blood-stream so that my body would have to grab something like calcium to neutralize the acidity, and if it couldn't find any calcium from what I'd eaten that day, it would go after calcium from my bones. (Remember Nicodemus?) Ah, to be completely responsible for everything we ingest!

Now, Becky not only glowed, but she was the perfect weight for herself. Weight was a nonissue with her because weight becomes normalized on a raw foods diet. "This is because one only needs about half the calories, proteins, fats, and carbohydrates on a living food diet that they need on cooked food because 50 percent of the protein and 70 to 90 percent of the vitamins and minerals are not destroyed through the cooking process."

I stopped to look around at the audience of about thirty people. Most were senior citizens, healthy looking, on the thin side, and with straight posture. They were alert, taking notes, and asking pertinent questions—they were a pretty energetic crowd. They seemed like people who were actively making choices, not helplessly waiting for someone to tell them what to do. They were taking responsibility for their own care.

Becky's younger friend and protégé, Rachel, then showed people how to make breads and desserts the raw foods way, since these are things from a regular diet that people miss. We got to sample the results: very tasty! One of my favorites was Flax Crackers, which consisted of dehydrating a mix of four cups soaked flaxseeds, one-third cup Bragg Aminos, lemon juice, and seasonings for ten hours. Mm-mm! We also learned the trick to eating raw food in a cooked medium: let the broth heat up, and then add raw diced vegetables. The veggies will cool the broth enough to be eaten, yet they themselves won't cook over 105°F. Ta-da!

Then willowy Becky stepped back in and finished off with some other techniques to help the body, such as lymph brushing, which is stroking upward—from hands up the arms and from ankles up the legs—with something rough like a loofah to increase flow in the lymph system. She also recommended using a crystal body deodorant made of 100 percent natural mineral salts and using natural shampoos and soaps, since what we put on our skin goes into the body. Then this vibrant, joyful woman gave everyone her cell number, and we left with her booklist in hand.[127]

By the time we'd been there two hours, we had heard about cancer, cleansing, herbs, raw foods, macrobiotics, and essential oils for healing. It was all so new, I'm afraid most of it zipped over my head.

When we returned home, Scott simply said, "You were gone a long time."

(Yes, we'd heard that before.) Becky's class gave really great information, but it overwhelmed me. I had so much on my plate that most of the new information tucked itself into the back of my brain like crumbs waiting in a dark corner to be swept into the light when the right broom came along. I did start implementing some of the suggestions, but it would take a while longer for most of the information to register as vital instead of merely nice.

Emotions and the Psychosomatic Network

Dr. Candace Pert, an early user of the term "bodymind" and discoverer of how emotions are created by actual molecules, explained how daily emotional self-care is missing for most of us. Pert said, "The tendency to ignore our emotions is *oldthink*, a remnant of the still-reigning paradigm that keeps us focused on the material level of health, the physicality of it. But the emotions are a key element in self-care because they allow us to enter into the bodymind's conversation. By getting in touch with our emotions…we gain access to the healing wisdom that is everyone's natural biological right."

How do we do this? My friend Barbara Bertucci suggests, "Be gentle with yourself." Pert says to acknowledge and claim "all our feelings, not just the so-called positive ones. Anger, grief, fear—these are not negative in themselves; in fact, they are vital for our survival. We need anger to define boundaries, grief to deal with our losses, and fear to protect ourselves from danger. It's only when these feelings are denied, so that

---

[127] See Becky's Reading List, Appendix E.

they cannot be easily and rapidly processed through the system and released, that the situation becomes toxic."[128]

---

[128] Pert, *Molecules of Emotion*, 285. (See also ematosoma diagrams in Appendix D.)

CHAPTER 16

NUTRITIONAL IV

FEBRUARY

The elemental cesium high pH therapy package arrived—it felt like Christmas! Scott started taking the alkaline liquid with its all-important accompanying mineral supplements. His schedule was even more rigorous than it had been with the supplements that we had gotten from Nurse Lorna. Then there was the way it was consumed!

Nurse Lorna said, "The longer Scott can keep the cesium under his tongue (that is, sublingual), the faster it will absorb into his body." So he would sit there and make himself hold that tasteless, colorless liquid in his mouth as long as he could—ten, twenty, sometimes up to forty minutes! Some of the supplements were sublingual too—one was salty, one was sour, and one tasted like dirty dishwater. His willpower was astounding.

Nevertheless, Scott was very weak and always nauseated. The cesium itself could make him nauseated unless it was accompanied by certain mineral supplements. But some of those supplements were hard for him to get down because of a persistent nausea that had developed after his surgery, which had been about three weeks earlier. It was a continual "Catch-22." On this particular day, he sat on the couch with his head in his hands, in anguish because his mother had gone up to his sister's house in Salt Lake City.

"What does she have to do up there? They don't need her!" he lamented.

As I bent down to give him one of his supplements, my long hair brushed his skin lightly. He cringed and asked me to get it off, not being able to handle anything extraneous. In a further indication of how absolutely worn out he was, when his mom finally called that morning—the one person he had been wishing for—he flicked his hand away, unable to talk to her. I left him with cesium to hold in his mouth for several minutes and ran upstairs to look on the computer for Neal's number or for other treatments to accompany the cesium. Back and forth, up and down stairs, I called on the phone and checked on him, called and checked, called and checked.

The hospital called back. The tumor board (the group of doctors who reviewed cases monthly) had met, as the radiation oncologist had said they would. They did not approve his having radiation, apparently since the tumor was too close to the right lung. I sighed with relief to hear that he wouldn't be expected to go in for burning treatments.

One of my calls on this day was to a friend in Ohio. Dr. Stan was an integrative medical practitioner as well as a pediatrician. He and I discussed several modalities, including chemo. The choice he favored involved going to Germany.

"If it were me that had cancer, that's where I'd go," he said.

He wasn't the first person to mention Germany, where techniques other than chemo and radiation were available.

Thinking of Scott, down on his recliner with his head propped on two pillows in his lap, I said into the phone, "No, that's not possible. He's too weak."

"Well, one thing he probably needs right now is a nutritional IV."

"What's that?"

"It's not intravenous medicine; it's intravenous food. Nutrition. It sounds like he's not getting enough. He probably needs more hydration too."

"That would really help. I wish there was something close."

To my astonishment, he said, "There is, right there in Provo."

There was? Who would have known! I had to call Ohio to find out that help for my husband was available only two miles away!

~

Dr. Remington's Office for Advanced Medicine fit us in that very afternoon. Scott was so weak, it was all he could do to sit up for the two-mile ride. An M.D., Dr. Remington integrated alternative therapies with Western medicine. He had practiced in our town for as long as I could remember and was, in fact, the very doctor I went to once to get rid of candida. It's too bad we didn't check into some of their other treatment choices for cancer because they had several. But we'd gone in only for intravenous nutrition, and that's all my brain and Scott's strength could accommodate right then.

They settled him comfortably on a recliner while "Infusion 907880" slowly dripped into his system for two hours to stem what Dr. Remington diagnosed as "malnutrition and dehydration." (Dr. Stan was right.) While he did this, I filled out nine pages of history and paperwork and paid our $165 for the M.D. exam and $70 for the drip. Insurance considered this IV optional, so the whole amount was paid out of pocket. To me it didn't look optional; it looked lifesaving! It was amazing how much better he was when he finished. He was almost a new man. He stood up straight, his eyes were shining again, and he felt stronger.

> *Insurance considered this IV optional, so the whole amount was paid out of pocket. To me it didn't look optional; it looked lifesaving!*

That evening, when people came to visit, he praised me: "Yes, Elaine is the one who found it."

I glowed under his recognition, feeling again that we were a team. Divide and conquer: my job was to find ways to help him, and his job was to heal!

∾

Before bed, he used some of his newfound energy contemplating his upcoming and dreaded chemotherapy appointment. Greatly influencing our thinking about chemo was a book we had read with Scott's mother, *Questioning Chemotherapy* by Dr. Ralph Moss. Moss was a Ph.D. about seven years older than Scott who had begun his career in the 1970s as a science writer at Memorial Sloan Kettering Cancer Center. He started out as "an enthusiastic believer in chemotherapy" in a time of "great hope" after President Nixon had signed into law a "war on cancer" with the National Cancer Act of 1971.[129] However, the longer Moss was around the business, the more misgivings he had. He saw many things that didn't add up, and this fascinating first book was his honest effort to address what he saw.

Dr. Moss said that chemo was perceived as quackery in the 1920s, yet by the 1970s had become America's (and much of the world's) cancer treatment of choice. Moss noted that part of the evolution came from society—people wanting a "magic bullet" for cancer after seeing how effective the magic bullet of penicillin was for treating infections. Part of the evolution came from the media[130]—newspapers and magazines finding that publishing hopeful reports pleased people and increased their readership.[131] And part of the evolution came from the media in a *different* form—newspapers and magazines promoting fear "that was then relieved by the good news of impending

---

[129] Moss, *Questioning Chemotherapy*, 5. Moss's impeccable research is bolstered by the 408 references in his appendix, as well as the 210 references in his newest book, *Cancer, Incorporated* (New York: Equinox Press, 2020).

[130] The media wrote glowingly about chemo cures and clinical trials, as shown by *Time* magazine's April 25, 1994, cover, "Hope in the War Against Cancer," where the headline was in two-inch-high red letters. Moss, *Questioning Chemotherapy*, 26.

[131] A study in the *Journal of the American Medical Association* (*JAMA*) showed that "when reporters were given both positive and negative stories on a new drug, about half of them chose to write *only* about the positive findings, and none of them chose to write solely about the negative results." Ibid.; "Proclaiming the imminent cure for cancer is as good for the media business as it is for the chemotherapy business." Ibid., 24.

drug breakthroughs."[132] So it turns out that chemotherapy was not always standard, common, traditional, or conventional, and that it was not all it was stacked up to be.[133]

> *Chemotherapy is basically ineffective in the vast majority of cases in which it is given.*

An important aspect of the therapy was how words meant different things to practitioners versus nonmedical people. For instance, "remission" to families of loved ones equated to "cured," but to doctors it only meant "about three to five more years of life." "Disease-free survival" to *families* meant "free of cancer"—exactly what families want! But to *oncologists* it was "essentially a measure of the time *until* recurrence."[134]

As far as effectiveness, Moss indicated that time hadn't changed the results much. "After almost a quarter century of effort (from 1971–1995)...the list (of treatable malignancies) is almost identical to what it was twenty-five years ago![135] (Bringing this up to date, Moss reported in 2020, "Fewer than half of the cancer drugs actually extend survival, even by as little as one month."[136] "Chemotherapy is basically ineffective in the *vast majority* of cases in which it is given.")[137] Of course, there are some cancers that respond well to chemotherapy (childhood leukemia and Hodgkin's disease being two),[138] but Moss further indicated "chemotherapy has reached the limits of its usefulness" for

---

[132] In 1994, the Scripps Research Institute in La Jolla, California, issued a press release that an experimental drug had shown promise in chicken eggs, not even rats or mice. But the Scripps news release claimed, "This approach not only is expected to eliminate primary tumors but also will likely prevent the metastatic spread of tumor cells by eliminating their access to the blood supply." Reporters would pick up on the last quote ("will likely prevent"), not the first ("shown promise"). Ibid., 26–27.

[133] The mass media and the oncology profession were locked in a codependent relationship. The doctors and Big Pharma companies needed skilled writers to interpret science for the layperson and publicize new treatments. The writers needed cancer doctors for access to breaking news and for jobs and freelance assignment. Moss, *Cancer, Incorporated*, 41.

[134] Ibid., 87.

[135] Moss, *Questioning Chemotherapy*, 81.

[136] Moss, *Cancer, Incorporated* 116.

[137] Ibid.

[138] Ibid., 163.

most advanced solid tumors of adults.[139] He quoted Senator Hubert Humphrey, just before his death from bladder cancer, calling chemotherapy "bottled death."[140]

> *The word "remission" to families of loved ones equates to "cured," but to oncologists it means approximately three more years of life.*

And as far as statistics go, they could be twisted to mean almost anything. A glowing report of over five thousand women receiving benefit from chemo for their breast cancer lost its luster when the full report showed that almost sixty-five thousand *other* women were treated with the same toxic drugs and *none* of the other women derived *any* benefit from the treatment.[141]

After just this brief review, Scott raised his eyebrows in dubious consternation. "When's the chemotherapy appointment?"

"Two days."

"Well, we'd better be ready for it."

---

[139] Ibid., 116.
[140] Ibid., 164.
[141] Ibid., 91.

CHAPTER 17

CHEMOTHERAPY APPOINTMENT

FEBRUARY

Scott talked optimistically about his cesium treatment and about wanting to live, but there was also an undercurrent about death. His grandmother had had a heart attack at age sixty (although she lived to age ninety-seven), and his father had died at age fifty-five from the heart attack he'd suffered at age fifty-four. The idea of a heart attack was an incessant worry to Scott. Another person he thought about a lot was Rex E. Lee, former U.S. solicitor general, president of Brigham Young University, and a personal friend of ours. Rex had been able to live an additional seven years after his diagnosis of terminal cancer. He was an inspiration to Scott, but a haunting figure as well. Scott couldn't help conjecturing, "Will I end up dying young— like Dad, like Rex?"

It was to stave off that eventuality that Scott wanted so many treatment choices investigated from both Western and Eastern origins. Though many other people choose to have chemotherapy, Scott didn't have a high opinion of it for his type of cancer. As soon as he had received a diagnosis, he had printed off fifty-eight pages on leiomyosarcoma from the American Cancer Society and the National Cancer Institute and had put them into a binder. One of the sentences he highlighted *and* underlined in all that information said, "The tumor's *response rate* to chemotherapy or radiation treatment is not high. The success rate is on the order of one third of the tumors showing response... *The cure rate*, however, is very, very low."[142] He instead wrote in his journal, "There are a *lot* of other treatments available. I am lucky, because I have choices."

Scott continued to have me rehearse sections of Ralph Moss's book to him. This time it involved the issue of money. What about the business side of chemotherapy? Most of us don't know anything about it.

In his 1995 book, Dr. Moss estimated that cancer was a $7 billion industry.[143] (To bring it to modern terms, it is now a $150 billion industry with an estimated 1.8 million new cases just in 2020.)[144] Moss said that from $5,000 to $65,000 per patient was spent on cytotoxic drugs, and that cancer hospital admissions generated two to three times the billing of non-cancer admissions, like stroke or heart attack.[145] (Moss's latest book states that cancer admissions now generate four times the revenue of what non-cancer admissions give[146] and that eleven of twelve FDA-approved cancer drugs cost $100,000 a year or

---

[142] www.leiomyosarcoma.org.

[143] Moss, *Questioning Chemotherapy*, 73.

[144] Moss, *Cancer, Incorporated*, 158; Samantha McGrail, "Cost of Cancer Care Reaches Nearly $150B Nationally," HealthPayerIntelligence, healthpayerintelligence.com/news/cost-of-cancer-care-reaches -nearly-150b-nationally.

[145] Moss, *Questioning Chemotherapy*, 74.

[146] Ibid., 77; healthpayerintelligence.com/news.

more.[147])[148] Moss's 1995 book listed out-of-pocket expenses[149] such as travel, hotels, childcare, additional sicknesses, and loss of work pay to be in the tens of thousands of dollars (and by 2020 that had not improved).[150] I concluded reading Moss's chapter: "The war on cancer is big business, and chemotherapy has become a major profit center for hospitals, doctors and drug companies."[151]

Scott looked up tiredly from his recliner while he patiently held cesium in his mouth. I waited for some acknowledgment of this information that we had previously read. He nodded and said, "Go on." Scott was so fatigued I couldn't imagine he wanted more, but I forged on a bit longer, reading highlighted parts of Moss's book concerning ethics.

Besides being a huge profit center for any facility, chemotherapy offers the darker angle of profit. The editor of the *JAMA* stated, "(It's) a marvelous opportunity for rampant deceit. So much money is there to be made that ethical principles can be overrun."[152]

> *At all costs, the public must be convinced that chemotherapy works, and that it is in their best interest to be quiet, take their medicine, and leave the thinking on such abstruse matters to those who wear white coats.*

Moss warned,

Did you hear this on the evening news? Of course not. Nobody in a position of authority will tell the public that toxic drugs are sometimes inappropriately

---

[147] McGrail, "Cost of Cancer Care"; Asbestos.com, 2019.

[148] By 2020, drug costs were no longer based on what it costs to produce them but on what the market could bear. See Moss's *Cancer Incorporated*, page 158 and for the example of Kymriah's actual production cost is $20,000, while the other 95 percent or so is profit. Another modern change is creating "new" drugs with a new name at twice the cost of the old drug but with no greater effectiveness, because it's basically the same as the old drug. See Moss's *Cancer Incorporated*, pages 58 and 73, and examples Zaltrap and Keytruda.

[149] Moss, *Questioning Chemotherapy*, 74.

[150] McGrail, "Cost of Cancer Care"; Asbestos.com, 2019.

[151] Moss, *Questioning Chemotherapy*, 80.

[152] Moss, *Questioning Chemotherapy*, 80.

administered, because it is financially beneficial for a great many people to do so. Quite the opposite. At all costs, the public must be convinced that chemotherapy works, and that it is in their best interest to be quiet, take their medicine, and leave the thinking on such abstruse matters to those who wear white coats. In my opinion, patients will do so at their peril.[153]

Another statement was just as chilling:

Dr. Ulrich Abel of the University of Heidelberg remarked [that] people take it for granted that if a notoriously toxic and expensive treatment cannot cure, it must at least have some beneficial effect on the patient's prognosis. But they are wrong.[154]

> *People take it for granted that if a notoriously toxic and expensive treatment cannot cure, it must at least have some beneficial effect. But they are wrong.*

One telling aspect was that many oncologists choose *not* to have chemotherapy when they themselves develop cancer. "An oncologist from Sloan Kettering was quoted, 'Do anything you want—but no chemotherapy!' He sent his own mother to Germany for 'unconventional treatment.'"[155] (As a personal reinforcement of that thought, the surgeon who had removed my enlarging thyroid in 1973 had investigated chemotherapy because of his wife's cancer. When he found Scott had leiomyosarcoma, he advised me, "Don't do chemo! It doesn't do any good."[156])

"Wow." Scott swallowed his cesium and then downed some supplements. "I'd forgotten how many inherent problems there are with chemo."

As we went to bed, I pondered Moss's information again. I thought, "Do newspapers *intend* to be deceitful? Do oncologists? Do hospitals? Do companies?" Well, I don't know about companies, but as for doctors, I don't think

---

[153] Ibid.

[154] Ibid., 32.

[155] Ibid., 40–41.

[156] Merrill Wilson in discussion with the author.

so. The doctors I know are wonderful, benevolent people who go into their field in a genuine effort to benefit mankind. They are caring, compassionate individuals. However, the business of chemotherapy nowadays *has* become a fertile ground for deception, fraud, and ego. And the public marches on, unaware of any problems concerning it. Scott, Mom B, and I were just as unaware until we did a bit of reading.

~

The day came for the dreaded chemotherapy appointment. We'd had three golden, un-chemo-fettered weeks in which Scott had been free to use cesium and to have vibrational healing sessions with Holly. They were his choice, they were doable, and they seemed useful to him. He could choose to use chemo, of course, but his fear of the appointment was that he would merely succumb to the expected pressure. Scott's mom offered to come down from Salt Lake; she felt the same way we did and wanted to protect him as much as she could. Scott assured her that the two of us would be fine.

As we got ready, Scott looked at me and said, "Do you remember that guy in Moss's book, the one who had a hard time leaving the clinic?"

I nodded. "Yes. He said that only after he'd agreed to start the chemo protocol did the oncologist let him be!"[157]

We'd already seen what "in-charge" doctors could be like from the radiation appointment with Dr. Hayes. "Well, I don't want that to be us." What he meant was that he wanted to retain more control. Using his meager strength, Scott helped me formulate a long list of questions.

(I would recommend that anyone going to a doctor's appointment take their questions and make sure they are answered. The physician is hired by you and is in service to you. You definitely want to know his or her opinion, but it's your appointment. Even more than that, it's your life. You are in charge.)

---

[157] Moss, *Questioning Chemotherapy*, 32.

Scott again assigned me to be the person the doctor dealt with. I appreciated his trust—it's one of the things I'd been *wishing* for—but after that experience with Dr. Hayes, the thought of talking to another oncologist scared me silly. Sensing my reticence, he gave me a priesthood blessing just before we left the house. Part of that blessing was to be strong and to hold to what we knew was true from what we'd read; that is, not to give in to the anticipated pressure to start chemo. Again, perhaps Scott would *choose* to have chemotherapy. I remembered those words that had come into my mind:

"Scott will make a choice; once chosen, it will be irrevocable."

I still assumed they meant that he would pick a treatment choice that would lead him to some end, but the treatment would be *his* choice. It would be a thought-out decision, not just default because it's expected, it's pressured, and because the majority of Americans do it.

∼

Dr. Lancaster, tall, energetic, and good-looking, was the main chemotherapy doctor at our local hospital, the Utah Valley Regional Medical Center. A nurse met with us first, and then he entered, donned in traditional white. He looked at the chart and looked down at my seated husband.

"Leiomyosarcoma, is it?" he questioned rhetorically.

"Yes," I answered.

"And it looks like radiation has not been recommended."

"That's what the tumor board said."

"Well, that's to be expected. The liver doesn't tolerate radiation well; cancer's more resistant than the liver is. You'll kill the liver three times by the time the cancer dies!"

"The surgeon indicated that Scott's cancer possibly started in the liver," I said.

Dr. Lancaster shook his head. "I'd say not. Leiomyosarcoma is a cancer of the smooth muscle. The liver has no smooth muscle. This cancer probably started in the bile ducts, or diaphragm, or in the liver's blood vessels."[158] Looking at a scan, he stated, "The cancer has replaced the right lobe of the liver and extended up the vena cava and out the chest wall."

He then told us about the success-rate statistics for sarcoma. "There is a possible 20 to 30 percent shrinkage, but complete remission is rare. A decreased tumor size will give a better quality and maybe quantity of life. For this kind of cancer, the agents (in other words, the toxic chemicals administered) are Gemzar and Taxotere. The two combined showed a 53 percent response, the best I've ever seen in papers. He won't be nauseated." Looking back at Scott, he smiled and said, "Yes, you'll lose your hair. But this doesn't permanently damage the immune system. The chemo has some bone marrow toxicity, which is totally reversible."

Despite what he just said, I indicated a reluctance to have chemo because it destroys the immune system.

Turning to me again, he said, "This cancer will reach a critical mass— millions of cells—and will kill him long before the lack of an immune system does. I think this one [i.e., Scott's tumor] has been there a while. He'll need to complete three cycles to make a dent."

After explaining the procedures—how many times a week he would come into the hospital for a cycle, drug levels, the expected side effects, what part insurance would pay, and so on, he said enthusiastically, "Well, shall we get started?"

He was all but jumping up to order the drugs brought in when I said levelly, "We're just here to investigate whether he would like chemotherapy. He's not starting it today."

I know it looks like just two sentences on paper, but they were hard for me to say. It is hard to oppose another person's opinion and energy when that energy is so directed and focused.

---

[158] Dr. Merrill Wilson later checked a physician's online register and found that zero cancers have started in the diaphragm. For all of us who speak or sing or breathe, it is a comfort to know what a stout organ the diaphragm is! Merrill Wilson in discussion with the author.

My words stopped him in his tracks. Obviously, he was not used to having people question his decisions. Nonplussed, he forged ahead, suddenly gone TV salesman—touting all the latest bells and whistles of chemo and what we would regret if we didn't accept his offer today. Except his offer was a product that would run poison through my husband's whole body.

He looked at us expectantly, assuming his words had changed our minds. They hadn't.

"We're just investigating," I said a little stronger.

Scott nudged me and whispered, "Tell him we'll let him know."

"We'll let you know if he wants to start."

He looked at us as if we were crazy—small children incapable of perceiving the truth—and said, "You'll want to get this started sooner than later."

Scott started to get up to leave, advising me softly, "Thank him. And be nice."

"Thank you for your time," I said.

"Well, let me know!" It was more of a command than a farewell.

As I walked Scott slowly back to the car, he said wryly, "That didn't go too badly."

Indeed, it had been less traumatic than I had thought it would be!

CHAPTER 18

RESEARCH AND CELL-SPECIFIC CANCER TREATMENT

FEBRUARY

As February proceeded, Scott felt horrible overall: the surgical incision healed with itches and prickles; persistent nausea cut into his energy and ability to eat; and holding the tasteless cesium in his mouth was detestable, although he did it. Overriding the discomfort of holding this substance in his mouth for long minutes was the pain in his side that was like having hot coals under his skin. When sleep came to him, it was an all-too-short relief.

Scott had now used three main treatments: cleansing, surgery, and elemental cesium high pH therapy. Being Scott, though, he wondered if those were all he could do and if they were the *best* he could do. He kept after me to thoroughly check treatment methods. I didn't know precisely what I was searching for on his behalf, but it was in the direction of a multidisciplinary approach—something that was more than chemo, more than surgery, more than—I didn't know what.

If we wanted something that was more encompassing than just chemo, surely that clinic in Mexico that I had called when my sister had cancer was a candidate. I looked online. To my surprise, their website was not as impressive as I remembered. Their treatment sounded dubious. Phrases stated, "This treatment *might* help..." or "This is *not* endorsed by..." Where was the certainty? The energy? The uniqueness? I thought, "Travel all the way to Mexico for what? It doesn't sound like they offer much anymore." I discounted that clinic and moved on.

I heard about the amazing MD Anderson Cancer Center in Texas and talked to a woman who had high praise for it. When I talked to someone at the facility, though, I found that their protocol for Scott's leiomyosarcoma was chemotherapy, and the chemotherapy used the same agents (Gemzar and Taxotere) as our local hospital. Their spacious center integrated other modalities, however. On-site specialists provided care with nutrition, emotional release, massage, and so on. Apparently, one could just walk across an atrium from the chemo appointment to the other professionals, with the scheduling juggled by one doctor. It sounded pretty good, but the drawback was the cost—$50,000! Unfortunately, we had just changed our insurance prior to the twins' missions, and our new policy didn't cover out-of-network facilities.

I went downstairs to tell Scott during dinner. Actually, I was the one who ate; he sat back in his recliner, holding cesium in his mouth. Twenty minutes later, when he could finally talk, he asked me many questions. He was always involved in what I had found. In this case, he was pretty downhearted about the cost at MD Anderson and the fact that we had just changed our insurance. After much discussion he directed, "Keep looking."

Over the course of the month, I contacted many more facilities. Some I found online and some I found through a network of people who believed in natural healing. (Hint: natural food stores are excellent places to start one's search for people or facilities that utilize integrative healing.) It was amazing how one lead would turn into another, and that lead would yield yet another. Once I started investigating the world of alternative treatments for cancer, there were more methods than I had imagined! We felt that many of them were answers to prayer. After all, our daily motto was:

Search diligently, pray always, and be believing, and all things shall work together for your good.[159]

> *Natural food stores are excellent places to start*
> *one's search for integrative healing.*

Several people again mentioned Germany, but I didn't contact any facility there. I called Tulsa, Houston, Reno, and San Diego. In all those places, however, when chemo was used as their primary source of treatment for leiomyosarcoma, it was always the same agents (Taxotere and Gemzar in combination or Adriamycin) that our local hospital utilized. It didn't make sense to travel away, incurring living expenses as well as the hardship for Scott in traveling, unless a great deal more was offered than what was available right here.

Every search for a facility took time in finding the right phone numbers to call. Every call took time to talk to the people in charge and find out what they had to offer. It took time after every conversation to think about and decide if this was an avenue that Scott could explore. The internet wasn't as Bing- and Google-friendly then and data wasn't nearly as readily accessible. All the while, the man I was doing this for was downstairs, and the computer and phone were upstairs. I was grateful for Scott's mom to be with him when she could be here. Nevertheless, I felt like I was missing out. Lots of times when I came down, they were talking about tender, deep topics, and I almost felt like I was interrupting.

One of the books Mom B read to him was a gift she'd given him, written by Neal A. Maxwell. Elder Maxwell, as he was called in the Church of Jesus

---

[159] Doctrine and Covenants 90:24. (I already cited this the first time I quoted it in Chapter 14.)

Christ of Latter-day Saints, had been academic vice president at the University of Utah prior to being called as an Apostle in the LDS Church. He was himself a cancer patient. Elder Maxwell's tremendous insights were always phrased beautifully, such as "God will tutor us by trying us *because* He loves us, not because of indifference!" and "Because our lives are foreseen by God, He is never surprised by developments within our lives. The sudden loss of health, wealth, self-esteem, status, or a loved one—developments that may stun us— are foreseen by God, though *not* necessarily caused by Him."[160]

Maxwell also built upon C. S. Lewis's analogy about God's "building a palace" when all we wanted was "a decent little cottage."[161] He described three different kinds of "remodeling" that cause suffering:

Type I is because of our own mistakes;

Type II is because of others' mistakes, and

Type III is the tribulation and suffering of the righteous.[162]

I saw later that Scott or his mom had underlined one of Maxwell's most important points: "whether or not an omnipotent God gives us a particular trial or simply declines to remove it. The outcome is obviously the same either way. God is willing for us to undergo that challenge . . . It is in our weakness and extremity that God's power is fully felt. Only when . . . we are helpless is His help truly appreciated."[163]

> *Only when we are helpless is His help truly appreciated.*

Elder Maxwell's words percolated in Scott's mind as he pondered the big things like God, trials, change, miracles, and forgiveness.

∾

---

[160] Neal A. Maxwell, *All These Things Shall Give Thee Experience* (Utah: Deseret Book Company, 1979), 28.

[161] Ibid., 29. See also Introduction.

[162] Ibid., 29–32.

[163] Ibid., 31.

I spent a lot of time on the phone and internet, but not much was truly panning out. The truth is that what we were looking for didn't seem to exist in the United States. Time was running out. Our neighborhood doctors, with furrowed brows, were warning me to do something fast. They didn't need to remind me; I could tell.

I looked through my scribbled paper in my sister's cancer folder to see if I'd missed anything important. Sideways, down in a corner, I saw the letters CSCT, and hope sprang in my heart. CSCT stood for Cell-Specific Cancer Treatment, a cancer center I'd heard about during an alternative health meeting. The sister-in-law of one of the inventors (ex-sister-in-law, she had corrected) had been at that meeting and had said that the CSCT device eradicated cancer cells without harming normal cells. After such an astounding statement, she was given the floor.

The CSCT device eradicated cancer cells without harming normal cells.

"My brother-in-law was part of a group of scientists in Tennessee who had a friend who died of cancer. It made them so mad; they thought they should have been able to do something to save him. So, two of them went to work for years and came up with a machine that works through magnetic arms and electromagnetic waves. The treatment doesn't hurt. One little gal actually got a tan on the beach while she was receiving treatment for Ewing's sarcoma."

Someone in the audience laughingly asked, "Where's the tanning beach in Tennessee?"

She replied, "Oh, they're not in America anymore. After they used it successfully for a while, they were "invited" to leave. The center is now in the Dominican Republic."

～

As I thought on that meeting, I remember how intrigued I'd been by her statements because Scott and I dealt with magnetic technology for healing (although we handled static magnets, and at a much lower gauss than CSCT undoubtedly used). The first time I had *ever* heard about magnets used for healing was an expensive, high-gauss treatment in Texas. A fourteen-year-old girl from Cedar City, Utah, had not found help anywhere for her ailment. She had hobbled into the clinic in Texas on crutches, and $7,000 later she walked out perfectly fine.[164] I was in the middle of grad school when I read that, and I was absolutely flabbergasted!

Even though the idea was new and I found it so unlikely, it turns out that magnetism "reestablishes order in the energy system and thereby allows healing to take place."[165] It makes sense; magnetism is one of the forces, like gravity, that holds together our earth and our bodies. As an example, the photo of a bruise forming two concentric circles shows that the healing was not random; the healing followed the round form of the round health magnet. Not only that, the health magnet caused the healing to advance more rapidly, as seen by the light-colored healthy skin in the center.

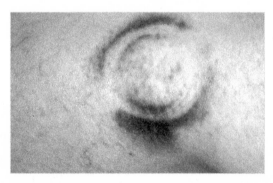

Bruising on a leg is affected by a round health magnet

After five years in our business, Scott and I had seen and experienced numerous benefits ourselves. One experience I personally had was while pickaxing some tenacious hollyhocks for an hour. I had placed a flat health

---

[164] "Magnetic Healing," *Deseret News*, September 3, 1997, C1.
[165] Valerie Free, *Complementary Healing: Magnetic Therapy* (Connecticut: MLMC, 1997), 7.

magnet (about the size of your splayed hand) on my lower back during that strenuous hour, and afterward I didn't have any bad effects. But the next year when only a few of the same persistent plants popped up, and I knew I wouldn't be outside as long, I didn't bother to put that large magnet at my back. Bad choice: I ended up in a world of hurt for three days afterward!

Health magnets and other energy technologies like far infrared were generally used for prevention and increasing overall wellness.[166] The magnetic device that the woman in the meeting had talked of, however, was different. As I looked at those four letters—CSCT—jotted down the side of my sister's folder, I realized they evoked thoughts such as "safe," "noninvasive," and "uncompromised immune system." I rummaged around in more papers and, amazingly, found one of their brochures I didn't even know I had. It had a phone number from the company. I ran downstairs to see if Scott remembered the meeting where the ex-sister-in-law had spoken.

Scott's mom was back and was rinsing dishes at the sink while he was occupied holding cesium in his mouth. I kissed him gently on top of his head so as to not disturb his concentration, and then I grabbed a sandwich for lunch. A while later, when it looked like he was getting to the end of his "holding" time, I asked if he remembered hearing about CSCT at a meeting. He nodded, and I read to him from their literature: "Cancer cells can be precisely targeted and destroyed by physicians using an energy beam. Their cancer treatment approach is simple yet radical: kill the cancer cells with magnetic energy from the CSCT-200." He nodded again in recognition.

I went on. "Do you remember the story of the fourteen-year-old girl? She got a tan on the beach during her eighteen treatments! When she flew back to New England with her mom, MRIs and CT scans revealed no signs of cancer." I read, "While at the hospital (in Connecticut), the girl, April, and her mother found themselves in the midst of fourteen children milling about. Each had a bald head and a very pale, whitish complexion. The mother thought, 'Why

---

[166] Read about far infrared waves that induce greater health in Whang, *Reverse Aging*, 79–89.

can't they just get a CSCT machine in here and help these kids? Why put them through all this? I felt almost guilty sitting there with a nicely tanned, healthy teenager who was spared all of this.'" April was currently healthy at age twenty.[167]

I quoted another statement from the brochure: "The therapy is designed to kill active cancerous cells in a patient's body, even after metastasis has occurred and even in Stage IV cancers, without causing any damage to healthy cells. There are no side effects and no aftereffects."[168]

I continued. "I have a phone number for them. Do you want me to call?"

He swallowed then and said, "Yes. Call them."

As I zipped upstairs, I heard him call behind me: "And try to find Neal's number. I've got a question about the cesium."

~

The CSCT brochure cover proudly proclaimed centers in "England, Tijuana, and the Dominican Republic." I only had the number for Tijuana, but that was okay because that center was the closest. To my astonishment, the person who answered the phone was in Canada. I was confused for a moment until he assured me that he was, indeed, the phone contact for the Tijuana office. The fellow's name was John Anderton. He answered all my questions and then some! John was a naturopath, a scientist, and the contact person for the center. He was also a past patient who'd had two kinds of cancer—skin and brain. Both had been eradicated by Cell-Specific Cancer Treatment. The latter was impressive because brain cancer was especially hard to conquer. John explained, "CSCT uses magnetic waves instead of chemicals, which have a hard time crossing the blood-brain barrier; so CSCT works, and it's safer." He chuckled wryly, and said, "We actually got rid of the brain cancer more easily than the skin cancer."

---

[167] CSCT brochure (England, Mexico, Dominican Republic), 1–2.
[168] Ibid.

I began asking questions, and John started rattling off answers, many of them with scientific words and phrases that I barely recognized. I figured my brilliant husband would understand, so I grabbed a sheet of paper and quickly wrote whatever he said. John was so excited to talk to someone interested about CSCT that he talked for a solid hour!

He said that this process was good for any kind of sarcoma or cancer. It located cancer cells; it didn't care what kind they were, how they were labeled, or where they had started. He told me about the CSCT machine. The machine worked somewhat like radar, but the "blips" it found were cancer cells that stood out from normal cells because of a unique characteristic: ionization. In the brochure, the director, Michael Reynolds, said that a cancer cell was "like a beacon:"[169]

> Normal cells make use of at least 90 percent of their nutrients, but cancer cells are highly wasteful, crude, and inefficient metabolizers, leaving behind about 80 percent of the raw materials. Perhaps as a result of this, they give off an excessive amount of ions, far more than normal cells. It is this excessive ionization that the Center's device is able to pinpoint.[170]

John explained the process to me. The patient lies on a table, and a device with an array of permanent magnets passes over the top of the person. It doesn't touch the person, is painless, and is done in an open room—there is no claustrophobic, confining feeling for the person. "The machine goes on diagnostic mode first, and any cancer is marked on the patient's body. What we don't know is whether it's one cell or a thousand, but the site gets marked."

"How is it marked?" I asked.

He laughed sheepishly. "With a normal purple marker."

I chuckled too, envisioning purple "pimples" all over someone's body.

"Later that day or the next day, the machine's frequency is changed—kind of like tuning to FM from AM—and we start killing the cancer cells. The old

---

[169] Ibid., 6.
[170] Ibid.

doughnut-shaped ring, the CSCT-200, had a focal area that was harder to control. Our new Zoetron with two magnetic arms is more precise. One arm lifts and locks the cells in place."

"Kind of like the iron filings my dad gave me to play with as a child?" I asked. "When you passed a magnet under the paper holding them, they stood up straight, like soldiers."

"Yes, kind of like that," he agreed. "The other arm, the one at ninety degrees, rotates at 120 times per second. You see, there is an iron-rich sludge left in cancerous cells, and these cells are lifted and twisted sideways. They literally swirl themselves to death."[171] This only happened to the cancerous cells; that's why the facility was called Cell-*Specific* Cancer Treatment.

He went on. "It is possible that the Zoetron therapy may be able to reduce the level of cancerous tissue in your husband's body to a point where the immune system, even though currently compromised, can take over the job of controlling the remaining level of cancer." He said it generally took around thirty hours of treatment to get rid of all the cancer cells, and that takes two to three weeks. The process was paced so the body has time to eliminate the toxic cancer cells.

Also extremely important were clinicians in a nearby network to help with diet, detoxification, and immune therapy. This was definitely a multi-disciplinary center!

John pointed out, "Cancer isn't the *cause* of disease. It's a whole lot of trouble, but not the principal source of toxicity. *Food supply plus polluted environment plus troubled spiritual or mental state—that's what equals a toxic soup that lets cancer get a foothold.*" (There was that idea again about the mind having something to do with physical health.)

---

[171] "First there is an array of low-strength permanent magnets that create a steady electromagnetic field. Second, there is an electromagnetic coil that passes through this array. The result is a complex interacting electromagnetic field [that can be] manipulate[d], somewhat like fine-tuning a radio. This fact explains why the device's core technology in scientific jargon is called a frequency-modulated, pulsed electromagnetic field." Ibid.

"Food supply plus polluted environment plus troubled spiritual or mental state—that's what equals a toxic soup that lets cancer get a foothold."

John was not happy to hear that Scott was on OxyContin and mentioned in passing that drug companies give $2 million to medical schools. He was happy, however, to hear that we had started detoxification and immune enhancement two months ago. In speaking of cleansing and detoxing, he referred to Dr. Christopher—the master naturopath who Becky and Dr. Schulze admired—so that was nice to know they were all on the same page.

"It is of the greatest priority that you seek out the appropriate health advisor in your home area and keep working on detoxing. As cells are destroyed, your husband needs to eliminate those waste materials."

John told us we need the nutrients that actual foods give us, not just isolated components. "Garlic has four hundred compounds," he said, "and we use *all* of them, not just one. So we don't want to take a garlic supplement; we want to take garlic." He also agreed with those who said that sugar was part of the "toxic soup" that lets disease get a foothold. "Sugar is acid; it leaches calcium and undermines the immune system for at least four hours after. It also slows metabolism, making it harder to lose weight." He said that he happened to know that the highest per capita sugar consumption in the U.S. was in my state. Ouch![172]

Feeling fairly comfortable with the hour's information, I took a breath and asked the big question: "What is the cost?"

John said it was a flat fee of $10,000. What a chunk, and all out of pocket![173] (To put money in context, though, conventional treatment of cancer, from diagnosis to death, can often cost $350,000. Even if the patient only pays 10

---

[172] "A study from the Hershey Co. found that Utahns lead the country in candy consumption. Residents of the Beehive State buy sweets at a rate that is nearly double the national average." *Deseret News*, May 14, 2015.

[173] Ten thousand dollars is a typical amount for many treatment centers in Mexico. Americans have a misconception that their chemo or radiation treatment is free because it is covered by insurance. Yet for every procedure, a person will pay roughly 10 percent or more out of pocket.

percent of it, that's $35,000 out of pocket.) John surprised me by saying that there was a full refund policy if a patient were deemed to receive no benefit by CSCT.[174] I thought that was very honest of them. I wasn't worried about Scott's being accepted, though. I knew he was a perfect candidate for them. Other than this tumor in his side, he was extremely fit.

I continued. "Where does a person stay this whole time?"

"There are places near the center where you stay." Well, that would mean more money.

As a last disclaimer, John said that the Zoetron machine killed all the cancer cells currently in the body but couldn't do anything with cancer that might crop up in the future.

John faxed us the application and encouraged us to hustle it in so that my husband could get on their list as quickly as possible.

I hung up and went downstairs to share with Scott everything I had written down. Sure enough, Scott understood it all. From his science background, he understood "glucose skipping the Krebs cycle"; from his chemical engineering training he understood "excites and heats particles by hysteresis"; and from his Air Force radio training he understood "radio-frequency oblation." *Everything* that scientist John said made sense to engineer Scott.

I marveled later that my husband never once doubted the information I relayed from John. So, here's a question, and it's a valid one: I am in Utah talking to a man in Canada about a pretty incredible machine from Tennessee that was now shunted off to the Dominican Republic. How does one determine whether a person you're talking to is honest? A large part of the answer is the tone of voice. Since I'm a voice teacher and an actress, I'm attuned to the sound of people's voices. People who want to share precious information have an innate excitement to their voices, which John had. Likewise, people who are protecting themselves have a subdued, restrained cautiousness to their voices, like Rosa and Nurse Lorna both had.

---

[174] "In the event that the CSCT device is unable to confirm my original diagnosis, the patient will not be admitted for treatment and any fees paid will be refunded in full." CSCT brochure.

Two other important parts of the honesty puzzle are delivery and vocabulary. We all know the mechanical sound of a telemarketer—someone who doggedly moves on to the next line in their script regardless of what you just said. (We could tell lots of jokes at this point!) John wasn't like that; he changed direction in direct response to my queries. That means he knew his material; it wasn't some memorized script.[175] As far as vocabulary, someone trying to pull the wool over your eyes would not talk freely but would use a prescribed set of words (i.e., words not of their own vocabulary, but words given to them by someone else). Because the words they were using were slightly unfamiliar, they might even sound halting in their speech. John did not halt, he didn't repeat, and he didn't "dumb down" scientific terms. (Did he really think I understood "viscosity in the cells" or "significant metabolic disruption"?) John just talked the way John talks.

After sharing what he had said, Scott and I discussed the process, the cost, transportation, and living expenses. Then Scott listed the pros and cons out loud. Pros and cons—that's how he always made a decision. He would make two lists—usually on a whiteboard—and whichever list had the most items, that's what he chose. That's how he chose to return to graduate school; that's how he decided to start a home-based business; and that's how he decided to start his chemical engineering career at BYU rather than at other facilities that offered. When he finished talking, he looked at me knowingly, his dark eyes glinting like tiger-eye gems. The pros of this program hugely outweighed the cons.

"What do you think?" I asked him.

He smiled broadly then, openly hopeful. "Maybe this is the miracle we've been looking for. Fax in the application *today*."

He stayed on me until I filled out the lengthy application and faxed it

---

[175] Listening to delivery is actually how I made it through graduate school with six children when the older two were on missions. I didn't have time to study the way I had when I was in college, so I paid attention to the things that the teachers' voices emphasized (speaking higher, speaking stronger, or repeating), and sure enough, *those* were the things that were on the tests!

in. John had said Scott sounded like the perfect candidate and that it would only take three days to process. Just three days. We sat back excitedly to wait.

CHAPTER 19

THE MIND INFLUENCES BEHAVIOR

FEBRUARY

So much was happening! Scott was feeling better from his nutritional IV, and his mom was helping him take all his powerful supplements. We'd faxed in his CSCT application, and Holly was coming every three days for a session with him.

Scott enjoyed Holly, with her soft words and gentle touch. She always made sure to tell him what she was doing, asking often if he was okay, because she sensed that the energy work she was doing was a little out of his comfort zone. I think Holly sensed his ambivalence better than anyone. She knew that Scott, in his home-based business, used energy technologies in the form of objects you could hold in your hands. But she could tell that *this* arcane and unseen part of science—this *feeling* of energy without holding any device in your hand—made him mentally squirm, like he didn't know where he stood. Actually, that would describe many of us!

Holly also knew he was trying to understand. She frankly praised his efforts at getting outside of his sequestered "engineer's box" and entering the relationship-based world that a home-based business required. Like us, she had attended many a lecture by Wayne Dyer, Bob Proctor, Jim Rohn, Joel Barker, and others whose aim was helping entrepreneurs to be relationship-oriented, to act differently than they had before, and to *believe* differently so that they could lead a business. (What a daunting task those speakers have, to help any of us turn dreams into reality by changing "the six inches between our ears"!)

The work that Holly was doing in energy sessions is often referred to as processing, or Three-Dimensional Therapy sessions (mind-body-spirit). A session allows access to problems, situations, and beliefs deep within a person and then helps to process through them and to let them go if the person chooses. While the facilitator is working with a person, the person's mind processes thoughts on an intellectual level while the body, unbeknownst, processes vibrations on a cellular level. Even after the session, the body continues to internally process what has been done. The result is growth, progress, and relief as old negativities are released and new paradigms are formed.

> *While the facilitator is working with a person, the person's body, unbeknownst, processes vibrations on a cellular level. Even after the session, the body continues to internally process what has been done.*

Many times—perhaps most of the time, as before stated—situations are buried in the subconscious. We don't even know they're there! (Thus, the title of Karol Truman's classic book *Feelings Buried Alive Never Die*.)[176] Conditions may even have come via our DNA, passed on to us at birth, and thus are generational. They become a paradigm of how we approach the world, but we can't fix or change them because, again, we don't even know

---

[176] Truman, *Feelings Buried Alive.*

these problem-paradigms exist!

A true story that shows how something lodges subconsciously in the brain and then causes subsequent choices came through a fellow I'll call Michael. Michael was a thirtysomething man who was an assistant to a national lecturer. He made good money, and he liked to buy shoes with his earnings. Michael owned thirty pairs! One day he realized that all his shoes were slip-ons, except for one pair. Now, *he* had bought these shoes; they hadn't just walked into his house. "Why," he wondered, "have I chosen to buy, almost exclusively, shoes that don't have laces?"

He put that question to himself and left it there for a few days or weeks. At last, a picture of a Thanksgiving when he was just a little boy came into his mind. He had worked for a long time in his bedroom figuring out how to tie his shoes. Successful at last, he bounded elatedly into the room where everyone was and proudly announced, "I can tie my shoes!" An uncle reached down, undid a lace, and said, "Do it again for us." But now the little boy was under pressure. He heard the sudden silence in the room, and he felt every eye watching him. He tried and tried and tried, but he couldn't retie his shoe. He ran back into his bedroom crying.

Now this does not seem like a horribly scarring experience. If any of us were the uncle, we wouldn't have thought twice about the situation. I like to think that his uncle was just joking, like any of my four sons might do. But it wasn't a joke to the little guy. It was important enough that it stayed in his psyche for more than thirty years! When he realized there was a pattern here of his own making and could think through what had caused it, he could then let it go.[177] Of course, some things are easy to let go, like a desire for a certain

---

[177] Of ideas staying in the psyche, K. K. Bajaj explains, "The cells of our body are always regenerating themselves. So why is it that a liver cell riddled with cancer in January would still be riddled with cancer in June? Dr. Deepak Chopra said all of us have 'phantom memories' stored inside our cells. The degenerated cell [contains] a traumatic memory of some unpleasant incident in life. Before that degenerated cell dies, it passes that [unpleasant incident] on to the next cell generation being born. Thus, the cells keep replicating themselves, passing on traumatic memory from one cell generation to the next and so on." K. K. Bajaj, "Miracles of Drugless Cellular Healing," *Investors India*, February 2020, https://www.magzter.com/stories/Investment/Investors-India/MIRACLES-OF-DRUGLESS-CELLULAR-HEALING.

shoe. Others are not, and we go down kicking and screaming before we'll let something go out of us.

> *It was important enough that it stayed in his psyche for more than thirty years!*

When I think about "kicking and screaming," I think about a processing session I had through the Institute of Healing Arts.[178] I went with a list of thoughts and questions to a facilitator named Tara who used modalities advocated by the Institute's founder, Pam Robinson. I liked the methods Tara used. Anytime she saw that I was mentally holding on to something that wasn't useful, she asked me if I could take that little bit of negativity and assign a shape to it. I could. She asked if it had a color. It did. Then she asked if I could put it in an imaginary basket off to the side. I mentally did that too. The basket became filled with mismatched oddities—an orange triangle, a green box, a reddish-orange ball, a ghastly amoeba-shaped mass that was puke yellow-green, a brown bundle whose shape I really couldn't identify.

After a while, Tara said, "Someone enters the room now. This person is the grandest, most noble person you know. It could be Mohammed. It could be a teacher. It may be your grandfather. Who is your person, Elaine?"

Of course, for me, it was the Savior, Jesus Christ.

Tara quietly said, "He's come for your basket. Can you give it to Him?" Tears sprang to my eyes. No! I didn't want Him to have that! Of all people, I wanted Him to have the best basket—the happy times I'd read to my children, the fun times we'd cooked together in the kitchen, my music, my love of colorful spring flowers, of rivers and trees and colors in the autumn. I wanted Him to have—then I thought, "But that's why He came. He came to take the bad away."

Reluctantly and rather embarrassed, I said, "Yes, I'll let Him have it."

And as soon as I said "Yes"—the *instant* I decided to let Him have it—the

---

[178] "Biofeedback energy worker Deepak Chari tells of the process that identifies negative emotions that are being stored in the body." Pam Robinson, *Institute of Healing Arts Newsletter*, Fall 2011, ihaofutah.com.

basket with its odd shapes vanished! It was gone, as if it had never been! My burden was lifted immediately, and in its place was lightness and contentment. I truly felt that my spirit had touched Heaven because it felt lighter, happier, and more peaceful.[179] Others might discount this mental exercise as not real because it happened only in the mind, but what is in the mind is perceived as real, and therefore *is* real to the psyche. Besides, what Tara did seemed to access God, and that made it especially real.

~

Holly knew that Scott had made changes but that he would make even greater improvement by better understanding how thoughts influence behavior. She listed five specific ways that the mind sends out directives unconsciously. She even made a chart that an orderly engineer's mind would appreciate.[180] Holly encouraged Scott and me to take a step back and look at the ways we responded to others to see if we could identify any of the four negative areas that were driving us and to increase positive thoughts in the fifth area.[181]

Thoughts influence behavior.

Scott *was* changing. He was working on being "creative, not competitive" and focusing on "an abundant, infinite supply" rather than feeling that life was limited and narrow.[182] Actually, as soon as Scott had started his own business, his brother-in-law, Kurt, had noticed that he was becoming more outgoing, confident, energetic, and compassionate. Scott's circle of caring for his family and church members had expanded to the people he worked with as he helped

---

[179] As an interesting note, at a later session, I had a couple of shapes in my basket that I wouldn't give up at that time. I knew it was stupid—purposely keeping negativity—but I felt like I had to be honest.

[180] See Appendix C, Holly's Chart of Five Categories Showing How Scott Felt.

[181] "Changing the feeling (i.e., the root of the unrest) changes the thinking (the result)." Karol Truman in discussion with the author, December 5, 2016. An avenue of change is through her script: Truman, *Feelings Buried Alive*, 95.

[182] Scott's personal seminar notes from You Were Born Rich.

them, watched them, and worried about them. It was really very sweet; he truly loved those people who looked to him for help. Now I wondered, would he really be able to change in these areas Holly had suggested? Because change is what it's all about! One man talked about change in terms of light and dark. He actually explained *how* to change:

> Dissonance…is like darkness in a room. It does little good to scold the darkness. We must displace the darkness by introducing light.[183]

Dissonance…is like darkness in a room. It does little good to scold the darkness. We must displace the darkness by introducing light.

Five Ways the Mind Unconsciously Gives Directives

- Self-fulfilling prophecies
- Negative broadcast messages
- Emotions, which are feelings and thoughts
- Faulty core beliefs
- Positive statements

The classic book by Karol Truman that Holly had recommended was written to encourage change. (Watch out if you start highlighting; you might highlight the whole book!) Near the beginning, Truman admonished, "It is imperative that we learn to identify negative feelings and thoughts. This is necessary before [it becomes] automatic, and we are able to be happier, more cheerful, more appreciative and more caring much of the time."[184] Motivational speaker and philosopher Wayne Dyer put it simply: "Change is what it's all about! If you change the way you look at things, the things you look at change."[185]

---

[183] Wilford W. Andersen, *Ensign*, May 2015, 55.

[184] Truman, *Feelings Buried Alive*, 6.

[185] Brainyquote.com/quotes/wayne_dyer_384142#.

Several times in his life when Scott did identify a change that was needed, he did so in a very unusual fashion: he just switched—abruptly, absolutely, and 180 degrees! An example of this was how he yelled passionately and vehemently at basketball games, which he did for well over twenty-five years. On the day he stopped, I even heard him say, "I think it's terrible how people yell at the refs." Wow, Scott!

Well, the change that was occurring now was going much more slowly, but I was so proud of him that he allowed himself to talk with Holly about his struggles and conflicts! Trying to figure out his age-thirteen mystery had opened up something in him that allowed him to keep exploring his past, even with someone he didn't know well. It was pleasant to hear them: she with her gentle nonjudgmental charity and he, feeling safe, telling her things he wouldn't normally share. He told her of his frustration in getting a Ph.D. without much guidance, of his difficulty as a newly hired assistant professor who spent inordinate hours working on a marvelous brochure (one that the university used for years, by the way) only to later discover that any other teacher would have given it only a cursory touch as it didn't create any progress toward tenure. He told of being assigned his first year to teach the most difficult undergrad chemical engineering class there was because a seasoned professor of sixteen years wouldn't touch it. (Scott said, "It was like teaching Spanish because they'd found out I spoke Japanese.") The negative student comments from that class were a stain on his record, and that was part of what contributed to his lack of continuing status. The hurt was still there in his voice when he told her how he felt when that happened, and how the wind had been taken from his wings. He hadn't had the heart afterward to continue trying for tenure.

Just like Holly's chart showed, there were such burdens on his shoulders! And Scott took responsibility for everything, working his hardest to make things happen in so many areas. I thought of all the places where the "buck stopped" with him: our home-based business; paying the mortgage; maintaining the house, yard, and cars; church responsibilities; the family; and now as a consultant at the university rather than as a professor. (I had no idea how much he protected me until he was gone and the buck now stopped with me!)

In addition, there were *so* many things he did to care for other people. He didn't see them as burdens, but he did have to schedule them in. His work was flexible enough that he was able to go to all of our children's sports games— he never missed one. And for a church assignment, he and one of our sons were "home teachers" to a ninety-year-old lady and her family, as well as a widow, daughter, and granddaughter in another family, visiting monthly to see how they were doing, helping if needed, and bringing a Gospel message. He worked in the Scouting program, making each month's meeting more special and fun than the last. He was also the oldest son in his family of origin, and he felt a great responsibility toward his divorced mother. And of course, everything, in all these areas, had to be done fully and perfectly. He gave and gave. One of the most important ways he gave as a father was by staying in a career that was not entirely fulfilling for him so that he could provide for his family. (At one point he had decided that being in the medical field would be more fulfilling, and he was prepared to go back to school. However, that was the autumn that the twins were born, and with five children ages seven and under, neither one of us felt right about his pursuing a different career. So he stayed in engineering, which wasn't as fulfilling to him, but where he really was a good breadwinner.) In so many other aspects of life, though, he was unprepared for the burdens he shouldered. Like any of us, he just did the best he could.

> In so many other aspects of life, though, he was unprepared for the burdens he shouldered. Like any of us, he just did the best he could.

~

As Holly was leaving, she asked Scott if he had made any headway with figuring out what the age-thirteen experience was that he was still carrying. He shook his head. He'd really thought about it, but he'd come up empty.

"Keep working on it, Scott," she said, smiling. "It's important."

As soon as she'd left, he thought more on it but only came up with typical memories from awkward early teenhood. None of them resonated with the truth that it was the emotion that his body had held on to. He had me call his mom back down to the family room.

"Holly's asking me to think of something that happened to me when I was about thirteen," he told her in consternation. "I've thought and thought and can't think of anything. Can you?"

She surprised us by saying immediately, "I know what it was."

Wide-eyed, we listened to her story.

Scott's father, Blair, managed his father's (Scott's grandfather Sheldon's) Seagull Motel in Salt Lake City. When Scott was a young teenager, he worked there too. The motel represented both good and bad. Some of the good was learning to swim there (every kid's dream on a hot summer day!) and earning money by working there. But the bad was the constant tension his father exuded in working there. You see, a crazy lawsuit in 1951 had cost Blair $10,000. Since his father had paid the debt, Blair was required to work at his dad's motel to pay it back. High-strung Blair felt chained to the motel. Blair loved his children and was a great father to them, but he often seemed frustrated with life.

One particular day, Blair could not find some keys to the motel. It took over half an hour to drive clear across town from the west side to their house on the eastern foothills, and another half hour to drive back to the motel, so coming home in the middle of the day was a big deal and further added to his stress. "Finding those keys was vital to your dad. Both of you started looking frantically through the house. I think he held you responsible for the loss. He finally found the keys and stormed out the door to his car. You raced after him calling, 'Dad, wait! Come back.' He didn't even acknowledge you. He threw the car into reverse and gunned it down the driveway and down the road with you standing on the lawn calling after him. You fell prostrate on the grass sobbing, and I stood in the doorway and watched the whole thing."

A profound sadness settled over all of us as Scott nodded that it was, indeed, the right story. We pictured that slim young boy being left behind by the man whose opinion mattered most. Both Mom B and I went to him to stroke his hair and hug him, as he became again, for a moment, that thirteen-year-old boy.

Examples of How the Mind Unconsciously Sends Out Directives

1. **Self-fulfilling prophecies** are ideas or feelings that fuel the subconscious mind's desire to always be right. My favorite illustration is from child-development professor Elliot Landau.[186] I have paraphrased his story about a preschool-aged boy I'll call Johnny.

   > Johnny sat in the back seat of their car drinking a soda while his mother drove and his grandmother sat in the front passenger seat. Johnny was a sweet little boy, very obedient and a delight to be around. His grandmother turned around and beamed at him, saying, "What a good boy you are." Unfortunately, she said that at the precise moment the car braked suddenly, and he spilled his drink. Johnny's eyes widened with alarm; he *wasn't* a good boy. He *knew* he wasn't a good boy because spilling his drink was bad! Thereafter he became rebellious, and he acted out a lot. He changed because he had to justify the truth as he knew it—that he was a bad boy.

2. **Negative broadcast messages** are subconscious ideas or feelings that are sent out to others through body language. The message may be "I'm a lousy person" or "Everyone is above me" or "Everyone is below me." As a personal example, one time our daughter Katie came home after attending both dance and piano lessons on the same day, which was an unusual occurrence. *Both* of her very nice, very religious teachers had sworn at her. She was understandably upset. However, it was *so* uncharacteristic of either of them to swear that instead of giving her sympathy, I chuckled, "You must have had a sign on your forehead that said, 'Kick me!'" For

---

[186] Elliot Landau (1925–1991), writer on child development in the *Deseret News*, family therapist, author, and teacher at the University of Utah's Graduate School of Education for more than thirty years.

some reason, on that particular day, she'd broadcast a negative message that said, "Make me your victim."

3. **Emotions** (or what Dr. Bradley Nelson calls "trapped emotions") are feelings surrounding an issue that a person has unconsciously held on to. Amy Scher, an energy worker, lists the top ten most common emotions that get stuck: anxiety, disgust, grief, and feeling criticized, unsupported, unsafe, overwhelmed, worthless, helpless, and conflicted.[187] In the case of the forty-two-year-old woman that Dr. Nelson helped, the emotion that manifested itself was sadness; she was grief-stricken at being left after both her divorce and her father's death.[188]

4. **Faulty core beliefs** are the embedded paradigms that tend to make us act a certain way, like Michael's unconscious desire for slip-on shoes. It is a core belief that causes a person to believe that life has to be a certain way. All of us live by core beliefs. Perhaps the most famous story about core beliefs is that of the Swiss watchmakers. Paraphrasing author and lecturer Joel Barker's telling of it:

   In 1968, the Swiss held more than 80 percent of world profits for finely made watches. In 1967, researchers from Switzerland invented revolutionary quartz movement and presented it to Swiss manufacturers. It was rejected because it didn't have a mainspring, it didn't need bearings, it required almost no gears, it was battery-powered, and it was electronic. It couldn't possibly be the watch of the future. So sure were the manufacturers of that conclusion that they let their researchers showcase their useless invention at the World Watch Congress that year. Seiko took one look, and the rest is history. Between 1979 and 1981, fifty thousand of the sixty-two thousand Swiss watchmakers lost their jobs.[189]

5. A fifth area was composed of **positive statements** that encourage one to let go of the negative and embrace positive change. Positive thoughts are like affirmations: "I am calm, quiet, and relaxed" or "I let go of feelings of despair and loneliness." In a similar vein, see the affirmations on the following page.

---

[187] Amy B. Scher, "The Top 10 Most Commonly Stuck Emotions in the Body," Amybscher.com/top-10-most-common-trapped-negative-emotions/.

[188] Nelson, Chapter 13, "Vibrations are Unseen Energy."

[189] Joel Barker, *Paradigms: The Business of Discovering the Future* (New York: Harper Business, 1992), 15–18.

AFFIRMATIONS

~

I am loved because I was born.
I am safe feeling my feelings.
I am a balanced and vibrant fourth chakra.
I am safe to give and receive love.
I am loving myself and sharing that love.
I am forgiving.
I am forgiving.
I am forgiving.
I am loved and supported by God.

—Carol Tuttle[190]

Today you are you! That is truer than true!
There is no one alive who is you-er than you!

—Dr. Seuss[191]

I am enough. I have enough. I do enough.
What others think of me is enough.

—Terry Cole-Whittaker[192]

---

[190] Carol Tuttle, "Root Chakra: Open and Heal Your Muladhara for Safety and Security," Carol Tuttle, https://ct.liveyourtruth.com/root-chakra-open-and-heal-your-muladhara-for-safety-and-security/?_kx=kOPcP WApBzlz7TDGZdMsvi0-nHDYW2-HkkeGeaoFvb8%3D.fektq7.

[191] Dr. Seuss, *Happy Birthday to You!* (New York: Random House Books, 1959).

[192] Terry Cole-Whittaker, *Live Your Bliss: Practices That Produce Happiness and Prosperity* (California: New World Library, 2009), 115.

CHAPTER 20

MESSAGES FROM BEYOND

FEBRUARY

Mom B's revelation about Scott's age-thirteen experience solidified a conclusion I had reached concerning a discontent Scott had with life; it was that I, his wife, was *not* the source of his unease. Over the years, I saw that the changes I had made to improve our relationship did little to alter his censures. No matter what I did, I never measured up. Finally, I realized: it wasn't me! It never had been. It was Scott's own internal discontent.

The next step of discovery was to find out "discontent with whom?" It wasn't with his mother. As the oldest child, he had a strong bond with her and felt protective of her. It wasn't with his grandfather, the one who accompanied Scott to his Eagle Court of Honor, took him on trips and to amusement parks, and let him swim at his motel. There was a strong bond there. The person I felt was the cause of his discontent was his father, Blair.

Black-haired Blair was a cool guy—slim, handsome, and athletic, lover of boating, Hawaii, ukuleles, and his children. His overdrive energy helped him to earn a Ph.D. and become a champion tennis player (singles and doubles) and skier (along with Scott, he had taught our older children to ski). He was the personnel director of Granite School District in Salt Lake City, Utah, and actually signed my checks when I taught elementary school in his district for three years, although I didn't know that at the time. When Scott was one year old, Blair had served an LDS mission in Hawaii, leaving his wife and child back in Utah for two years. Husbands leaving families to serve missions had been a practice of the LDS Church back in the 1800s. Blair, as a married man, was only allowed to go on a mission because so many of the unmarried men were involved in the Korean War. He was in one of the last groups ever called to go on LDS missions *after* being married. I think because of his dad's being gone those two years, Scott lacked a bonding or belonging. I do know his dad's approbation was *incredibly* important to him.

I saw in Terry Warner's book (the book that had helped me so much) an explanation of Scott's relationship with his father. Warner would have called Scott/Dad a "primary collusion" and Scott/family "satellite collusions."[193] Warner explains collusions this way:

> We concentrate on *their* misdeeds in order to have proof that they are to blame and not us. And they focus on *our* misdeeds for the same sort of reason. Thus, we and they set in motion round upon round of edgy and sometimes hostile interactions, in which each blames the other and exonerates himself or herself.[194]

Dr. Warner likens these collusions to hooks that grab others unknowingly.

---

[193] We tend to export our way of being from our collusive relationships into other relationships. We may export anger, self-pity, suspicion, fear, sarcasm, or any other accusing, self-excusing attitude or emotion and thereby create a collusive satellite of another collusion carried on elsewhere. Warner, *Bonds That Make Us Free*, 273.

[194] Ibid., 82.

Because of our primary collusions, we often greet the world anxiously or angrily and do not comprehend how we became the way we are. We simply find ourselves beset by some inexplicable dislike, selfish desire, judgmental attitude, uncontrollable fear, despondent feeling, explosion of temper, or other mood, preoccupation, or impulse, without being able to explain why. We can't see that we have any responsibility for having this attitude or feeling. It seems to rise up in us whether we like it or not, like an alien force not subject to our will.[195]

> *We often greet the world anxiously or angrily and…*
> *we can't see that we have any responsibility for having this*
> *attitude or feeling. It seems to rise up in us whether we like it*
> *or not, like an alien force not subject to our will.*

Warner indicates that this is true for the vast majority of us, not just a few people. His book is full of interesting and workable examples in which we see ourselves.

After I realized that many of our problems probably had to do with Scott and his father's relationship, I became mad at Blair. Even though he was dead and gone, I was angry that problems I felt he had created by divorcing Scott's mom the month after we married were now surfacing in my marriage and my children's lives.

One day after this discovery, when I was frustrated with life, I was sitting and pondering, feeling "justifiably" piqued again as I thought about it. At that moment I felt unseen hands rest gently on my shoulders. This was peculiar. What soul from Heaven would this be? Somehow, through their size and weight, I could tell they were the hands of a man, and the gesture was familiar enough that it seemed like a family member. So, whose hands were they? Not my dad's; he would never use that gesture. Scott's grandpa? No, the former tax reformer and speaker of the house in Utah's legislature would be firmer. Who was it? Ahh, I realized that these were Blair's hands. I felt that this sweet

---

[195] Ibid., 274.

gesture of his hands on my shoulders was an assurance of his love for me and was his way of apologizing for the anguish he knew I felt he had caused. That was a tender mercy to me to feel those unseen hands and the care toward me and our family that they represented.

~

Another heavenly experience had occurred one month before Scott realized anything was wrong. Scott and I had attended the fiftieth anniversary of the founding of the engineering department at BYU. Permanent pictures of chemical engineering professors were displayed in order of hiring, and Scott's photo was up there with everyone else's, and still is. That was a proud moment for him. Perusing the display, I noticed that the second picture was that of my brother-in-law. He had died a year before my sister had died. I'd forgotten that he had worked at BYU. It was lovely to have this special tie to both of these great men in my life at this celebratory function.

During the entertainment following the banquet, my thoughts were suddenly turned away from the singer and drawn toward the air by my side. A thought came into my mind, and I replied back in thought. Another thought came, and when I responded with sudden, stinging tears, I realized these weren't just thoughts: I was having a conversation with an unseen being. A real give-and-take conversation, just in the mind. During the third exchange, I realized this unseen being was my sister, and I felt that she was standing there with her husband, who was one of those being honored. I cried out mentally, "But I *miss* you!" as if my heartfelt emotion would bring her back! She simply replied, "But I'm happy." That stopped my tears abruptly. How can you be sad when you know someone is happy?

How I treasured that touching of spirits, that brief contact with my sister, the kindest, most gracious person I have ever known! That occurred one month before Scott's ordeal began. I know that Heavenly Father knew that Scott already had cancer; perhaps he allowed my sister to come to let us know that life after death can be good.

I know Heavenly Father knew that Scott already had cancer;
perhaps he allowed my sister to come to let us
know that life after death can be good.

~

Visitors often came to the house. Everyone was sad that this was happening to Scott, but they were very supportive of him. Family, neighbors, and church members brought good wishes, proclaiming, "We are proud of your resilience. You remain in our thoughts and prayers," and "Hang in there!" They brought lovely cards with reinforcing sentiments about the Savior: "He is the light and the life of the world; yea, a light that is endless that can never be darkened."[196] A fun older couple, Nola and Clyde, said, "Scott, some people work hard first and then play later, and some people play first and then have to work later. With your music and chemical engineering, you've done both at the same time!"

The bishop came often, sometimes with his wife. On one visit, though, instead of commiserating, he queried, "Scott, how has this illness blessed you?"

Scott drew back, surprised. After a pause, he responded, "I never realized before how many people care about me! It has been a real treasure to find that out. Also, to feel the love of my family. They are wonderful! I truly love them. They're the best thing I have."

The bishop smiled knowingly. "It's amazing how these experiences, awful as they are, bring out some special and beautiful aspects."

His wife added, "And they bring us closer to Christ."

I smiled to hear Scott's answer. Prior to his surgery, he had not bothered to put into words very often the love he had for his family. His "love language" was *doing* things for others—and that he did; he *lived* for his family.[197] But words? Not so much. The positive energy of these words, however, manifested the change he was going through.

---

[196] Mosiah 16:9, Book of Mormon.

[197] Gary Chapman, *The 5 Love Languages* (Chicago: Northfield Publishing, 2010).

When I think of blessings, I think now about the song by Laura Story that my daughters sing.[198] Story's message is that our hardest trials actually bring us *to* the Lord's tender mercies. Like the Apostle Paul observed, "We glory in tribulations, knowing that tribulation worketh patience, and patience, experience, and experience, hope."[199]

Scott went on. "That's what I'm finding. As hard as this is, this tribulation turns me to Christ. I trust God's plan completely, and I feel a real reliance on my Savior at this time. I think a lot about what He has offered me through His Atonement." Scott then had me read to them something his mother had been reading to him from the book by Neal A. Maxwell:

> Without the ransoming atonement of the Savior, we would be stranded souls, doomed to die with no hope of the resurrection or of individual immortality. We were literally purchased by Jesus.[200]

> *Without the ransoming atonement of the Savior,*
> *we would be stranded souls.*
> *We were literally purchased by Jesus.*

With his wife nodding her head in agreement, the bishop added, "We surely are dependent on the Savior. It's hard for a lot of us because we want to do everything on our own."

Hope, calmness, and serenity suffused the house and stayed even after the bishop and his wife left. The next visitor, Dr. Dan, was one who also came frequently. He was one of our pediatricians as well as having a calling in our ward as the leader of the adult men. His church leadership position required two counselors, and he surprised Scott when he asked him to be one of them. Scott felt extremely humble and grateful to be considered for this calling.

---

[198] Laura Mixon Story, "Blessings," *Blessings*, INO, 2011.

[199] Romans 5:3–4, KJV.

[200] Maxwell, *All These Things*, 23. (He hath purchased [us] with his own blood. Acts 20:28.)

"We'll wait to appoint you after you're well, though," tall Dr. Dan said with a wink. "You don't need any extra burdens right now."

Scott was thrilled to think of working with Dan in that assignment. *I* was grateful to have Dr. Dan at our house for a different reason. I had wanted to talk to him in his role as a health professional, one of several in our neighborhood. I stopped him by the front door and said, "I have to tell you, I feel awkward around you doctors because the techniques that we've been doing are so unusual. I have felt that I would receive disapproval from all of you, and so I've avoided you. I'm sorry."

He smiled down at me from his towering height and assured me that what Scott and I did was up to us, and the doctors in our neighborhood wouldn't think any less of us because we were doing some different things. That short chat relieved me greatly.

~

A couple of nights after that, Scott received a visit from two older friends, Sally and Walter. They came as soon as they heard about Scott's illness. They greatly admired Scott and were sad to hear of his affliction. They asked about our missionary sons in Romania and Hungary, saying, "This is probably hard for them to be gone right now, but the Lord has ways of blessing them." They let Scott know how they valued him, what a good job he and I had done raising a wonderful family, and how they knew that what mattered most to Scott were his family and the Lord.

Scott bore his testimony to them, telling them that he knew the Savior lived and that his family was eternal because of ordinances that bound families together. They presented a plaque in beautiful calligraphy.

An

Eternal Family

Is a circle of strength

and love. With every birth

and every union, the circle grows.

Every joy shared adds more love.

Every crisis faced together

makes the circle

stronger.

The sweet sentiment of the plaque made us think of our growing family. Courtney, our granddaughter, had turned a year old, and a new baby would be born to their family in April. Davis, our oldest grandson, would turn one in May. And those three were just the start of the grandchildren![201]

Somehow the course of the conversation turned to the afterlife. With Walter nodding, Sally matter-of-factly told Scott her firsthand account of it. You see, this diminutive, gray-haired ball of energy—then age seventy-seven— had died when she was thirty-two years old. Her story is given here with her permission.

> I had dropped off my three children at an afternoon church activity when I entered an intersection and a car came barreling through and hit me broadside, sending me into a telephone pole. My little Volkswagen was bent in half, and I was crushed into the window, shattering it. It brought such pain in my head that I just couldn't stand it, and my spirit left my body.
>
> At that moment I heard beautiful singing, and the music propelled me through a dark tunnel where there was a bright light at the end of it. Standing in the center of the light was a man who was the source of that light. He glowed as bright as the sun at midday. As I left the tunnel and went into that light, I was engulfed in this light that was so peaceful, warm, and loving that I realized it

---

[201] At the time of printing, Elaine had eighteen grandchildren.

must be the Savior. He said, "Look," and I turned back toward the car and saw that mangled body and the blood on my collar. I thought, "Oh, she looks a mess."

We moved fast and effortlessly by a recital hall where there was a rehearsal of a chorus just concluding. A lovely girl came out and said to me in surprise, "Sally! What are you doing here? You are supposed to be on Earth to find me when I come!" I shrugged my shoulder like, oops, here I am! I didn't know what to tell her. (By the way, I did meet her on Earth several years ago. We knew each other instantly!) Then the Savior said to follow him, and quickly we were in a park, a meadowlike place. The grass was so vibrant and alive; the flowers were so many colors, even colors that I had never seen on Earth. Then the Savior stood with his back to a white fence. Facing me, he said, "Look," and He presented to me videolike pictures of my whole life, from birth to the present. It only took a few seconds to see it all. I saw some things there that I wasn't too proud of, and I told him how embarrassed I was and how guilty I felt to see them. He said, "Those were learning experiences, just like in school when you learned two plus two is four. Have you learned from your mistakes?" "Yes, I surely have!" "You have repented. Will you do them again?" I said, "No, never," and he assured me, because of the Atonement and my repentance, I was clean every whit. My sins were wiped away as if they'd never been. That was the most heavenly thing to know—Jesus and His Atonement made everything all right again!

There were other things I saw—some of my family … but I'll skip to the end. The Savior said, "Now you must decide. You can stay here or go back right now." Up until that time, our conversation was all mental; this, however, he said with his voice. I vacillated because I was so happy in that place of peace and love.

"Decide now," he urged again, and again I vacillated. I wanted to go back to Earth to be with my husband, to raise my three children, and to have another promised daughter, but the peace and love were so hard to leave.

Then, with utmost urgency, he directed a third time, "Now!"

I thought, "I want to be with Walter!" and just that quickly I was put back through my forehead again, just as at birth, and it hurt, just as at birth. I found out later that as I was going back into my body, I was in the ambulance, and they were using the defibrillator to get my heart going again. I was in so much pain after that, that for six months I wondered why I had chosen to come back!

~

I had heard Sally's story before, but it was new to Scott. He was amazed, and his body became more relaxed during their visit. Maybe it was listening to her story; maybe it was thinking about the Savior; maybe it was the comfort and support that he felt from this caring couple, but I was happy that he felt more peaceful.

"Scott, I know that Jesus knows what you're going through," Sally said.

"Yes," Scott concurred. "I've even thought that maybe I 'signed up' for this."

"Could be," gentle Walter, a former educator, nodded. "In any case, the Savior's love and redeeming power are there for you. We know that the purpose of this life is to come to Christ. You've done that. You live a good life; you love the Lord and your family." Walter encouraged Scott to rely heavily on the Savior and do whatever He wanted him to do.

Sally encouraged, "You're a good man, Scott. Just keep working with the Savior on this. He will make everything work out."

As Scott went to sleep that night, his thoughts were on a world beyond this one.

CHAPTER 21

LEIOMYOSARCOMA APPOINTMENT

FEBRUARY

Scott was still so excited about the prospect of Cell-Specific Cancer Treatment (CSCT) that he considered skipping his sarcoma appointment a couple of days later at the Huntsman Cancer Institute. Even the thought of CSCT's diagnostic scan being done in an open room excited him. He had been confined in a narrow tube during his recent PET scan up in Salt Lake with his arms lifted painfully over his head for an hour. Scott only consented to go to this appointment because Huntsman was the flagship of Utah cancer centers. Huntsman also was the only hospital that specialized in sarcomas, which apparently needed to be treated differently than other cancers. Scott's appointment was with Dr. Deirdre, one of the sarcoma specialists.

The hour-long drive up to Salt Lake almost did him in. Mom B came with us, so while I parked, she found a wheelchair and then helped me wheel him in. She waited with him while I filled out a voluminous amount of paperwork.

He was having difficulty breathing again, and it had only been a month since his surgery. That awful tumor had remobilized, and the golf-ball-sized bulge had grown to half-a-grapefruit size, preventing him from putting his arm straight down. I looked at it with a certain amount of horror; you just didn't want a person's body to look like that.

I'd already seen some horrific pictures of sarcomas at the library of the Huntsman Institute. A short time before, when Scott had had his PET scan at LDS Hospital, Mom B and I had driven up to the Huntsman Institute to see what it was like. The Institute's entry was impressive—a glimmering wood foyer with its philosophy etched on tall, imposing walls: *Hope through Research, Hope through Education, Hope through Care.* The gleaming wood gave an atmosphere of warmth and hope, and the clean lines of wall and furniture gave a feeling of professionalism and efficiency. It was very beautiful. All of the people who worked at Huntsman—receptionists, nurses, doctors—*all* took time with us, looked us in the eye, and were very solicitous. Huntsman was definitely several cuts above a normal hospital. In fact, founder Jon Huntsman (who donated more than $341 million of his own money to the Institute after its founding in 1995) proudly stated, "Except for my family and faith, there is no cause more important to me than fighting cancer."[202]

When we walked into the library that first time, the librarian had apologized. "There are fewer sarcomas than other kinds of cancer; I'm afraid we don't have that many books about them." The books that were there, however, had photos like nothing I'd ever seen before. Sarcomas often grow on the outside of the body, on appendages generally, and the images showed arms and legs with lumps on bumps that piled, bulged, and bounded on top of each other. When one had stopped growing, ending up as hard as a table, another grew on top of it, and then another and another. Bubbly mounds engulfed a shoulder, encasing the arm as the sarcoma greedily spilled into new masses. Lumpy knobs on children's thighs made the kids look like mini-Quasimodos.

---

[202] Jon M. Huntsman, "Huntsmans Give Another $41 Million to Huntsman Cancer Institute: Donation Fills Patient with Hope," *Deseret News*, April 22, 2011.

Bumpy, grotesque mounds on adults' arms and legs made them look like huge gray beasts in a bad sci-fi movie. Oh, these tumors shouldn't be here; they shouldn't be allowed! Indeed, one of the common ways to deal with sarcomas is amputation.

> *Oh, these tumors shouldn't be here; they shouldn't be allowed! Indeed, one of the common ways to deal with sarcomas is amputation.*

Sarcomas are quite rare, accounting for about 1 percent of all cancers in adults, or four in every thousand. Scott's type was even more rare; his type affected about four people in a million.[203] A radiologist at LDS Hospital commented to me, "I've never seen a sarcoma in that area (the diaphragm and rib cage) in the ten years I've worked here." A researcher said, "Because of its rarity, few doctors know how to treat it, and it [therefore] attracts little research."[204] Diagnosed in fewer than thirty thousand people worldwide, leiomyosarcoma is found in the smooth muscle cells of involuntary muscles. As I mentioned earlier, *leio* (pronounced ly-o) means smooth, *myo* means muscle, and *sarcoma* is a malignant tumor. The Greek word means fleshy growth. It is a resistant cancer, meaning that it is not generally very responsive to chemotherapy or radiation. Even now, years after Scott's cancer experience, there is no cure for this rare cancer, and the literature says it could reappear anywhere and at any time. Some of the literature tried to sound cheery, but I could read between the lines—it was obvious that leiomyosarcoma was a tough beast to conquer.

Finally, we were ushered into a room with Dr. Deirdre, the sarcoma oncologist. What a sweetheart she was—competent and kind! The focus of her attention was Scott himself. She made him comfortable in his wheelchair, checked the room's temperature, got him a drink, and asked him how he was doing. She was gentle and soft-spoken, with a sense of humor and a merry laugh. Even as sick as he was, she addressed questions to *him*, looking intently

---

[203] National Leiomyosarcoma Foundation, www.nlmsf.org.

[204] "Leiomyosarcoma," Wikipedia, https://en.wikipedia.org/wiki/Leiomyosarcoma.

at him rather than at Mom B or me. Kind and capable, she epitomized the sarcoma center's mission statement: "To provide compassionate, comprehensive, state-of-the-art, interdisciplinary care of patients of all ages afflicted with benign and malignant tumors of soft tissue and bone."

We told her, respectfully, that we didn't think much of chemotherapy from the reading we'd done, but we were here to look at all sides. She congratulated us on our openness to do so, saying, "Many people who want to do alternatives won't even listen."

She looked at the test results that had been faxed to her. "Kidneys are normal; liver, ammonia level is normal. Albumin-protein is low—malnourished. That's to be expected; the cancer is taking away a lot of your nourishment." She smiled with a little joke: "Leiomyo: this looks like smooth muscle gone bad."

Concerning chemotherapy, Dr. Deirdre said, "I'd go slowly; I wouldn't want to push you over the edge. Previously, chemotherapy hasn't been effective for sarcoma; surgery was the best. Well, you've had surgery. Chemo is still not great for sarcoma, but it's getting better all the time. I wish chemotherapy were better. The best numbers are 35 to 50 percent of tumors that respond." (My translation of that was, chemotherapy is a long shot for your type of cancer, Scott, remembering that the word "respond" does not equate with "cure.") I appreciated her honesty as she continued. "Historically, this is hard to cure, but I always go into therapy optimistically, with full intent to get rid of the cancer. Sarcomas are an orphan field. There are not many of us who have studied them or specialized in them. I have only a handful of colleagues nationally. The agents that we typically use are Gemzar and Taxotere."

Scott looked up wearily. "Those are the same chemicals our local hospital uses."

Dr. Deirdre nodded. "We're working hard to find new agents." She mentioned some clinical trials that were on the horizon and then looked straight at him. "If you do nothing, death is certain. We know it's growing back by your symptoms."

When we told her that Scott was taking cesium chloride and mentioned

Dr. Brewer's papers, she tilted her head in interest and said she'd take a look at the literature. She continued talking about alternatives. "Time is an issue. It is good to have options and hard to have so many. I think it's wonderful for patients to make their own choices. That's what I do with myself. Many people looking for alternatives are looking for something natural. A lot of chemos were discovered from nature. One of the new clinical studies concerns sea urchins. They have a novel mechanism against cancer; maybe it holds promise for sarcoma. What we've found so far has undergone scientific rigor. People in academics aren't out to get you, and it is not financially based." (That was an interesting statement, considering that we had read Dr. Moss's book that discussed both of those issues.)

Speaking of finances, by some magic, Dr. Deirdre was able to get Scott on insurance with her, even though the change we had made for our twins had made it seem impossible.

She talked a bit about medications and told him, "Take *something*. Don't let the pain get out of hand. It's not a contest!"

Then she told Scott what she could do for him if he were her patient. First, they would put him in the university hospital, even today, right now, if he wanted. They would stabilize him nutritionally. In a few days they would start chemotherapy. She frankly recognized that chemo ruins the immune system. "What we're banking on is that the chemo will get the cancer before it gets the person." She also admitted that there were side effects, but, assuming them to be well-known, she didn't linger on them. We already knew the odds were low with this type of cancer, and she didn't concentrate on numbers or percentages. She said, "You are not a statistic; you are you, and you can be one of those who lives. So, if you become my patient, I will always treat you as if you are going to live. I will even tuck you in at night!"

We all chuckled as she continued: "We can do pain and nausea control, peripheral issues that will help your quality of life. I want you to see all the options on the plate." She finished by thoughtfully saying, "We are an option in all this. In ten years, I'd love to say, 'We are the one.'"

When she left the room to let us think, Scott and his mom started talking animatedly. Dr. Deirdre was so comforting and positive that she left hope in her wake. The two of them reviewed all the positive things they were hearing. They became quite excited. After a bit, they noticed that I was not contributing to the conversation.

"You're awfully quiet," Scott stated perceptively. "What do you think?"

I actually wasn't quiet; I was seething. I didn't want to say what I thought. I didn't want to be the one to ruin the happiness they'd built up, but I couldn't believe what I was hearing. I remained silent and dour because I couldn't think of any nice way to say what I was thinking.

Both of them turned to me. Scott said again, "I want to know what you think."

"I think," I looked at each of them, "that both of you have forgotten what we've been reading for the last five years! When she said a 35 to 50 percent response, that didn't mean cure. That just meant the tumor shrinks a little bit. She's offering you a bed, not life." Looking at Mom B (I can't believe I talked to my mother-in-law this way), I said, "I think you just want him to be comfortable." Looking at Scott, I said, "And I think you are too sick to think straight anymore. Chemo is still chemo. I don't think it will save you. Do you?"

> *"She's offering you a bed, not life."*

I had burst their bubble as surely as a kid stomping on a beetle. I felt I'd crumpled their dream like an old gum wrapper thrown in the trash. But I had to answer honestly since Scott had asked.

His mom acquiesced. "It's true, I haven't read as much as you. I guess you're right."

I reminded them again, "We're after something that builds up the immune system while the cancer is being attacked. I know what she offers seems warm and cozy, but I don't think it's enough. It's not my decision, but I think you two have been swayed by her niceness."

It was Scott's turn. It was his decision. He could have said, "I want the fluffy bed. I want to be tucked in. No more hot/cold showers for me. No more stuffing down nutritionals in the middle of vomiting. No more holding cesium in my mouth for forty minutes. Ahh, just to be taken care of." To be honest, he was so tired. His soul so badly desired to just have someone else handle his well-being. But he didn't. When Dr. Deirdre came back, he told her, "No, but if I decide to do chemo, it will be here at Huntsman with you."

As we got in the car and coasted slowly out of the concrete parking garage, he looked back longingly at the medical center. If not for his agreeing to my resolve, he could be tucked away in there right now.

~

The agonizing trip and the appointment had exhausted Scott's meager reserves. Still, as soon as we pulled into our driveway, he reminded me to call CSCT.

"They said they'd call us," I said.

"They also said three days," he countered. "They should have called today by the latest. I want you to call them."

He was right, of course. Obtaining treatment was urgent. His three-week postsurgery grace period was over, and he'd just turned down an offer to do chemotherapy. One of the surgeons at church had even told me with a dire voice, "You've got to do something now!"

I found the CSCT number and called. John answered the phone, but very quietly this time. I didn't catch on at first to his tone of voice and just asked him if Scott had been selected for the program.

"Look, I shouldn't be talking to you," he murmured surreptitiously, as if he were checking for spies over his shoulder. "Our facility was shut down today."

That got my attention. "By whom?" I asked, distressed.

"The U.S. Federal Trade Commission."

"How?" I asked incredulously. "I thought that's why you were in Tijuana."

Sardonically he replied, "Let's just say that Uncle Sam has a long arm."

I shook my head in disbelief as he continued, sounding like a mother dog whose pups had just been taken away. "They took everything—the equipment, the computers, even the records." The story was Allen and his lab all over again. I could hardly breathe because of my anguish for them.

"What did they accuse you of?"

"False information. The internet has made a gray area. We tried to be as careful as we could on our site, but I guess it wasn't good enough. The ironic thing is that they now have the *very* records they need to show that what we did was effective and safe! But they'll never look at them."

I was so stunned I couldn't say a word.

He said again, "Look, I shouldn't even be talking to you. I'm glad you called me, because I don't have your number anymore. They even took our contact list."

Still sounding fearful, he finished our conversation as quickly as he could. "I'm sorry for your husband. He would have been perfect. I have to go. I won't be able to talk to you again."

A moment after hanging up, I remembered that there was supposed to be a CSCT Center in England, so I called John back for that telephone number. The phone rang and rang. True to his word, John Anderton never talked to me again.[205]

I stood in a daze. The room was murky and overcast, a dark cloud having formed while I was phoning. I felt like a tall city water tank drained of liquid, standing mutely over a drought-stricken town. I felt as empty as a metal canister, open on both ends with absolutely nothing in the middle. After *all* the treatments we'd found and *all* the time that had gone into researching—time that was seeping out of my husband's life—there was *nothing* to show for it.

---

[205] An email came a week later announcing the closing of CSCT. Its wording was vastly different from John's. "In a joint law-enforcement action announced Thursday, officials from the U.S., Canada and Mexico worked together to bring down a company that was offering a useless and expensive cancer therapy to desperate patients. The FTC in coordination with officials from Canada and Mexico charged CSCT with making false claims that its magnetic device, called 'Zoetron' can destroy cancer cells. 'This is one of the most reprehensible scams that we have seen,' said the director of the FTC's Bureau of Consumer Protection." February 20, 2003.

No green tea. No radiation. No MD Anderson. No Germany. No chemo. And now no CSCT. Other than cleansing and cesium (and I *still* hadn't been able to get hold of Neal), we were back to square one. I felt so lost.

When I told Scott, he was extremely disheartened. CSCT had sounded so good. Strangely, he didn't turn to the sarcoma appointment we had just had. Instead, he said, "Well, we'd better find something."

Our bishop came by that evening to see how Scott was doing. On his way out, I stood by the front door explaining some of the research I had done for Scott, and the immune-building approach we were trying to find. I told him how devastated we were at this latest news and how utterly drained and despondent I felt.

I imagined that he would be shaking his head, thinking to himself, "What are these people doing?" Instead, his response surprised and cheered me. "I admire all the research you have done for your husband, Elaine. I couldn't have done it. But since your first choice is not an option anymore, you go with what you feel is the right thing to do. Pick something, Elaine, and just move forward."

Just move forward. I would. Tomorrow I would start over.

PART TWO

CHAPTER 22

ENTER BECKY

FEBRUARY

In the morning I intended to look yet again for Neal's number so Scott could ask him something about the cesium therapy. Why couldn't I find it? He'd asked for it a couple of times already. It seemed like I was a chicken with its head cut off—running downstairs to juice things for him and give him supplements according to his schedule, running upstairs to check the computer for information and ideas, and grabbing the phone to call yet another facility or answer a previously made call. I appreciated Mom B because she had time to sit and talk to him, which I didn't seem to have.

Scott, however, had a different assignment for me: call Becky. I hesitantly called her. She'd had such a high persona the night she'd taught the raw foods workshop that I figured she might not even take phone calls. I was wrong. She not only took my call, she said she'd come right over. That was like having the head of a hospital, the dean of a college, or a firm's top executive give us their personal time—and at our house! She was so far above us in her knowledge, expertise, and experience that I was totally surprised by her offer to come over. I was even more surprised when she stayed and graciously talked with us for three hours.

The three of us—Scott, Mom B, and I—sat in our family room with Becky. She was so vibrant, bubbly, and alive—someone you want to "be" when you grow up. Light surrounded her when she entered, just like it had when she'd given her lecture.

Becky was delighted to meet Scott and just as solicitous of him as Dr. Deirdre had been. Even though he looked ill, she was able to see through the physical weakness to recognize in him a great man. Becky briefly told her story to Scott: how she'd had cancer, how she had investigated the methods used by different people who had overcome their cancer, how she had mainly used Dr. Christopher's method, and how she'd gotten well.

By way of reference, she mentioned several people with whom she was now working. Kelsey was one, a friend who had ovarian cancer. "Eleven months ago, she was diagnosed with a stage IV cancer. They wanted to take out five organs, and they gave her two months to live. They considered her dead. Now, as long as she stays away from anything cooked, her body stays alkaline and keeps the cancer abated. As soon as she decides to cheat even a little, even a cracker, the sugars allow the cancer to grow." Becky was happy and excited for Kelsey's future.

Another friend of hers, Jill, had been working with Becky after Jill's first round of chemo. "Yes," Becky answered our questions, "we can still work if the body has had chemo or radiation, but it's harder. Then the body has to get rid of the effects of the chemo or radiation as well as the cancer and normal toxins that accumulate. It's a lot for the body to do." Unfortunately, in Jill's case, her husband was a physician who didn't understand Becky's methodologies at all. He took Jill off Becky's program and put her back in chemotherapy. Becky's compassion was touching, and with a sad face she declared, "I don't think Jill will make it now. I think her immune level has been brought so low that she won't be able to recover." Indeed, a couple of months later, I chanced upon Jill's picture in the obituaries. It is ironic how willingly her husband and family mourned her but were not willing to let her try something new that might have saved her.

> *It is ironic how willingly her husband and family mourned her but were not willing to let her try something new that might have saved her.*

It was only now, in having Becky spend these three hours with us, that I began to understand the nature of her work. Teaching raw foods cheerily at the health food store was just the tip of the iceberg. She ministered to many people, all of whom were deathly ill. She and her protégé, Rachel, massaged essential oils into their bodies to give them higher energy, gave them herbs to increase their nutrition and counter difficulties, and especially gave them hope. Most of the ones who stayed with her program got better.

"This natural healing is not easy," she warned. "It's harder than having chemo kill your immune system and then dying. That's hard, but it's an enduring kind of hard. This is work. And yes, it'll hurt! This is *not* for the faint of heart." (All of us know that going through chemo or radiation is not easy; I saw that with my sister. Going through those takes a heroism of staying the course. What Becky was indicating is that holding yourself together while you are being *acted upon* by oncologists is a very different task from *choosing to act* in your own cancer treatment.)

> *"This is not for the faint of heart"…*
> *Being acted upon is a very different task from choosing to act in your own cancer treatment.*

"You must be committed. Scott, are you committed?"

Herein lay the crux of the whole picture. If he was committed, she was confident that he could get well. If he wasn't, then eventually he would die, despite all the things she or anyone else might do in the interim.

To these rigors, Scott nodded and said, "I'm committed." Yes, he was up for the challenge, and I was overjoyed! That dual promise from the Spirit surfaced in my mind once again:

"Scott will make a choice; once chosen, it will be irrevocable."

I knew that once my husband made up his mind, he followed through. I thought of his earning his doctorate when he felt like he'd been stuffed in a closet and told to come out three years later with his degree. I thought of his wanting to change careers to medicine, only to stay in what felt like an unfulfilling profession because he took seriously the responsibility to earn a living for his family. I thought how he'd once driven the Winnebago for thirteen hours straight for his grandparents. I thought of the cars he'd rebuilt, the hours he'd taken to learn banjo and guitar, the painstaking way he memorized his stories to tell, as well as the time and care he lavished on our home business. No, he was not opposed to hard work, and he said so. When a man like that said he was committed to a program, hope was on the horizon as bright as a sunburst!

All right, Scott was game, and Becky was ready to go! She continually reassured him, "Scott, you're a smart man. You can do this!"

After commitment, the next item on her list was to build up Scott's body. She was happy with the high-nutrient shakes he'd been receiving, but she worried that there was too much sugar in them. She felt more comfortable with juicing. She herself drank fresh juice—no canned, bottled, or concentrated juices bought in the store. She juiced mainly vegetables.

"We need to build him back up. The fastest thing that will do that is juices— one hundred ounces a day. I know that's a lot, but juicing gives a person far more nutrients—after all, how many times do you have five oranges or five apples or eight carrots at one meal?" she asked merrily. "The nutrients go right into the body because juicing eliminates the fiber; it shortcuts the digestion process. For someone who needs emergency nutrition, this is the way to go."[206] She gave him a schedule, complete with how many calories and how much protein, iron, calcium, and different vitamins each meal gave.

"Do you have a juicer?"

---

[206] Jay the Juiceman corroborates this: "Made fresh and consumed on the spot, juices, which contain about 95 percent of the food value of the fruit or vegetables, instantly release nourishment to the body through the bloodstream." Jay Kordich, *The Juiceman's Power of Juicing* (New York: Warner Books, 1993), 15.

We did. I showed it to her.

"This juicer is okay, but he'll have to drink the juice within a half hour of juicing. This machine throws oxygen into the juicing process, and oxygen starts breaking down the nutrients. A better juicer is the Champion, but this one will be all right for now." Then she reiterated to both Mom B and me, "This will be a lot of juice in one day, but he needs it."

To Scott she said, "I want you to walk barefoot for ten minutes a day out on the grass. We need to release static electricity and obtain energy right from the earth. Our cars, buildings, homes, and even our rubber-soled shoes shield us too much from Earth's energy." (Becky was an early advocate of a new therapeutic technique called "grounding," in which the body absorbs healthy antioxidants from the earth through bare skin.[207] Luckily, there was a thaw in Utah that February, and there was grass showing to be walked on.) She also knew that Scott needed the tranquility the out-of-doors provided.

Other things she wanted Scott to do were lymph brushing, jogging, or using a mini-tramp twenty minutes a day, deep breathing three times a day, and wearing only natural fiber clothes, since skin needs to breathe and synthetics hold in toxins. She suggested rubbing essential oils on that protruding tumor at his side, saying, "Rosemary, thyme, oregano, and tea tree oil kill cancer."[208]

> "An honest look is essential for anyone
> wanting to truly become whole. We must work on the
> mind, body, and spirit—the whole being."

She also wanted him to "take an honest look at negative emotions and actions" and suggested Karol Truman's book (as Holly had) as a way to assist in the process of clearing unproductive thought patterns and core beliefs.

---

[207] For more info, view the documentary *The Grounded* (1:04:46) and read *Earthing* by Ober, Sinatra and Zucker, 2014.

[208] When a plant is cut, it "releases oil in order to clean the break, kill bacteria and start the regeneration process. Essential oils enhance and support the building of the immune system." D. Gary Young, *An Introduction to Young Living Essential Oils and Aromatherapy* (Utah: Essential Press Publishing, 1996), 6.

Becky said, "This is essential for anyone wanting to truly become whole. We must work on the mind, body, and spirit—the *whole* being."

Next, Becky wanted to know what we'd done in the treatment-seeking process. Scott turned that discussion over to me. I told her that every facility I had called used either Adriamycin or a Taxotere/Gemzar combination for chemotherapy. No facility offered a multidisciplinary approach that I was somehow envisioning.

Becky agreed that an integrative approach would be a wise decision. We told her we'd been to Huntsman and how kind Dr. Deirdre had been. She nodded. "I'm glad she was. She should be, working with people in such extremity." (Becky's clients, by the way, were always "friends" or "people," never "patients.") She looked wistful and said with an inside knowledge that I didn't have, "Huntsman would like to be more integrative, but right now there's nothing more they can do for you than any other chemo clinic. They're basically a glorified chemo clinic right now."[209]

She grew thoughtful, muscle checked, then smiled broadly. "There *is* a facility that I think you would like. It's very integrative. It's called the Optimum Health Institute."

I told her, "Several people mentioned that during my phoning."

She nodded. "They're held in high regard. They've been around for more than thirty years—a good track record. They are one of the premiere teaching organizations on natural healing. There's one in California and one in Austin."

Scott and I looked at each other. "We'd go to California."

Becky saw the Optimum Health Institute (OHI) as an extension of herself because their philosophies were the same. Both of them valued wheatgrass juice, positive thinking, and raw foods. "Living foods for living bodies, dead foods for dead bodies," said their founder.[210]

---

[209] A different report of the Huntsman Institute: "Huntsman Cancer Institute Made the List of Top Fifty Cancer Hospitals in a National Ranking of Medical Facilities Released by *U.S. News & World Report*," *Deseret News*, August 2, 2016.

[210] Steve Meyerowitz, *Wheat Grass, Nature's Finest Medicine* (Massachusetts: Sproutman Publications, 1999), 33.

*"Living foods for living bodies,
dead foods for dead bodies."*

Becky told us about the founder, Ann Wigmore. Sick and dying, Wigmore had revitalized her blood and healed herself by eating anything green and chlorophyll-rich since chlorophyll was the closest thing there is to the molecular structure of human blood. Ann had been inspired by her grandmother's teachings about the healing powers of herbs and weeds (things available to her Lithuanian peasant grandmother, with which the grandma had healed wounded soldiers in World War I). After healing herself, Ann helped a few other people, and that grew into multitudes being aided—Ann was always working to bring people back to basic truths designed by nature. Ann's original retreat, the Hippocrates Health Institute, had been opened in Boston in 1958; next to that, OHI was the oldest wheatgrass retreat center in the world.

OHI also emphasized taking responsibility for your own health, as did Becky. Most importantly, both Becky and OHI desired to create an environment within the body where the self-healing body could get to work and expel this horrible thing. That's what we wanted too.

"If that is what you want to do, the best place to do it is at the Optimum Health Institute. That's what they *do*; they help the body get to an optimal level." Becky gave glowing reports of their abilities. "One woman was brought in on a stretcher and left feeling well. It is marvelous what they can do there. People are healed all the time." Becky said they had one-week to three-week educational programs. "You should do the three-week program to get the full benefit, Scott. You'll come back a new man, and I'll help you too!" She ended by assuring him, "Scott, you won't be the worst one there."

She left us to think about OHI, but I think the deed was already done. The crux—the major concept that ruled us—was that the body is designed to heal itself if put in the proper environment. This facility offered natural sources for that environment, staff support, and supremely healthy food, such as a constant supply of wheatgrass juice.

Scott prayed with me about Huntsman and about OHI. When you're praying like this, you try to put your own thoughts on hold—shove them into the background—and just "listen"—sense—for some sort of internal response (like what Clayton Christensen explained in Chapter 1). My internal response was interesting. When I listened to Scott praying about going to Huntsman, my internal response was like a low EKG—almost a flatline. In contrast, my heart leaped when he prayed about OHI, absolutely leaped like a Mexican jumping bean! What was I supposed to think about two such different internal responses? I had to go with my feelings.

As I picked up the phone to call OHI the next day, Scott looked at me and asked, "Are you sure?"

I shrugged. "I told you my response when you prayed."

Scott nodded, and we put our money down. We were going to OHI!

CHAPTER 23

TWO PRAYERS

FEBRUARY

Scott's life for almost two months now had been spent in his recliner since he couldn't lie flat in a bed anymore. Also, no more driving up to work and back, no more learning Japanese or practicing instruments. He spent his time quietly listening to his mother read, absorbing elemental cesium through his mouth, and thinking. Apparently one of the things he was thinking about were miracles.

He believed deeply in Jesus Christ and in the miracles that had been cited in the Bible, such as Elisha's ax floating on the water, the widow of Nain's oil that never ran out, the water at the wedding in Cana being changed to wine, and Jesus' raising the daughter of Jairus, to name just a few. He could not get those miracles out of his mind and called our stake president to come see him.[211] President Monte came on a Thursday night.

---

[211] An LDS stake president is the leader over a fairly large geographical area, similar to a Catholic diocese. www.mormonnewsroom.org.

Scott asked him, "We believe in the miracles that are in the Bible, don't we?" He knew the answer was yes, but just wanted to hear confirmation.

The president answered, "Yes, indeed we do."

Scott continued, "Can we ask for miracles in our own life?"

President Monte replied, "Yes, we can."

Scott asked humbly, "Will you ask the Lord for that miracle? Would you ask Him to heal me?"

President Monte answered, "I will need to fast for that." Perhaps he was thinking of the Savior's admonition to his disciples that "this kind goeth not out but by prayer and fasting."[212] "I will ask my counselors to fast with me. Obviously, you can't, Scott, but will all your family who can, fast?"

He looked at me, and I said I would call all the children and extended family to invite them to join in a family fast for Scott on Sunday.

The following Sunday night the president, with one of his counselors, came back as promised. Scott and I would be leaving soon for treatment at OHI in California. In the living room, our little family group consisted of Scott, Mom B, Katie, and me. The Spirit of the Lord came peacefully into the room as President Monte laid his hands on Scott's head and gave him a beautiful blessing. Interestingly, he talked sometimes to Scott in the prayer, and sometimes to the Lord. He encouraged all four of us to visit together afterward and to write down any parts of it that we remembered. Gratefully, we remembered quite a lot.

> Heavenly Father knows you and loves you. He knows what you're going through and has heard the pleadings of your heart. May you live to see the day when your posterity will number many, and may God give you peace through this episode. He sent his Son to atone for everybody. We are weak, and Thou art strong. We are little, and Thou knowest all. Sometimes laws are suspended so that miracles can happen. I pray for that miracle. I administer a blessing of healing through your

---

[212] Matthew 17:21, KJV.

faith in Jesus Christ, and if you are not "appointed unto death"[213] that you will live a long and healthy life. You will see the day when your posterity numbers many. I bless you to find the best help available, whether through doctors or other sources. I pray for every part of your body [and he listed them]. You are surrounded by a loving wife and others who love you. We love you. There are many who pray for you. Have peace. I plead for his life, but not my will but Thine be done, on earth as it is in Heaven.

We felt very peaceful with an increased faith. The phrase that jumped out at me the most was "a blessing of healing"—so similar to the other blessings he had received! The part that was specifically different about this one was the phrase "unless you are appointed unto death." That was disturbing, but it was only one phrase in a whole prayer full of positive pleading to restore all his bodily functions, so I found myself tucking the phrase into the back of my mind. I knew it was there, but unless Scott told me that's what he intended or felt he was "appointed to," then I would happily just let it stay in the back.

> *The phrase that jumped out at me the most was "a blessing of healing"—so similar to the other blessings he had received!*

Scott's mom had the marvelous idea of requesting them to give me a blessing also while they were at our house. The president had the counselor step forward, and he gave me an exquisite blessing. I felt my heart expanding like a fledgling butterfly opening wet wings. I felt sunlight enter my soul. It was a short prayer, so I was able to remember it.

The Lord loves you *[I thrilled to hear that!]* and knows your situation. I bless you to release old thoughts and to open to the love of your husband, who loves you. I bless you with peace and with the ability to work with people, both doctors

---

[213] Doctrine and Covenants 42:48: "And again, it shall come to pass that he that hath faith in me to be healed, and is not appointed unto death, shall be healed."

and others in the alternative health world. I bless you to handle the temporal workings of the household. This is a growing experience, to understand and make the Atonement of the Savior more effective in your life.

We thanked the stake president and his counselor, who had cared for us, fasted for us, and come to our house to give us the Lord's blessings. These two prayers helped us to move forward peacefully and surely.

CHAPTER 24

OPTIMUM HEALTH INSTITUTE'S FIRST MEAL

FEBRUARY

We had one more day before leaving for the Optimum Health Institute. Mom B and I borrowed a Champion juicer and spent a day juicing the combinations Scott needed. Our musician friend, Rebekah, and her husband brought dinner. Both the company and the food were a nice respite.

It was a very busy day. At midnight I was surprised to hear footsteps coming up the stairs. Who could it be? Sara and Allen wouldn't move in to be with Katie until tomorrow, and Mom B had already gone to bed. To my surprise, Scott poked his head through the door. It was extremely rare that he would come upstairs.

"I appreciate what you're doing," he said, "but I don't want you to drive to California unless you've gotten eight hours of sleep."

I was touched. Sure, he was probably thinking of the safety of all three of us, but he phrased it as being concerned about *me*—another of his lovely recent changes! His consideration felt as sweet as a child gently touching a flower petal. He went back downstairs to his recliner, and I hurriedly finished my preparations and then went to bed.

The next day, after loading jars of juices into boxes and into the trunk of the car, we took off. Mom B and I took turns driving to her house in Temecula, California. After ten hours, during which we left cold, gray winter behind, we were very grateful to get out of the car, and Mom B's husband, Lorin, was very grateful to see his wife again! We happily crashed for the night, and even Scott, with his persistent pain, got some rest on a main-floor couch.

In the morning, the drive from there to Lemon Grove was not far. Lorin and Mom B followed us so they could see what kind of place we were going to. All four of us parked and walked around OHI before dinner started. The grounds were lush and green, almost equatorial. Palm trees waved, bright bougainvillea draped luxuriously on walls, and huge succulent plants grew as solidly as furniture in the atrium between the central buildings. Even the red Spanish ceramic roofs of the townhouses where participants stayed seemed to welcome us, as did the bright green ground cover, colorful flowers, and decorative bench by each apartment.

Mom B looked around appreciatively. "My, this is lovely."

Lorin, Scott, and I nodded our heads in agreement. Having come from dry desert Utah, not to mention winter, the lushness and warmth felt like Heaven. The only drawback was stairs, many sets of stairs. There were stairs down to the Wheatgrass Shack and more stairs down to ancillary shops like Bonnie's Colonics. Scott tackled them gamely, albeit slowly, while older white-haired Lorin huffed and puffed.

When we got to the main hall, we were warmly welcomed by the director, Pam, and asked to sit at a large table for dinner. Later we would meet all the participants in person, but for now we just nodded pleasantly to each other. I couldn't figure out this crowd, though. They all looked pretty healthy to me, so I wondered why they were here. Where were the sick people Becky had talked about—the ones in need, the ones in cots, the ones who came for a miracle? Scott, with ponderous breathing and a gray pallor, was the only one hunched over the table and having a hard time sitting down. Becky was wrong, and I knew that Scott knew it too: he *was* the worst one there.

> Becky was wrong, and I knew that Scott knew it too:
> he was the worst one there.

Visitors were allowed to join in our first meal, so Mom and Lorin stayed and ate with us. None of us had any idea what to expect for the meal, but it certainly wasn't what they brought out. Even after they had served us, we still wondered! We eyed each other quizzically because this was like nothing we had ever seen. On each plate was a tennis-ball-sized sticky orange ball, six kinds of sprouts, a fluorescent purple cabbage dish, red tomato salsa, and two asparagus spears. That's it.

I knew there were reasons for everything they did here—after all, it was the *Optimum* Health Institute—and it was obvious that they were starting right away to teach us to eat more nutritiously than we had ever eaten before, but it looked so strange! It turns out that the orange sphere was a seed ball and was very yummy. The seed ball contained most of the protein the body needed, and the protein was more easily digested than meat. The sprouts gave our bodies the energy that bursts from newly growing things, in addition to more protein. Actually, many of the meals at OHI were similar to this one, and truth be known, I was never hungry the whole time we were there.

Lorin, a meat-and-potatoes man, declared, "That wasn't half bad. Weird, but not half bad."

After dinner, Director Pam shared OHI's philosophy—the very reason that all these "guests" were now gathered around the table. "This is a God-centered holistic program of healing, designed to help our guests achieve the optimal balance in body, mind, and spirit. You're here to change your life. Many people have changed their lives. If there is a cure, it is *you* who will find it. *You* who will do it to your own body. *You* who will cure yourself. You've come to a safe and sacred space to let healing occur."[214]

She said that the first week emphasized eating live, raw, organic vegan dishes, as well as gaining tools for cleansing and creating inner harmony. We would deepen our understanding of all that during the second week as well as being taught how to grow wheatgrass in our own homes. During the third week, we would be able to ferment, chop, blend, shred, dehydrate, and juice foods, which would be made for the second-weekers.

A staff member then told us that *all* of us have health challenges, some of which have been labeled by society: bipolar disorder, cancer, diverticulitis, ADHD, multiple sclerosis, and diabetes, to name a few. With a smile, she said, "Here at the Institute, we believe that these conditions are the body's way of giving you notice that what you've been doing hasn't been working! But we

---

[214] See Optimum Health Institute Newsletter, Winter 2013.

don't label them; to us they are 'health opportunities.'"

So, what most of us perceive as difficulties—even insurmountable difficulties—OHI perceived as opportunities for individual change and growth![215] I kept looking at Scott, as he hunched over, holding himself together. He smiled at me and nodded wearily as he agreed with the concept of a "God-centered healing program." However, "health opportunities" and "the body's way of giving you notice" didn't seem to register at all with him. If anything, he looked a little puzzled.

> *"Health opportunities" are the "body's way of giving you notice" that what you've been doing hasn't been working!*

Guests were strongly encouraged to *learn* what to do, and then *they* cured themselves. She said, "Optimum Health Institute does not, and never has, cured people." Our two officials told a few stories of guests who had cured themselves by coming to the Institute. What medical science calls "spontaneous remissions" were simply called "miracles" at OHI. One story was of a woman who had a health opportunity that society would identify as cancer in her liver and lymph nodes. The first week here was tough for her, the second week better, and the third week great. Her husband had supported her for the nine months afterward that it took her to eliminate her challenge. Her doctors were shocked! Another person had come with a tumor on the knee, and four months later had no tumor.

To help facilitate these miracles, they told us to go down to the Wheatgrass Shack as often as we wanted. "It's open 24/7!" they exulted. And, just as Becky had said last week, the director lauded Ann Wigmore's work, saying that the grain of wheatgrass contains all the elements of which the body is composed—a perfect food. Another proponent of wheatgrass juice stated,

---

[215] This is the same reasoning Maggie Sale used when she stated that "the beauty of thinking holistically is that you don't have to know anything about the condition you are attempting to resolve" but rather to place the body in an optimal environment.

"Fifteen pounds of wheatgrass is equivalent to 350 pounds of the choicest vegetables... [There's] more vitamin A than supplied by 84 ounces of food and more vitamin C than is supplied by 30 ounces of [recommended] fruits and vegetables."[216]

Wheatgrass juice was also recommended in a specialized way: as an implant. An implant is sort of a backward enema. Whereas the enema is inserted into the colon for the purpose of flushing waste *out*, the implant is inserted into the colon for the purpose of putting nutrition *in*. Instead of having to pass through the digestive tract, an implant allows nutrition to go *right* into the body. They smiled. "Wheatgrass juice has a direct shot into the liver through the veins."

Director and staff recommended two ounces of wheatgrass juice twice a day, preferably taken alone. They then shared the week's expectations, saying, "We will give you everything you need for nutrition this week (because wheatgrass juice has everything you need). We ask that you not use any of the supplements you've brought."

Scott and I looked at each other in consternation. His supplements weren't just happy little give-you-a-boost-of-vitamin-C tablets; his were life-giving and part of his treatment. They weren't add-ons, appendages, or accessories; his were powerful substances designed both to attack the cancer and to build up his immune system. This would be a supreme sacrifice; we'd have to think about this.

Then they got to the responsibility part that Becky had said she advocated. They said that a huge part of change and growth was each individual's taking *complete responsibility* for his or her whole life—from physical condition to mental framework. OHI was a teaching facility, and they reiterated that the best way to learn was to go to classes. Over and over they stressed, "If you don't change what brought you here, you'll go back to it." Director Pam reemphasized their philosophy on self-healing: "Life is a gift. Change negative

---

[216] Meyerowitz, Wheat Grass, 47.

thoughts to positive; stay focused on the positive. By the weekend, you're going to feel better than you have in years!"

> *"If you don't change what brought you here,*
> *you'll go back to it."*

So far, so good. Then came the bombshell. The director stated, "We will not advise you on any medical condition."

"What?" Scott and I both looked at each other in distress. We had known we would learn about new food, new classes, new information, and new perspectives. We had *not* known that we would be at a facility with no medical personnel on-site! Scott, Mom B, Lorin, and I were all alarmed. How could they justify having a facility open to extremely ill people and not having medical practitioners on hand? We felt a little better to learn that the director herself was an R.N., but her function here was administrative, not nursing. Scott made sure I booked a personal appointment with her. Unfortunately, it would not be until the next afternoon.

"Try the classes first, and then we'll talk," Director Pam advised with a smile.

Scott turned to me and murmured, "Let's call Becky. She said she'd help. This isn't what we expected."

With sad eyes, I reported, "Remember, she's on vacation with her family this week. And they don't have a cell phone." Even though there was kindness, beauty, and support all around us, we suddenly felt like an oasis stranded in the middle of a desert.

As the evening ended and Mom B and Lorin prepared to drive back home, they indicated that they were not sure that the Institute was a good thing for Scott at this time. Scott told them that he and I would talk about it, and then we slowly walked back to our townhouse. We discussed pros and cons. On the con side were the lack of medical help, not being able to take his supplements, and not being able to contact Becky. On the pro side were Becky's recommendation and the fact that other people had cured their cancer by doing this program.

Scott prayed that night, telling the Lord, "Much prayer, fasting, and thought has brought us here. 'I go,' as the scripture says, 'led by the Spirit, not knowing beforehand the things which I should do.'"[217]

Feeling led to this place, Scott chose to give OHI a try. He decided that if he was going to participate, he would do the program the way they wanted it done. I reluctantly put the cesium and other supplements in the fridge. The juice Mom B and I had lovingly juiced for him he might still be able to use since the first couple of days at OHI used detoxing through juices. We went to bed, though, wondering what the week would bring.

The Amazing Qualities of Wheatgrass Juice

Following are some of its uses:

Double-strained as an eye or nasal passage rinse (aiding also in red eyes).

As a rinse four to five days for an abscess in the mouth; as a cleanser to dissolve earwax.

As a foot soak (because nutrients come into the body through the soles of the feet).

As an implant (to put wheatgrass's high nutrients into the body the quickest way possible).

As a poultice, particularly on a cancerous area, or on cuts, bruises, rashes, or burns.

As a weight reduction aid just before meals or as a sleeping aid just before bedtime.

To stop pimples, acne, or blackheads, by applying wheatgrass juice on a bandage.

As a hair rinse to get rid of dandruff and make hair shiny.

To stop bleeding gums, tooth pain, and sore throats.

To help congested nasal passages and inflamed mucous membranes.

To stop itchy skin, poison ivy, sores, boils, and insect bites.

---

[217] "…and I was led by the Spirit, not knowing beforehand the things which I should do." 1 Nephi 4:6, Book of Mormon.

Ann Wigmore noted other ways wheatgrass juice and its sister, Triticum barley, aided her guests, who gave her testimonials of relieved high blood pressure, diabetes, obesity, gastritis, stomach ulcers, pancreas and liver troubles, asthma, glaucoma, eczema, skin problems, constipation, hemorrhoids, diverticulitis, colitis, fatigue, female problems, arthritis, athlete's foot, anemia, and (even) bad breath/body odor.[218]

---

[218] Meyerowitz, *Wheat Grass*, 34.

CHAPTER 25

LITTLE IMPROVEMENTS

FEBRUARY

S cott started Monday morning with a bang! He was ready to give 100 percent. First up was an exercise class amid the atrium's luxuriant greenery. He stretched, squatted low, and reached high the best that he could in time to the music. He threw thin, bony arms in the direction the teacher did, but I could see it was a struggle. Out of the corner of my eye, I watched the racquetball champ—the guy who dove for balls like a crazy college kid, the guy who was indefatigable, the guy who gave college athletes a run for their money—struggle to lift his arms during simple calisthenics. On the one hand, it was admirable; on the other, it was pathetic.

Breakfast was juice. It didn't agree with him, and he struggled to keep it down. The juices we'd brought from home didn't affect him this way, but for some reason this juice did. By the time of the first class on detoxifying at 10:00 a.m., he felt so horrible that the only way he could attend was to lie on the floor by the wall at the back of the room, a cardboard container in hand should his breakfast decide to revisit the world.

The first educational class reaffirmed that OHI wanted to help us detox mentally as well as physically. The first way to achieve a mental change was through having a positive mental attitude and focusing on your goals and solutions rather than on your problems.

The teacher said, "These concepts sound so simple as to be bypassed! Yet how many times a day do we think or say, 'I'm really worried about...' or 'I can't ever seem to...' or even worse, 'I wish they would...' Those statements focus on problems instead of what we can *do* about them! When you write down your goals, the reticular activating system helps your brain pay particular attention to things that can help you attain your goal."

Even from his prone position, Scott wrote a few notes, beginning with "Thoughts are the blueprints of what we attract into our lives." When we were asked to write three goals as well as to keep a gratitude journal, Scott wrote, "My goals: Detoxify body; Nourish; Get on the road to recovery from my cancer. I'm grateful that I was able to sleep several hours last night. I thought I was going to be awake and uncomfortable all night, but God heard my prayers and worked a miracle." Remembering that it was nigh impossible for Scott to lie flat to sleep and that his rest was usually interrupted by discomfort of some sort, a decent night's rest was, indeed, a miracle.

When the lunch juice came, Scott shook his head. No way was he going to chance it.

For the afternoon class, he just lay down again on the floor at the back of the room with his cardboard container nearby to handle his nausea. He wasn't listening; he was just biding time until we could go to our appointment with Pam. Finally, 3:00 p.m. came, almost twenty-four hours after we'd first heard the distressing news that no medical personnel were on-site. Now he could add to his list of frustrations that he couldn't keep down the food they gave him.

However, Scott's angst and pain took a back seat to Pam's compassion when we were finally ushered into her office. Her diminutive body calmly bent toward Scott's weakened one, and the first thing she did was get to know him. She found out that he was a father, a chemical engineer, a mathematician, and a musician. Pam listened intently to his concerns. She asked that we wait a day or two on the nausea issue—enough time to let his sick body acclimate to the diet. She was sorry that we had assumed that medical help would be on-site and indicated that the reason they were able to stay in the business of helping people all these years was because they weren't a medical facility. They were a teaching institution—they offered education; participants provided the cure. For Scott, though, she said (almost in an undertone) that she would make her nursing skills available should we need them. That made him feel more secure, and as far as he was concerned, the appointment was over.

Pam wasn't through yet; she had more than Scott's physical condition in mind. Her eyes shone in her delicate face with a deep understanding born of years of helping people, including tending her own husband before he had died the previous year. Leaning forward at her desk with slim hands folded, she tried to shed more light on OHI's position.

"Here at OHI, experiencing optimal eating styles is just a portion of what we do. Two-thirds of this program is mental, emotional, and spiritual." She restated what the morning detoxifying class had taught—that work here at the Institute involved both physical and emotional aspects. "You're much more than food, Scott! God had to get your attention through this cancer. Men tend to think, 'I am my job.' You are more than your job, Scott, even though math and music are unique and high callings. You have a right to be you; you have a right to speak up. You *have* accomplished; you are a divine creation of the Creator."

"God had to get your attention through this cancer."

This was a fabulous conversation, and I thought, "Finally, we're getting to root causes instead of focusing on facades or false beliefs." But then I happened to look at all our faces, and I saw different expressions in all three pairs of eyes: Pam's shone with love; mine were bright with hope; Scott's were merely perplexed and fatigued.

Then, with tremendous compassion shimmering in her voice, Pam looked softly at him and said, "It's hard to be perfect in an imperfect world." Bingo! How could she know him so well, when we'd just met? She continued, "But the only thing your family and the Creator want is love—noncritical, nonjudgmental love. Let things go; it's hard for you, but really so simple."

> "The only thing your family and the Creator want is love—
> noncritical, nonjudgmental love."

I'm sure she noticed—but it didn't seem to faze her—that Scott looked totally baffled, not to mention exhausted. He'd been doing his best to participate and to wait all day, he'd been sitting on a hard chair in her office for over half an hour, and now his physical ability to sit was gone. He nudged me meaningfully to excuse us from her office, and I told her we needed to go.

Just as we were leaving, she asked one final question. "Scott, what would the payoff be if you got well?"

> "Scott, what would the payoff
> be if you got well?"

His eyes cast about as he tried in vain to register her query. But his acute pain and unease had made him oblivious to everything she'd said. As I shut the door behind us, he looked at me in consternation.

"What was that all about? I went for help, and she just talked. 'What would the payoff be?' Well, I'd be well! I don't even understand what she was saying."

I understood, though. She was trying to help him to accept life without having to be perfect. To let go. To be more "human." As I gently walked him back to our townhouse, I hoped that he would come to learn what she knew.

∽

Scott missed a fascinating 7:00 p.m. class on brain states because he spent the whole time in the restroom. While the rest of us learned about alert Beta, relaxed Alpha, meditative Delta and deep-sleep Theta, I kept looking in that direction, wondering if he'd ever come out. For an hour and a half, he alternately threw up or waited to do so.

In the middle of the night, Scott needed me to help him get to the bathroom. He was too weak and exhausted to get up himself. Even though he was slim, his man-bones were certainly bigger and heavier than I was. I tried unsuccessfully a couple times to pull him up. Finally, I counted, "One, two three!" and heaved him up. I balanced him and then set him off. Part of his waking so late at night was just being scared of what the future might bring. And now there were three blisters on his protruding "knob." Who knew what that meant?

"What are we *doing* here?" he groaned as he fell back into bed. "This isn't doing any good."

I could tell that he was scared and hurting, but prayer had led us here, so why would we want to turn our back on the Lord? This facility seemed like the best place to be right now, and the leaders here indicated that sticking with their program usually yielded wonderful, even miraculous, results. After all, I'd been calling agencies and facilities for a month; we hadn't found another place that centered around natural health in all its aspects. I thought we should give OHI a little more time and just look for tiny improvements that made him feel better and healthier.

I answered, "We don't know that, Scott." I reminded him of the prayers that had brought us here. "When you prayed about going to Huntsman, I felt a polite little 'nod' inside. But when you prayed about this place, my heart leaped up with a huge grin on it. What am I supposed to think about that? It felt like a gauge gone off the scale!"

"Well, we *are* trying to listen to the Spirit," he concurred.

"That's what I think we've been doing. We're just looking for little improvements day by day; let's give it a chance."

I kissed him as I tucked him back in, then did some negative-energy release work as Holly had taught me. My journal recorded, "His mind and body are wreaking havoc with him." And this was just day one.

On Perfectionism

- Perfectionism is "too much" of a good thing! Unrealistic expectations placed on others creates unhappiness and disappointment. Nothing's *ever* good enough. It backfires on you: if you're a know-it-all, you alienate people.
- Unrealistic expectations lead from one thing to another. We then *fear* taking new actions, and that leads to procrastination, which leads to paralysis.
- Excellence works, instead of having to feel superior. Excellence is good; having to always be the "best" can be detrimental.
- Life is a boomerang; what you throw out comes back. (Or like a sower—what you sow, you reap.) The bumps in the road let us know how rich we are. Life is striving—that is, a journey—not strife. It's a process. Like a sculptor, we mold and we carve out life. Forgive yourself if it was icky. Life is what you make of it. It's all an inside job. Life's not a problem; it's a process, an opportunity.
  Calvin Coolidge is reported to have said, "Having problems is not a problem. The problem is in thinking the problem is a problem—that is the problem."[219]

---

[219] Notes from a class at Optimum Health Institute, February 2003.

CHAPTER 26

WHAT IS IN THE MIND WILL FIND RELEASE

FEBRUARY

Tuesday morning was gray with a cool rain. Scott didn't exercise today. In fact, he didn't get up. "Oh dear," I thought. "If we're looking for day-to-day improvements, staying in bed is probably not it." I remembered what they'd said the first night—the learning, and thus the changing, came by going to classes, so I begged him to reconsider. But no, he simply would not get up. And he couldn't imagine lying down again on the floor in the back of the room for classes. He did rally enough to ask me to take notes for him.

Today's class, taught by an R.N., was a discussion of water, because "the act of digestion of solid foods depends on the presence of copious amounts of water."[220] We were happy to find that OHI used the same books that we did, such as *Your Body's Many Cries for Water*, which confirmed concepts we'd learned through our wellness business. Our teacher emphasized three main points about water:

1. Often when we reach for food, it is hydration, not hunger, that is triggering the body's need.
2. Just because something is liquid (a beverage) doesn't mean it is *hydrating* the body. The body uses *more* liquid in processing tea, coffee, and soft drinks, for instance, than the amount of liquid originally ingested!
3. Since the body is composed of at least 70 percent water, that much water needs to go into the body daily. An easy plan is to set out eight to ten glasses of water a day and not have any other liquid until the water is consumed.

I would add two more points:

4. Be sure of your water sources; the majority of bottled "spring" water is simply tap water—complete with chlorine, chemicals, pesticides, hormones, and even microplastics—it's not special water. And reverse osmosis or distilled water strip minerals, so depleting your body on an extended basis is not a good idea either.
5. Use the singer's creed: "Sing wet; pee pale." The second part means, if your urine is pale, then you are getting enough water. If it is dark yellow, you're dehydrated. Easy.

> "Chronic dehydration is the root cause of most major degenerative diseases."

Author Dr. Batmanghelidj said that diseases such as reflux, inflammation, allergies, arthritis, and low back pain were caused by lack of hydration.

---

[220] F. Batmanghelidj, *Your Body's Many Cries for Water* (Virginia: Global Health Solutions, 1992), 29.

"Chronic dehydration is the root cause of most major degenerative diseases."[221] The crazy thing is, ingesting water does not automatically hydrate because not all water (such as our municipal water, laden with chlorine) gets *into* our cells.

The class was reminded that "water regulates *all* functions of the body."[222] Another way of stating it is that *every* activity of the body—every electrical connection between synapses, every joint that moves, every thought that is thought—occurs in a water medium. That's a *huge* concept! Our R.N. teacher mentioned again that water is not just a beverage; it's a nutrient. Water *feeds* us with nutrients our bodies need. And she mentioned that soda drinks do not even equate to water. (And this was years before energy drinks were on the market, and they are even worse than sodas.)

Elaine's Thoughts on a Nurse's Lecture on Soda Drinks

Our teacher said, "Humans love to drink our waste." Gag, why would someone say that? She went on, "It concerns the wonderful, symbiotic relationship that the Maker of this world set up between plants and people. Plants give off oxygen as waste, and humans use that; humans give off carbon dioxide as waste, and plants use that. So, when people drink soda drinks, which contain carbon dioxide, they are ingesting a waste product! That goes for beer, sparkling juice, sparkling water, and champagne. Soda is the number one grocery item in America. This sounds like something that should be in Ripley's Believe It or Not!"

As I understood the nurse's lecture, the soda causes burps, which eliminates some of the soda in gas form. The rest of the soda goes through the body (again). The phosphoric acid pulls electrolytes out of the body, and the phosphorus binds with calcium, thus pulling needed calcium out of our bloodstream and causing calcium to *have* to be released from the bones. Thus, much pediatric osteoporosis, which builds up through

---

[221] Ibid., 11.

[222] Ibid., 19.

age thirty-five, is preventable, as is childhood obesity and diabetes. *The biggest single thing we can do to increase our health is to eliminate soda drinks.*

When I was a little girl in the 1950s, milk and water were our standard beverages at meals. My mother would buy an occasional orange soda or root beer for us during trips in the summer. Both of those patterns were quite typical of the time. Why did that occasional use become full time for people nowadays? Only a few reasons come to mind: convenience, coolness, and campaigns. Notice that *none* of these reasons has a thing to do with health! Manufacturers of soft drinks don't care that their products are nonessential at best and hurtful at worst. They just care about their bottom line—money—and so they continue to put out cleverer and more compelling advertisements. And we continue to fall for them!

It was nice to know that the PiMag water unit Scott and I used and sold was highly thought of by the Institute. This PiMag water unit was so highly energized, by the way, that it created auras—or electromagnetic waves—that were visible when taken with Kirlian photography.[223] (Google "Pi water" and "auras" for an image.) I actually think of this aura picture *every* time I take a drink—knowing that I am drinking in *energy* as well as hydrating.

∾

After lunch, a sweet, soft-spoken fellow named Roland came with me to our townhouse so he could talk with Scott. Most of us would label Roland's "health opportunity" as M.S. The Institute had helped him marvelously. When he first came, he couldn't walk more than a few steps before tiring. Now he was one of the Institute's helpers, giving and working all day long, albeit at a slower pace.

Roland spent a long time with Scott, with the result being that Scott got up, dressed in loose gym clothes, and came to the afternoon class. I looked

---

[223] Shinji Makino, *The Miracle of Pi-Water* (Japan: IBE Company, 1999), 12.

at that as nothing short of a miracle! Scott curled up on the floor again with his little cardboard container, but he came.

The afternoon class, taught by another R.N., was a review of elimination that reminded me of eighth grade health but was far more detailed and far more fascinating. It added to things that we'd learned via the Schulze videos, such as a person should eliminate waste sometime after *every* meal! Our nurse teacher said, "The desired peristaltic action of the colon works best if one can pay attention to elimination as soon as one feels the desire. There is a 'Roto-Rooter' action; there's *supposed* to be!" She said the colon is supposed to be about two inches in diameter but gave the example of one famous star who was found to have a colon four inches in diameter after he'd died of a drug overdose. She mentioned another person whose colon, on death, weighed forty pounds, whereas the colon itself weighs four pounds. It seems that we humans usually go about our lives—busy with plans and meetings, people and problems—taking our amazing bodies for granted. I bet most of us don't think twice about how these bodies of ours function, these remarkable bodies that let us do all the things we want to do. Our nurse's class sure made you think!

Our teacher then talked about the liver. Scott paid attention to this since his cancer involved the liver. She told several OHI miracle stories. The last was of a schoolteacher who came to OHI in need of a liver transplant and, using a continual supply of wheatgrass juice as suggested, ended up not needing the transplant. Then our teacher shifted direction as she said,

> The liver is responsible for nausea and fatigue; it "talks" back to you! Send loving thoughts to it and visualize healing light going into it. The Chinese say that anger is stored in the liver.[224] Forgiveness, then, is needed. Let things go. If you keep hurtful things, you are the one who suffers.

---

[224] Also from the Chinese: grief is stored in the lungs, fear in the kidneys, and worry in the spleen.

"The Chinese say that anger is stored in the liver."

As seamlessly as a leaf grows out of a twig, our Optimum Health teachers all had the ability to transition from talking about physical processes one moment to emotional or spiritual ones the next. It was amazing! They were able to pull together an overarching oneness with life—a connection with the universe and God, as in the words of a twentieth-century healer:

> With infinite care (God) made the leaf so that every tiny cell therein can absorb the sun. With the same care He made us so that every cell within our frames can absorb Him. God is not a far-away sovereign but is actually the medium in which we live—the very Breath of Life![225]

Scott became somewhat of a focal point for our fellow participants at OHI. It was apparent to everyone that his health was the most precarious, and many of the forty to fifty guests took time to greet him and talk to him. (Even the ones who didn't say "Hello" carefully stepped over him while he was on the floor.) Scott managed enough energy to be gracious to them. It pleased me to see how they really liked him and to watch him being enfolded in this new "community." All the guests were classy individuals. Among them were older participants like Naaz and the Cohns from California, Bruce from Canada, and Lucille and George from Florida. There were younger participants like Big Tom (a giant, lovable teddy bear) and Little Tom (a wiry fellow). There were energy healers, Hoberleigh and John, and a yoga enthusiast, Felicity. There were more, of course, and I found that most of them were not overwhelmingly ill but had come to recharge their spiritual and health batteries. A spirit of camaraderie suffused OHI; people were more interested in supporting one another than competing with one another. How welcome that was!

---

[225] Agnes Sanford, *The Healing Light* (St. Paul, MN: Macalester Park Publishing, 1947), 38–41.

Another facet of this setting was—how do I say it?—a plain honesty with no posturing. We were all on equal footing. For instance, I know that Mr. Bruce owned several businesses, yet here he was asking pleasantly about Scott and learning alongside everyone else. His money didn't make him different or set him apart. In fact, in this place, furs, fancy suits, dangly earrings, fake fingernails, and stiletto heels were all left behind. The Institute made no requirement to do so; guests just somehow must have felt that such blingy armor (or, as Isaiah stated, the "bravery of tinkling ornaments"[226]) wasn't needed. This beautiful setting somehow begged simplicity.

Scott perked up a bit after class and decided to try more juice for dinner, but since he'd spent a second afternoon lying on the floor, he announced he wasn't going to the evening class. A sweet gal named Autumn with big, luminous eyes who lumbered like her "opportunity" was cerebral palsy, lugged over a huge, cushy chair for him and begged him to stay. He couldn't very well turn down her efforts or her beaming smile and huge brown eyes. Several others chimed in, entreating him too, so he relented.

The camaraderie of the group continued in a class that taught more fully how one turned a health challenge into a health opportunity. Our lanky, jovial teacher said he had two vocations—one as a fireman, the other as a psychotherapist. He quipped, "You wouldn't think the one vocation had anything to do with the other, but actually you'd be surprised how firefighting can lead into psychotherapy!" A little bit older than some of our other teachers, he showed us his "true" vocation—that of jokester! He kept us in stitches with his one-liners: "I have entered the snapdragon part of my life: part of me has snapped, and the rest is draggin'!" and "I'm old enough that I no longer buy green bananas." You just had to shake your head and smile! He said, "I'm still around because I decided, 'What fits my busy schedule better: exercising one hour a day or being dead twenty-four hours a day?'"

---

[226] Isaiah 3:18, KJV.

Our teacher's main purpose was to teach us to be true to ourselves. "All we have to offer other people is the quality of relationship we have with ourselves." That relationship included taking responsibility for *everything* in our lives, finding peace through losing ourselves in whatever the moment required, and feeling a new love for ourselves through laughter. It turns out that Norman Cousins had a basis for using ten minutes of laughter and a positive attitude to combat illness![227]

> *All we have to offer other people is the quality of relationship we have with ourselves.*

Our teacher talked of problems and about allowing change to occur in our minds: "Having problems is not a bad thing—not facing them is. Or, to put it another way, having problems is not a problem; the problem is in thinking the problem is a problem." This witty guy had so many witticisms, but they were true. With laughing eyes, he pointed to his head, chuckling, "It's all an *inside* job!"

He even told us that we could change past painful events by giving them happy endings, and that would change our perspective of the events.[228] He quoted one of my heroes, Christopher Reeve, who said after his paralysis, "It'd be so easy to die. But I look at this as another chapter in my life."

∾

Then, like a preacher using a scriptural text for his sermon, our teacher turned to a book written by Dr. Lawrence LeShan entitled *Cancer as a Turning Point*.[229] Dr. LeShan's book was used extensively at the Institute because his philosophy aligned with OHI's: cancer is your body giving you notice that you need to change some things. Back in 1947, Dr. LeShan had begun gathering

---

[227] http://en.wikipedia.org/wiki/Norman_Cousins; Anatomy of an Illness (1979).

[228] "If we don't like what is being shown on the movie screen…the only real solution is to change the reel in the projector." Evy McDonald, quoted in Siegel, *Peace, Love and Healing*, 82.

[229] Lawrence LeShan, *Cancer as a Turning Point* (New York: Plume, 1994).

data concerning cancer, the immune system, and the mind "and went back into the childhoods of cancer patients to find the black seed that poisoned their psychology."[230] Thirty-five years and several thousand people later, Dr. LeShan wrote his book. The preface states,

> Thoughts and feelings do not cause cancer and cannot cure cancer. But they are one factor, and an important one, in the *total ecology* that makes up a human being. Feelings affect body chemistry (which affects the development or regression of a tumor), just as body chemistry affects feelings.[231]

I bought the book the next day at the Optimum Health bookstore.

Our teacher asked, "What is cancer?" Answering his own question, he said, "Not being your own true self." Then he reminded us to let life happen and not to take ourselves too seriously, smiling as he quoted Anonymous, that great master of wisdom: "Blessed are they who can laugh at themselves, for they will never cease to be amused."

"What is cancer? Not being your own true self."

He gave us plenty more reasons to laugh as he gave his take on some of Dr. LeShan's more unusual teachings. My favorites included "Do the things you don't want" and "See yourself as miserable and not worthwhile."

Seven Great Ways to Get Sick ☺

- Do the things you don't want.
- See yourself as miserable and not worthwhile.
- Fill your mind with dreadful pictures and then obsess over them.
- Avoid intimacy because you might get hurt (i.e., meaningful and emotional talk with another, or coming to someone with an open heart).
- Blame others for all your problems.

---

[230] Ibid.

[231] Ibid., xiv.

- Shun humor.
- Avoid making changes that might bring joy.

On a serious note, our teacher pointed out again that we don't give ourselves a destructive malady on purpose. We *do* want to have an awareness, though, that the mind and the body are connected: the body influences the mind, and the mind influences the body. If thoughts are continually sad or depressed, worried or angry, the body *is* going to respond in a negative way. Our teacher quoted Deepak Chopra, who stated, "Worry transforms itself from organ to organ. Each point in the body knows that there is worrying going on, and every cell remembers."[232]

> *"If thoughts are continually sad or depressed, worried or angry, the body is going to respond in a negative way."*

When class was finished and we got back to our townhouse, Scott and I got on our knees for our evening prayer. Among other things, he prayed, "Help me to participate more fully." I was grateful. That sounded positive. Still, I couldn't help sensing his mortality as I watched him again rock back and forth, back and forth with his head bowed over. In the middle of the night, though, when Scott needed to get up for the bathroom, he got himself up! That was an improvement. And he was still able to sleep flat instead of hunched over. Two small miracles.

---

[232] Chopra, *Quantum Healing*, 137.

CHAPTER 27

ALPHA AND VISUALIZATION

FEBRUARY

When the Wednesday morning class started, Scott was there! Seated once again in the overstuffed chair (because Amber shooed away a gal who had wanted to sit in it), he was greeted by friends as they walked past. Several pulled me aside and quietly said that they thought he looked a lot better. I agreed!

On Monday, the lectures had started us off with physical cleansing and detoxification. This morning's class once again concerned *mental* detoxification. Our teacher was a doctor who had taught this class every week for eight years. He said, "The body is self-healing. If you do not believe the human body can heal itself given the right circumstances, you are in the wrong place." Well, that was said without mincing words! His philosophy was "Health is every day. Yes, you can do things that aren't really healthy for twenty years, but then watch out! You get away with it for a while, and then you pay. It's the everyday lifestyle that makes the difference."

> "Health is every day. You can do things that
> aren't really healthy for twenty years,
> but then watch out!"

He went on. "The human body is the most sophisticated thing on the face of the earth. There are 50 trillion cells in the body, and the body replaces about 3.8 million new cells every second. "Imagine you have both a Ferrari and a Volkswagen; to which car would you give high-octane fuel? For humans, a soft drink or a taco is *vastly* different nutrition than an avocado or an apple."

First off, he wanted to show us how to get into an Alpha state where the brain and body could access healing and change. He asked us all to sit quietly and imagine different parts of our bodies releasing tension. Interestingly, the Alpha relaxation we learned here was almost identical to ones in voice workshops I'd attended. (*See "A Method for Relaxation" sidebar in Chapter 27.*)

He told us, "Alpha isn't something unknown and separate from us. Alpha is us, but in a relaxed state. There is information all around us. We want to get to this intuitive state, the Alpha state, for our answers."[233]

When he indicated that information all around us is *part* of us, I thought of a strange occurrence I'd had one summer in the woods. I was walking my bike up the hill from a lake that was far below our campsite. It was quite a steep hike, so I paused for a moment to catch my breath. When I stopped, my brain registered the word "eyes." Not an image, but the word "eyes." It dawned on me that someone or something was watching me. I slowly, carefully looked around. I finally saw a squirrel on the ground a couple of feet away from the trail, standing stock-still with haunches raised, looking straight at me. I find it truly fascinating that some intuitive part of me sensed the presence of that squirrel long before my physical eyes did!

---

[233] The brain waves in the different states are Alpha 8–13 Hz, Delta 1–4 Hz, Theta 4–8 Hz, and Beta 13–30 Hz.

Our teacher said that things we enjoy help us to get into that Alpha state: gardening, singing, sewing, crafts, reading, puzzles, playing with children, dancing, hunting, playing an instrument, running, or repairing vintage cars, to name a few. Maybe that's why time seems to disappear when we enjoy what we're doing—we have gone into an Alpha state! Scott paid attention to this because the teacher said Alpha would reduce pain. I paid attention because it made me feel relaxed and ready for new things to enter my life.

A second part of mental detoxification was called visualization. The concept seems simple but is extremely powerful. Visualization is envisioning an outcome before it is created. A good example from many years ago was when our seven-year-old son suddenly started doing dives he'd never done before off a board at the university pool—360s, backflips, and twists. I couldn't figure out how he was coming up with such amazing moves, until I observed him intently watching the college guys in the line ahead of him. They were vying to make the most creative moves off the board, and then the whole line would imitate what the first guy did. Our son internalized their moves through visualization, and then just let his body do what they did. After a while, the guys noticed this little kid doing what they were doing and happily included him in their "contest."

Visualizing an outcome before physical activity is initiated, like my son did, was a novel idea in 1974 when Timothy Gallwey wrote *The Inner Game of Tennis*. Later it became an accepted technique used in many fields, with sports and music being but two. Our teacher showed us how useful it could be for cancer.

"If your opportunity is one that society would label as cancer, try imagining Pac-Man running around inside your body and gobbling up the cancer. That's an excellent image!"

Here's a similar image from a woman who had breast cancer:

I imagined small, delicate birds searching my breast for crumbs. To my surprise my imagery took the form of the cancer being golden crumbs, filling in their richness. Each day the birds would eat the golden crumbs. It was amazing to me that I visualized the cancer in this form, as being crumbs too golden rich for my body. After the birds had eaten their fill, I would then imagine a pure beam of intense spiritual white light entering my body. I would then pray to God for guidance, renewal, and protection. (One morning I woke and could no longer find any golden crumbs.) An inner voice whispered, "There isn't anything there." I told my husband, "I wish they'd take another mammogram. I bet they wouldn't find anything." A week later the second mammogram didn't show any cancer.[234]

Scott asked me to take notes because it was all he could do to sit, listen, and try not to throw up. The most interesting thought of the day was, "Who are you?" Our teacher continued with questions that are good for all of us to think about: "You are not an answering machine; you are a *questioning* machine. What's important to you? What makes you get up in the morning? How can you choose to honor your passions? What is a goal you can have on the other side of this pothole called a 'health opportunity'? To whom or what are you giving away your power? Where do you lose energy? Where do you gain energy?"

> "What is a goal you can have on the other side of this pothole called a 'health opportunity'?"

As I walked back to our room in the townhouse, I was captivated with the idea that these were ways to eliminate insidious disease! *Any* of these questions may prompt deep soul-searching and hours of thought within us.

The teacher encouraged us to go through the Alpha script twice a day. Scott was too emotionally distraught to do it himself, so he would have me say it for him back in our room. I spoke slowly and evenly, giving him time to visualize a more peaceful body and hoping that he did.

---

[234] Siegel, *Peace, Love and Healing*, 113.

In addition to this, I gave him enemas, wheatgrass juice footbaths, wheat-grass juice implants, and wheatgrass juice drinks.[235] It takes a lot of juice to perform all those different functions, so I spent more time than I would have liked down in the Wheatgrass Shack, juicing for him. Scott hated the time I was away from him, but the juice was one of the main reasons we'd come to the Institute. When I told him we were out and I needed to juice more, he'd always plead, "Hurry, please."

Scott didn't attend the afternoon class. It was too much for him. He asked me again, though, to go and take notes. The discussion about different body systems led to a lecture on medications. The teacher said, "Medication is not good for you. It will never be." He further warned, "Advertising advises, 'Take a pill and go on your merry way.' Beware. Once you start taking medicine, you're in 'disease-care,' not healthcare. For instance, some nighttime cold remedies contain alcohol. It's not that they get rid of a stuffy nose; it's just that you don't feel it anymore!"

> *Once you start taking medicine, you're in "disease-care," not healthcare.*

The medication Scott was using was OxyContin. Our doctors had given it to him after surgery to control his pain, and he was still using it. One day, Hoberleigh, the calm and contented energy worker with long, wavy brown hair that was so shiny it could have been used in a shampoo ad, was helping Scott through the day with a little massage and energy work. Vibrant and peppy John, the other energy worker, walked over. Both said they were con-cerned with Scott's usage of OxyContin. At Hoberleigh's suggestion, I muscle tested him myself. Even with my low level of expertise, I received a response: OxyContin was hindering his progress. Hoberleigh and John both tested him and found the same thing.

---

[235] See sidebar The Amazing Qualities of Wheatgrass Juice, Chapter 24.

"Scott," Hoberleigh challenged him, "OxyContin isn't good for you. It's hindering your progress. You need to get off it, if you can."

At 6:00 p.m. and before bed, he switched to two Endocet. I was so proud of him for daring to make the change!

Night was hard again, though. The dark hours seemed interminable, as they often do for people who are ill. Night seems to magnify difficulties. He woke me at 4:30 a.m., saying, "I'm glad I look better, but I'm feeling worse." He was having a hard time breathing, the pain in his side was constant, and his ankles were weak. His current condition was so vastly different from his former athletic and energetic self that it was frightening. And he was so scared!

A Method for Relaxation

Lie on your back with your knees raised to flatten the small of your back. Eyes open or closed.

Feel your forehead and head "float" out behind you. Feel your eyebrows "fall" off your face to either side, then your eyelids, your cheekbones, your nose, "mustache," lips, and chin.

Let your scalp "puddle" onto the floor, then expand your neck, and then your back, and let them expand and "puddle" into the floor.

Let your knees "float" up to the ceiling, and let your feet and toes "extend" all the way across the room and out through the wall.

Breathe fully and relaxed, letting all the organs inside you relax.

Let your chest, rib cage, diaphragm, and abdomen all fall away, one by one, from the vertical center line in your torso (the aponeurosis).

Let your hips "fall" away from the center and stretch onto the floor.

Go back to your spine from top to tailbone and let it puddle under you.

Go back to your knees, calves, ankles, feet, and toes, relaxing them.

Imagine a wave of peace and tranquility washing through you from top to bottom.

Imagine all the cells and organs inside your body, down to the bottom of your feet, as very relaxed.

Breathe fully again. Bring to mind something for which you are grateful. When you've done that, your awareness bubbles up to the surface. You feel more present in your body.

Wiggle your fingers and toes as you begin to be aware of the room around you. Your eyes are open; you're awake, relaxed, and very present. Stretch if you want to.[236]

---

[236] The word "let" is used extensively here and in the Alexander Method of Relaxation. See health.harvard .edu and other sites for Mathias Alexander's (1869–1955) method of relaxation for performance enhancement.

CHAPTER 28

RENEWAL THROUGH TONING

FEBRUARY

It rained again Thursday morning, but this time Scott came to class, walking slowly through the drizzle. I supported him with one arm while holding an umbrella over him with the other. Midway through the morning, we left after a class to go for his first colonic. Slowly, we made our way down three sets of stairs to the shop. Darn, we had the wrong time. Back up we slowly came.

Around 11:00 we talked with Bruce, whose wife's friend had used Essiac tea. A neighbor of mine had also used Essiac for her cancer, so I was familiar with the name. Essiac was purported to do all sorts of good things—fight cancer, improve liver function, improve digestion and bone health, and so on. I called his wife in Canada and had a great conversation with her. It didn't seem like a strong enough substance to help him right at this moment, but it sounded worthwhile overall.

At noon, Lucille, a sweet elderly participant who was also an R.N., saw that Scott was having difficulty breathing. She lent him her oxygen tank with an extra breathing tube. What a woman! He rested in the common room while I phoned different facilities on the OHI phone to see if we could order him an oxygen tank. Ordering was difficult because of insurance, delivery, and distance issues, but I finally found a place that would send one out. When Scott thanked Lucille and returned her unit several hours later, he remarked to me that he didn't know if it had made any difference. So we didn't order one for him after all.

After the afternoon class, Hoberleigh asked Scott if he would like her to do an energy release for him, and he readily agreed. Her long, shiny hair glistened past her face as she bent her head and put her hand about an inch away from Scott's tumor, as Holly had done. Hoberleigh's method of getting rid of bad energy was different than Holly's. Instead of shaking it off, she directed it, or asked it, to go out the top of her head to Heaven, "where Jesus will know what to do with it." Hoberleigh also gently maneuvered her hands on that twitching shoulder and to his back. Her tools were her expertise, essential oils, and, most importantly, her heart. Scott loved being ministered to by her gentle touch. He even felt revitalized enough that he asked, "Isn't there an exercise class next?" He worked out (at a low level) in the fitness class before dinner!

At 5:00 p.m. we went back down to the colonics building, where the colon flush made him feel better than he had in a couple of days. He was then able to eat dinner, which was amazing; he hadn't really eaten all week! I mentally counted the improvements: sleeping flat, getting himself up at night, exercising, trying a less-addictive medication, going to classes, doing Alpha relaxation, and having a colonic. He was doing well. Then came the class of classes!

∽

It was Thursday evening, and we walked into a large, empty room. There were only a few chairs scattered here and there. The teacher sat on the floor but invited us to sit anywhere we wanted. Scott chose a comfy chair and I sat on the floor by his feet. Tonight, we would practice achieving harmony within our own bodies using tools we had not even considered: color, pitch, vowels, and body location. OHI called this method of balance "toning."

I bet many of us recognize systems of color coding like the one where red is powerful, blue is supportive, yellow is cheery, and white is logical and objective.[237] (A color code practitioner told me a story of a husband and wife who almost divorced during the house-building process; she wanted vibrant jewel tones and he wanted warm earth tones. The interior designer recognized that their disagreements were merely over color, and she was able to bring together the bright and the subdued in such a way that the couple was happy again!)

But the colors we talked about in this class were not like color coding. These colors were associated with locations (chakra points) in the body. In addition to color, each location also had a pitch and a vowel associated with it. (*See the Toning chart at the end of the chapter.*) The pitches or tones we used were healing sounds. Sound has power. All live beings respond to sounds: some sounds make us edgy; some sounds make us relaxed. Olivia Dewhurst-Maddock has an entire book devoted to healing sounds; its subtitle is *Heal Yourself with Music and Voice.* (It's another of those books that you don't dare start highlighting because you'll highlight every statement!)[238]

> *Music bypasses the conscious brain and goes straight to the subconscious. That's why music is so powerful!*

Back to the idea that sound has power: like pendulums that end up ticking in unison, the body entrains to the better frequency of what is being intoned, and the frequency begins curing the body. (I have seen sounds heal people at singing conventions, either with a circled group of caring people or with a machine that "sang" into people's bodies the frequencies they needed. This is

---

[237] Free personality tests are available on ColorCode.com.

[238] Olivea Dewhurst-Maddock, *The Book of Sound Therapy* (New York: Simon & Schuster, 1993).

called "frequency healing.") Our Thursday night instructor told us, "Singing is the best entrainment to balance and integrates the energies in your body. The tone just enters you—so powerfully, it goes right into your brain." (Music bypasses the conscious brain and *goes straight to the subconscious*. That's why music—for good or ill—is so powerful!)

Our teacher continued. "Physics shows that emotions can get locked in the body. Our body carries all the emotional responses we've never released. Unprocessed emotions keep your frequency low and cause blockages."

> *"Our body carries all the emotional responses we've never released."*

Each of us in the class intoned the same pitch on the same vowel for about five minutes, letting our minds be free to center in on the location and color associated with that pitch. As we were intoning our pitch, a story from one of my singing teachers, JoAnn, came to mind. She had undergone a similar exercise at a workshop in a large warehouse room, except they had intoned a single pitch together for a much longer time (almost an hour). After a period of time, JoAnn had heard chimes in the corner of the room up by the ceiling. But there were no chimes. The sound came from overtones—extra pitches or oscillations above the actual pitch—created as a result of the unity that her workshop class had achieved!

In our class, there was a listening stillness, a thoughtfulness, and a serenity that cocooned us. It was as peaceful as a shady afternoon beside a forest brook. They say that one needs stillness to hear God's voice and that our current world, fraught with worry, busyness, and constant noise / loud music / stimuli takes away that stillness. This setting brought back a pleasant, reflective pensiveness, and there was a subtle unity that linked us all by the end of the class. As for me, I didn't hear any chimes during the hour-and-a-half class, but by the end, I did feel calmer and more in tune with myself.

And Scott? Like a bird shaking rainwater off its wings, he shook off all our attempts to help him walk, and literally skipped down the three stairs exiting the building! He didn't walk, he *skipped*! Hoberleigh, John, and a few others around us grinned and burst into applause and cheers. Scott felt light. He felt joyful. He couldn't wipe that silly grin off his face. After the last few weeks, this was truly a miracle. It seemed that he had finally turned a corner!

> *He literally skipped down the three stairs exiting the building.*
> *It seemed that he had finally turned a corner!*

~

The next morning, people noticed that Scott sat in a regular folding chair instead of the big cushy one, and he stayed through the whole day of classes. Those were little improvements all around! Our friends encouraged him every time they walked past: "You have better color today!" and "There's more brightness in your eyes."

What they saw was true; he did look brighter and stronger. But also true was the horrible way he felt. He still threw up daily, the pain in his side never abated, and everything he did was done oh, so slowly. All too soon, he'd had enough of sitting. He went to lie down in the small common room. He asked me to save him from the likes of bouncy John, sweet, concerned Big Tom, and earnest Little Tom. All three men were wonderful, caring fellows, but their energy was too much for him in his fragile condition. Throughout the morning I shielded Scott from a chat about energy with John (who brought some ginger to make Scott's wheatgrass juice taste better), a scientology discussion with Big Tom (who generously gave us his own copy of the *New Age Bible*), and a religious discussion with Little Tom, who desperately wanted us not to be in denial about the possibility of death.

Of that last discussion, poor Little Tom looked confused when I told him that we had zero problems with dying, but that's just not where Scott was quite yet. Apparently Tom hadn't sensed that from us. Perhaps he expected a sense of desperation, almost pounding our chests and rending our clothes. Perhaps he mistook our calmness about the possibility of death for denial. But the discussion required either a complete explanation or none, so none it had to be. There was so much depth and majesty on this topic, you couldn't just say one word and be done.

Our view of death was much like that expressed in the poem "Gone from My Sight" attributed to Henry van Dyke at the end of the chapter. Like the poem expresses, we don't dissolve into nothingness; a person's soul continues after death, and it is only the perspective of those who are leaving a person or greeting a person that changes how they see the event. Of course, this perspective is made possible only through the resurrection of Jesus Christ, and the fact that He has promised everyone on Earth that they, too, will be resurrected. The scriptures tell us, "In Christ shall *all* be made alive,"[239] and "The spirit and the body shall be reunited again in its perfect form."[240] These thoughts do soften the blow of death.

But that's not all I would have wanted to tell Tom. If we have lived worthy lives, we will be able to live *with* the Lord. "God himself shall be with [his people] and be their God."[241] Wow! The smartest, cleverest, most loving, most daring, most engaging, most powerful person in all creation wants *us* to live with Him! And I really would have wanted to spend time with Tom reveling in God's most glorious and tender promise:

> And God shall wipe away all tears from their eyes; and there shall be no more death, neither sorrow, nor crying, neither shall there be any more pain: for the former things are passed away.[242]

~

That Friday evening, after slogging through a difficult and unusual week, Scott and I both looked forward to an evening movie in one of the Institute's large rooms. It was the only movie of the week, and we were excited to go.

---

[239] I Corinthians 15:22, KJV.

[240] Alma 11:43, Book of Mormon.

[241] Revelation 21:3, KJV.

[242] Revelation 21:4, KJV.

Scott had made tiny but consistent progress in just a week, so I was feeling fairly joyful and lighthearted. We were to be here three weeks; what might happen in that time?

Scott very much wanted a comedy, but the introspective *Pay It Forward* was the only movie offered. "I don't think this is doing any good," he said, sitting on a hard chair in the dark. Then I realized he wasn't referring to the movie, but to the whole OHI experience. My heart dropped again. It didn't sound like he was opening himself up to new experiences like the teachers had encouraged us to do. Not wanting to say any more right then, I just waited to see what he would do. He finally gave the nod to watch the whole thing. After the movie, his face looked less tense. All he said was, "That was a good message." I nodded in agreement.

~

Every morning, the participants and some leaders stood together in a large circle and shared information, love, and testimonies. We heard about people's experiences, and some of them really were miracles. It was Saturday morning, and the Institute was winding down as final classes focused on maintaining what we had learned throughout the week. But my focus was simply on Scott. He looked like he was winding down too. Despite Thursday night's respite, it didn't look like OHI was doing for Scott what Becky had indicated would happen. His breathing was labored, pain and nausea were constant companions, and life was so difficult for him right now as to almost preclude living. His eyes were haunted, and he looked like a lost soul.

He had tried this program valiantly, but he really needed to go someplace else. I spent quite a bit of time in the foyer talking with Roland and others about different clinics. Scott's health had declined so badly by this point that I could only consider driving him to San Diego or Tijuana, each of which was an hour away. It appeared that in Tijuana there were about thirty smaller and three larger clinics. One doctor there had a clinic that gave ozone treatments. Roland mentioned that oxygen was critical, especially to a person with cancer—oops, he meant a person with a "health opportunity." He said that blood carries oxygen, but when disease is present, less oxygen goes into the cells, and they become acidic. I tried calling the Mexican Ozone clinic over and over, but because it was Saturday, no one answered the phone.

Saturday evening's entertainment was a talent show before all the one-weekers left the next day. All day Scott had only eaten a breakfast smoothie that took him one and a half hours to get down, two wheatgrass juices with John's ginger and peppermint, a little lunch, and no dinner. He didn't feel any better than he had all week, but he doggedly insisted on participating in the talent show.

At 7:00 p.m., Scott set his hammered dulcimer on its stand in the corner and sat uncomfortably on a hard folding chair. He looked sharp in Dockers and a collared shirt instead of the sweats and T-shirts he'd been wearing the whole week. On this evening, his only concession to being ill was wearing sandals instead of his normal polished oxfords. Nevertheless, he shifted constantly on the hard chair, moving his legs and feet back and forth, turning and squirming, all hunched over. Part of him enjoyed listening to everyone, but the larger part of him was barely biding his time until his turn came.

The variety show was of high caliber. It turns out that these OHI participants from all over North America were very talented. Actress Debbie Reynolds had actually been one of those participants a few weeks earlier! Now one woman showed beautiful colorful embroidery she had done. One man read his own poetry. Another man stood and sang with a wonderful voice, and another played a guitar piece he had written himself. When my turn came, I sang a musical theater piece, accompanying myself since I didn't know who else might play the piano.

Then it was Scott's turn. As he stood up and moved his dulcimer toward the center, I held my breath. What would come out? He used to play entire pieces note-perfect (and there are so many notes in a dulcimer piece that it's difficult to do), but he hadn't touched it since our show in December. I needn't have worried. As soon as he started "Castle Kelly," the title piece of our Celtic CD, the audience was mesmerized. They were swept along on a series of repeated tones and passages and taken to a magical place in their minds. They heard castles and wind and water. They heard seagulls wheeling above and the burial ground of kings beneath. They heard green and stone and finally, mist. They erupted into a standing ovation when he finished.

I think their delighted applause was not only for the beautiful piece, but because they saw it as another OHI miracle. It wasn't a miracle, though. It was the incredible stamina of a man who makes things happen, the tenacity of a musician for whom "the show must go on." The beauty he could contribute, he felt he should contribute. In normal circumstances he would have stayed to answer people's many questions about the hammered dulcimer, but instead he asked me to help him leave quickly.

The night before, I had told Scott something that had flooded over me—how much I loved him. Twenty-eight years earlier, he had successfully wooed me by proclaiming, "I love you. I need you. I want you." And last night, I had repeated that back to him: "I'm not complete without you. I love you. I want you. I need you so much!" Back in our townhouse after the talent show, he asked me to repeat that to him. I did that gladly, along with many gentle hugs and kisses.

> *Something had flooded over me—how much I loved him.*
> *Back in our townhouse, he asked me*
> *to repeat that to him.*

GONE FROM MY SIGHT

~

I am standing upon the seashore.
A ship at my side spreads her white sails to the morning breeze
and starts for the blue ocean.
She is an object of beauty and strength. I stand and watch her until
at length she hangs like a speck of white cloud just where the sea
and sky come to mingle with each other.

Then someone at my side says: "There, she is gone!"

"Gone where?"

Gone from my sight. That is all.
She is just as large in mast and hull and spar as she was
when she left my side and she is just as able to bear her load
of living freight to her destined port.

Her diminished size is in me, not in her.
And just at the moment when someone at my side says:
"There, she is gone!" there are other eyes watching her coming,
 and other voices ready to take up the glad shout:
"Here she comes!"

And that is dying.

—attributed to Henry van Dyke

Toning

ENERGY CENTER	LOCATION	VOWEL SOUND	COLOR	PITCH
1st	Tailbone	Oo	Red	*A below Middle C
2nd	6" below Navel	Oh	Orange	B♭
3rd	Solar Plexus	Aw	Yellow	Middle C
4th	Heart	Ah	Green	D
5th	Throat	Eh	Pearl, Gray-Blue	E
6th	Between Eyes	Ih (like "lit")	Blue-Violet	G
7th	Top of Head	Ee	Red-Violet	G#
8th	6" above Head	Humm**	White Light	B

* The pitches start low and move higher incrementally.

** Alternate sound is Aum. In either, emphasize the *M*.

CHAPTER 29

PRAYER
OF SUBMISSION

MARCH

How quickly time changes things. Thursday night's miraculous turn of a corner only led to Friday's lying on the common room couch all day, and Saturday's energetic talent show was replaced by Sunday's inactivity. My journal of Sunday recorded, "Scott is very weak. He has no energy, so we barely talk about anything, let alone how he feels about the mental part of this program. He is diligent, however, in having me do the program for him faithfully, like Alpha and the visualizations, the two ounces of wheatgrass juice, wheatgrass juice implants, and footbaths. The feeling in our townhouse is very heavy and dejected. He went without OxyContin until 1:30 p.m., and then he asked for it. I have had to do everything for him today—dry him, dress him, give him his juices, etc." We had originally talked about going to a church meeting with some friends, but last night's activity took it out of him. We were content to stay in the townhouse.

Unbeknownst to me, however, Scott was doing more than just lying despondently on his bed; he was thinking and making important decisions. Three months earlier, he had written a Christmas letter to his children and grandchildren, expressing his love to each of them. "The realization that my life could be shortened has jerked me to a heightened awareness of the value of life, the Plan of Salvation and relationships. Life is a marvelous opportunity! I am very grateful to be alive. I plan to live a long time yet, but with the Atonement of Jesus Christ and the Plan of Salvation, death is not something to be feared, if we are prepared." *This* is what he was thinking about.

In the early afternoon, he asked me to pray with him. He knelt unsteadily by the bed, and I knelt by his side. He told me, with a quiver in his voice, "I can't imagine continuing on in this state any longer." He was thin, tumored, always hurting, vomiting, and completely miserable. He took my hand and began talking to Heavenly Father. I was honored to be there as he did.

"Dear Lord, I've had a good life. I've been able to do many things. I've helped six children come to a point where they are capable, independent, and faithful to Thee and to Thy church. Father, this can't go on."

Then Scott totally submitted himself to the Lord's will. It was amazing and beautiful. The room was radiant with light, and though tears coursed down my cheeks, my soul responded with openness and expansiveness.

"The room was blazing with power and Spirit!"

"If you want to take me, I'm ready to go. I won't stand in your way. Thou knowest all things, and knowest an eternal perspective. Thou knowest if it's better for me to go or to stay. Let me be where I can serve Thee best, where I can help Thy kingdom the best." Then, with a touch of pleading in his voice, but with not a hint of demanding like I'd heard earlier in the week, he said, "Help me to know what Thy will is. Make it plain to me. But Father, if I am to go, make it fast. Help it to be fast. I can't go on like this. If I am to stay, there needs to be a change."

He made some specific promises to the Lord if he should remain on Earth, among which were to "be a loving husband, so his wife feels that he is her friend. And to be the kind of father that his kids could look up to and want to emulate." It was the most heartfelt prayer he had ever offered in his life.

The room was blazing with power and Spirit. It was strong, alive, and hopeful. It felt full of forward movement, full of rejuvenation and power, full of dynamic progress. It even took on an amber yellow tint—the same warm, comforting color that indicated the presence of God at my mother's funeral.[243] I cried. I rejoiced. I didn't ever want that feeling to go away!

There was a change after that. The feeling in the house was lighter, enervated, and full of hope. Scott and I were both invigorated and infused with God's Spirit because of his genuine, 100 percent submission. I felt privileged to have manifested—right before my eyes—the single most important statement I've ever heard:

> The submission of one's will is really the only uniquely personal thing we have to place on God's altar.[244]

The submission of one's will is really the only uniquely personal thing we have to place on God's altar.

That was said by Neal A. Maxwell, the man whose books Scott had been reading with his mother. I've thought a lot about his statement. What do we have to give God? Not our breath—He gave that to us. Not our talents—He gave those to us. Not our possessions or our families—those are on loan from Him. Not even keeping commandments or forgiveness of ourselves or others—He expects that of us. Besides, as soon as we do something good, He blesses us, so we're always in His debt. Our will, our agency, is the only thing that is ours alone to give.

---

[243] See other examples of Heaven's Golden Light in Appendix A.

[244] Neal A. Maxwell, "Swallowed Up in the Will of the Father," *Ensign*, November 1995, 24.

That is a similar conclusion to what Holocaust survivor Viktor Frankl found in a concentration camp in Germany:

> Everything can be taken from a man but one thing: the last of human freedoms—to choose one's attitude in any given set of circumstances, to choose one's own way.[245]

~

A little later in the day, two young men, Jeff and Ruston—humble, faithful teens—brought the sacrament to us from an LDS chapel nearby, and that brought an exceedingly sweet feeling. They shared with us what some of the speakers had talked about in the meeting we'd missed. I shared with them the pictures of our missionary twins, because Jeff and Ruston were both planning to go on missions themselves in a couple of years.

At 5:30 p.m., Mom B and Lorin came over with their support and companionship. Mom B rubbed Scott's feet with peppermint oil and spoon-fed him some soup while Lorin napped and I called our kids on our cell phone. After a while, Scott called out, "You talk too long!" (So, in my opinion, he wasn't quite as meek as he'd been four hours earlier.) I didn't think we all needed to be rubbing his feet, and I had four sets of children to talk to plus emails from Aaron and Matt.

After Mom B and Lorin left at 8:30 p.m., my eyes landed on President Monte's blessing that I had typed out before leaving home and taped to the wall. One line that I hadn't remembered caught my eye: "I bless you to find the best help available, whether through doctors or other means." Scott was not feeling like OHI was working for him, but he still needed other treatment. I wondered, "Where was that 'best help available'? Could it possibly be Mexico?"

---

[245] Viktor Frankl, *Man's Search for Meaning* (New York: Pocket Books, 1959), 86.

CHAPTER 30

BLACK SALVE

MARCH

We told the OHI staff that the Institute was not working for Scott and we would not be staying. They kindly allowed us to stay in our townhouse until we could make other arrangements. The weekend had been a difficult time to contact people. Facility after facility was closed. On Monday, I was prepared to work on it all day while Scott rested in our room as much as possible. The only thing he did that was part of the OHI program besides having wheatgrass juice was to go down to his second colonic.

On our way, we stopped at the OHI common room, where I tried reaching the ozone clinic on the phone. Still no response. Going outside again on this marvelously sunny day, we walked slowly down several sets of outdoor stairs to reach Bonnie's Colonics. Cute, dimpled Bonnie welcomed us, her short, curly brown hair bobbing as she set up her apparatus. While she worked on Scott, she listened to our quandary about finding another place for him to go. With her hands busy, Bonnie motioned with her head to brochures in the corner from the New Hope Clinic in Tijuana, suggesting that we look into it.

"Oh, them," I replied, picking up a trifold brochure. "I looked into them for my sister several years ago; I even talked with their surgeon. Super nice guy. But when I looked them up online this year, their information had changed. They didn't look like they had much to offer."

Bonnie countered, "No, they are a really good facility. They do amazing things down there. Don't you know they have to phrase things indefinitely to stay in business?" She sounded amazed that I didn't understand the game. I *did* understand the game; I just kept forgetting that people had to play it.

She continued, "If they say anything like, 'We can cure...' or 'We have healed...' they'll be shut down!"

I said, "I thought that's why they practiced in Tijuana—to avoid being shut down."

"You'd be surprised what agencies lurk around to pounce on clinics and shut them down! They have to be overly careful." She told us of her own good experience at their clinic and then encouraged me: "Call them."

> "You'd be surprised what agencies lurk around
> to pounce on clinics and shut them down!
> They have to be overly careful."

I thought about CSCT and about Allen's lab, and how both had been shut down, even though both offered great benefits and neither was using harmful treatments. So maybe there was something to this New Hope after all. Scott finished his colonic, and we took the brochure back to our townhouse.

With a prayer in my heart and at Scott's urging, I went back to the common room to call. First, I called the large ozone clinic again. No answer. So I called New Hope.

To my delight, a pleasant-sounding man who simply called himself Stephen answered the phone. No title. No "doctor." Just a simple name. That was rather refreshing. I explained Scott's situation, and to my astonishment, Stephen said they could fit him in—right now! Hope leaped in my heart. Stephen was able to answer all my questions. He said that the Spanish-speaking surgeon was still at the lab, and he reiterated their philosophy that involved a multidisciplinary approach: they worked on building up the immune system and other systems of the body while simultaneously working to eliminate the cancer.

> *Their philosophy involved a multidisciplinary approach: they built up the body while simultaneously working to eliminate the cancer.*

Familiarity flooded back to me! All this time I'd been searching for something that was dancing at the edges of my consciousness but had never come fully into my mind. It wasn't until this moment that I realized I had come full circle; *this* was the method that I'd been looking for all along!

Stephen asked what kind of cancer Scott had, where it was, and how big it was. He whistled at the nine centimeter by four centimeter size and then said, "Well, I've dealt with worse."

I asked about the cancer-attacking portion of their program. They did use chemo if they felt it was right for that person, but they also used a variety of other methods. I asked about black salve, that elusive and expensive ointment that I had initially felt so drawn to. (I had found a lady who administered it who was scheduled to come over that very night to tell us about it.) Yes, they occasionally used black salve, although they preferred other treatments.

When I asked if they used cobra venom, his voice immediately lowered to a whisper. "Where did you hear that?" he asked softly and furtively.

"From Bonnie at the colonic shop at OHI," I answered in my usual voice.

His restrained response quieted me. "We don't talk about that on the phone."

Would my naivety never end? I could never get used to the rules alternative health practitioners had to live with!

I asked about Holographic Repatterning (now called Resonance Repatterning), which was mentioned in the pamphlet. He answered, "That's a method for changing the frequencies in the body using sound and light. It allows the body to completely eliminate certain negative thought patterns.

The creator of the system, healer Chloe Wordsworth, says, 'When you change what you resonate with, you change your life. You feel lighter, as if the burden's lifted.'"[246]

I nodded silently as he spoke. It sounded like a different form of the toning that had been so successful on Thursday or like those vibrational healing machines I'd seen at singing conventions. I then asked what they did for pain, one of Scott's main concerns.

"What's he on now?"

"OxyContin and Endocet."

"OxyContin is addictive, and it covers up the pathway we need to use for healing. We need to get him off that. But we have some other things. We *do* have pharmacies down here. To tell you the truth, when the tumor implodes, there is no more pain."

"Fair enough," I said.

They agreed to enter Scott into their clinic tomorrow, and he gave me phone numbers for a hotel near the clinic. I returned to our room with renewed hope and vigor.

"Guess what? You've been accepted! We're going to the New Hope Clinic in Tijuana tomorrow—and there is a doctor there!"

Scott was so relieved; he lay back and went to sleep for the rest of the afternoon.

~

The last person to meet with us before we left Lemon Grove was Cherie, the lady who worked with black salve. She'd been referred not only by Bonnie, but also by the local natural foods store's integrative treatment "underground."

---

[246] Resonance Repatterning creates changes in the body partly through light frequencies. Perhaps Chloe's work uses German scientist Dr. Fritz-Albert Popp's biophoton theory. He said, "We now know ... that light can initiate, or arrest cascade-like reaction in the cells, and that genetic cellular damage can be virtually repaired, within hours, by faint beams of light." MJ Pangman and Melanie Evans, *Dancing with Water* (California: Uplifting Press, 2017), 249.

At long last someone could tell us about this elusive potent salve!

Dark-haired, slight Cherie swept into the townhouse with a flourish, flowered scarf at her neck, carrying a scrapbook and supplies in her arms. Scott had been watching war news on TV, as he often did. (The mission in Iraq was a carryover from the war in Afghanistan, and by March 20 would become its own war.) Cherie straightened her dress and scarf and put her heels daintily together as she sat on the couch by Scott. She was careful and solicitous of him, but also cheery and happy. She could see that his breathing was labored and that he was doing poorly. After making sure he wanted her to be there, she began.

"I use an old traditional recipe from American Indians. My supply actually comes from a Native American on a reservation." The ingredients were indeed bloodroot, sheep sorrel, red clover, and the other things I had once bought to make it myself, but they were all ground to a fine powder and mixed with a binding substance. The dark reddish-brown paste was put into a tiny white jar. The cost was sixty dollars for half an ounce!

She told how it was administered: a dime-sized amount—no more than a nickel-sized amount—on the protruding tumor. It was rubbed on with an applicator rather than bare fingers. The whole point of black salve, it turns out, was to burn a hole through the skin. (Scott had screamed bloody murder when we'd applied his whole grapefruit-sized tumor with a garlic pack; imagine if it had been black salve!)

"Doesn't it hurt like crazy?" I asked in consternation.

"Sometimes it hurts a little. Sometimes just little pinpricks. One woman who had a tumor on her abdomen said it tickled. After the hole is created, it doesn't hurt at all, because the hole is already there."

"Then what?"

"Black salve is only for creating a hole, and that takes one to three days. Then you rub on a drawing salve to keep the edges open. The drawing salve you can apply with your fingers several times a day."

"Doesn't it get infected?" I asked.

"No, the drawing salve is sterile and acts as an antibiotic as well as drawing out the cancer. It goes into the roots and kills all foreign matter and draws it out." Cherie gave us some papers that explained more.

Black salve was not a gentle healer. In many cases it was a relentless substance that hunted down and penetrated all abnormal tissue. Pain, swelling, redness around the area, and sometimes fever were associated with its use. The salve went in and traveled the area to the roots, killing all foreign matter (i.e., tumors) and drawing it out. Black salve completely eliminated abnormal tissue and stimulated regrowth of healthy tissue.[247]

"People use black salve for other things than tumors," Cherie said. "They use it to get rid of moles and warts too. And it's used on animals—animals seem to mind it less than people do. Here, let me show you some photographs." Cherie opened her scrapbook and showed us photos of an older woman she had helped.

> *I imagine black salve is in the underground of*
> *America's cancer options because it sounds ruthless and scary.*
> *Our society must consider this method to be barbaric,*
> *figuring that months and years of vomiting, feeling cold,*
> *and going bald is much more sensible.*

The woman's cancer was just under her collarbone. The succession of photos showed the cancer coming out of the hole, layer upon layer, and fanning into a circle as it exited the hole. It looked exactly like a gray tissue flower. If the color hadn't been so ghastly, and the placement hadn't been so high up, it would have looked almost like a feathery, festive flower jacket pin. After ten days, the tumor had been drawn from the inside to the outside. When the drawing salve was discontinued, a scab formed, just like the body would create for any abrasion. Finally, the whole thing sloughed off, like any good scab does when it's ready to come off. The woman had a small round scar

---

[247] From Cherie's papers. See Lawrence Wilson, "Black Salve," http://drlwilson.com/articles/BLACK%20SALVE .htm.

where the scab had been—a small price to pay for getting rid of a cancer.

If we weren't supposed to be under a doctor's care tomorrow, we would have tried black salve right then. But we were at least happy to learn of its proper use, to see photographs, and to hear testimonials.[248] I imagine black salve is in the underground of America's cancer options because it sounds ruthless and scary.[249] Our society must consider this method to be barbaric, figuring that months and years of vomiting, feeling cold, and going bald is much more sensible.

To celebrate Scott going to New Hope tomorrow, Scott and I ignored juicing, sprouting, wheatgrassing, and seed pulverizing. We ordered in Chinese, and we both thought a meal had never tasted so good!

---

[248] For a variety of photographs of and information on this modality, search the internet for "black salve."

[249] See Appendix A for a summary of the Harry Hoxsey story, which used something akin to black salve.

CHAPTER 31

THE NEW "DANCE" AT NEW HOPE

MARCH

T uesday morning, Scott stepped gingerly through a light rain and into the waiting taxi that would drive us the hour to Tijuana. Too weak to support himself, he reclined his head and body on me. We rode in a companionable silence. Part of me was anxious and worried for him, but part of me was strangely content just to sit next to him and to feel his presence so warm against me. Apprehensive of what kind of a place we were going to, Mom B and Lorin drove behind us. Who knew what this clinic might be like?

We entered Mexico easily and bypassed all the children who pressed up against the cars, eager for handouts. Even though my heart went out to them, I was content just to leave the windows rolled up; Scott's need was greater than theirs. We continued past the market area at the border to a lovely section of town where there were well-kept buildings, beautiful flowers, and a central island of imposing statues in the middle of a street called Paseo de los Heroes, the Way of Heroes. I was surprised, though, when our driver stopped in front of a narrow five-story building saying, "Here you are." The medical buildings I was used to going to were large and imposing, so I couldn't imagine why he thought this smallish building was our destination. I questioned the driver, and he pointed to the white building, saying, "Yes, that is the address."

One of the doctors spotted us and hurried outside. Scott hauled himself slowly out of the car and started walking with halting steps through a gentle drizzle. A surprised look of concern flashed across the doctor's face, but then he was suddenly at Scott's side, putting his arm around him and carefully leading him up the walk. He coached Scott with a litany of positive, kind words. "Slow is good. We'll make it. You're doing just fine!" I smiled. I could tell right away from his beautiful Spanish lilt that he was the same surgeon who had been on the three-way call with my sister. It was unusual but nice to have the doctor himself supporting my husband's faltering steps.

> *There was something different and very lovely here: this, then, was truly the world of holistic healing.*

There was no elevator, so Dr. Jorge supported Scott while he walked up the cold white steps to the third floor. Entering the clinic, we met another man and his beautiful wife. It was Stephen, the man with whom I had spoken most recently. An accredited doctor of naturopathy, he was the owner of the clinic, and his wife worked with him. Because of his training and experience, I considered him a doctor, even though I knew his degree would not merit that title in the States. So that was it—just two doctors to run a medical center. I hadn't realized before how small the "smaller" Tijuana clinics were!

The first thing they did was put Scott on nutritional IVs. The surgeon said with concern, "He is so depleted, his body has nothing to build on. This is our first task."

He gently eased Scott onto a bed and tucked blankets around him, making him comfortable and warm. Mom B, Lorin, and I hovered near the edges of the bare, tiled room, chilly now with the rain drumming outside. Both

Stephen and Dr. Jorge continually talked to Scott, encouraging him and asking for his input. Scott responded wearily but positively. There was something different and very lovely here: the doctors didn't just "care for" their patient; they literally included him in all their choices. This, then, was truly the world of holistic healing. This was more than lip service to the concept of holistic healing; it was what these doctors *lived*. The doctors treated Scott and the rest of us with absolute respect and as if we were equals. A perfect example is once when I moved out of the surgeon's way, saying, "Excuse me. Am I in your way?" Dr. Jorge had smiled. "Maybe I'm in your way." These men were more like servants, helpers, big brothers, or uncles than unreachable practitioners placed on a pedestal so high that one couldn't even talk to them, let alone be heard by them.[250]

On closer inspection, I thought these men were greater than medical practitioners doing medical jobs. They represented a pinnacle in medical achievement because their methods comprised *both* Western and Eastern modalities—all the knowledge from the West and all the natural healing from the East. They even seemed to be a sum of everyone else we'd been working with: they were as intuitive as Holly, as concerned as our Provo doctors, as energetic as Becky, as insightful as Pam, as compassionate as Dr. Deirdre, and as ready to help as Chris.

Stephen invited Scott into this world of holistic healing by telling him, "We truly believe in the self-healing capabilities of the body and your participation in that healing."[251] Looking directly into his eyes, he continued, "You can get yourself better, Scott."

> *"We truly believe in the self-healing capabilities of the body, and your participation in that healing." Looking directly into his eyes, he continued, "You can get yourself better, Scott."*

---

[250] I believe that Western culture's expectation that physicians know everything and can do everything is grossly unfair both to them and to us.

[251] I noticed how New Hope's holistic healing principles followed the Four Tenets listed in LeShan, *Cancer as a Turning Point*, 133.

As they administered the nutritional IVs, the surgeon told us, "We have a plan, but again, these IVs are our first task." Then Dr. Jorge explained their plan to us. "Cancer is a complex, composite illness. The cancer eats the nourishment, makes the body acidic, and lowers the immune level on its way to the rest of what it does to invade the body. Our task is to build up the nourishment and lower the acidity so that the immunity can be strengthened." And, using the precise phrase he had on the phone with my sister, he said in a tone of awe, "Immunity—that's the horse we're counting on."

Stephen added, "Cancer involves the whole body, not just the specific location where it's situated. Cancer of the liver, for instance, is cancer of the whole body. The immune system is depleted and the whole body is acidic. At this clinic, we work on those issues as well as working to change thought processes and balance emotions. You see, once the cancer is eliminated, if thoughts and emotions don't change, it will recur."

There it was—their five-pronged, multidisciplinary approach to cancer:

- **Nourish**
- Increase **alkalinity**
- Increase **immunity**
- **Balance** thoughts and emotions
- **Attack**, that is, actively work to destroy the cancer

New Hope's Five-Pronged Approach to Cancer

- **Nourish**
- Increase **alkalinity**
- Increase **immunity**
- **Balance** thoughts and emotions
- **Attack** the cancer

Although both doctors were involved in the whole process, it seemed to me that Dr. Jorge's emphasis was making his patient less acidic, increasing immunity, and administering the attack method, while Stephen's was to increase nourishment and to balance the client's internal thoughts and emotions.

Stephen then made an astonishing statement. "I used to think that most cancers had an emotional component to them. I now believe 100 percent of cancers have an emotional component." There it was again—the idea that the mind influences the body or, as Dr. Candace Pert stated, "Your body is the outward manifestation of your mind."[252] Stephen's ideas were not new—his statement echoed Chris's, Holly's, Becky's, Pam's, and Bob Proctor's, to name a few—but his realization was startlingly clear-cut.

> "I used to think that most cancers had an emotional component to them. I now believe 100 percent of cancers have an emotional component."

Thinking About Barbara

I thought long and hard about Stephen's astonishing statement, particularly as it applied to my sister. At first, I thought his statement implied that there was something wrong with the *person*, and yet I didn't know anyone as kind, as gracious, as generous, as inclusive, or as thoughtful as Barbara. She was my hero; there was nothing wrong with *her*. She possessed every quality that would cause people to love and admire another person. Yet her *situation* did have challenges. She was a second wife (the first having died of cancer), two of the five children she helped raise had ADD/ADHD, and one daughter was intellectually disabled. When the kids were older, she considered going back to teaching, but the officials said that she would need to go back for *four years* instead of just taking a one- or two-semester refresher course to switch from

---

[252] Siegel, *Peace, Love and Healing*, 164.

junior high to elementary teaching—ridiculous! Finally, she mentioned to me on the phone several times that she stayed out of the way of the youngest boy, whose massive body filled a doorway by the time he was fifteen and whose behavior grew more unpredictable the older he got.

Clearly, she had situational issues that she dealt with, but was she really "dealing" with situations or was she "keeping" them? I'd say she was a keeper, as evidenced by her two bouts of ulcers. According to Karol Truman's list of "Probable Feelings Causing Illness" in her book *Feelings*, ulcers are related to "worrying over details, feelings of anxiety, fear or tension, and feelings of helplessness/powerless."[253] Hmm, that could describe Barbara. Even though she was absolutely loved and well accepted in her family, neighborhood, and church, apparently she *did* have some things in her life that were emotionally based that may have unknowingly contributed to her cancer. In fact, she was *so* giving and altruistic that something in Larry LeShan's book may have been written about her: "By her actions, she was telling her body that it was always someone else's turn and never hers."[254]

I turned back to speak to Dr. Jorge about New Hope's five-pronged program: nutrition, alkalinity, immunity, balance, and attack. "Which of the five do we do first?" I asked eagerly.

The surgeon laughed. "All. It's a dance. It has to be woven together at the same time, and that's what makes our work so unique, so hard, and so rewarding. We have to allow the body to work with its own processes. It is typical for people not to come to us until they're in their last stages of cancer, so we hope that the body will give us time to work."

> *"We have to allow the body to work with its own processes."*

---

[253] Truman, *Feelings Buried Alive*, 270.

[254] LeShan, *Cancer as a Turning Point*, 3.

Stephen said, "It's amazing that any of us in these clinics in Mexico even have the success we do! You should see the state people are in when they come!" He turned to Scott, grinning. "You look good, Scott, compared to some of them!"

Scott wryly smiled. "I'm sure I look just great."

Mom B asked when the tumor might be gone.

Dr. Jorge said, "We've seen regression in three weeks, with the latest about six weeks. These big tumors, about six weeks, then they just implode on themselves."

When Mom B and Lorin's questions were answered to their satisfaction, and when Lorin got tired, they went back to Temecula. Later, after the doctors had taken care of Scott, they surprised me by turning to me.

"Now, what are *you* going to eat for lunch?" they queried.

I shook my head. I hadn't gotten that far in my plans. But they didn't miss a thing. Dr. Jorge's wife had actually made me soup for lunch on this first day! The hot soup warmed me on the cold day and put off for one more day my chance of getting lost in Tijuana. Then they showed me nearby places where I could get lunch in succeeding days and hopefully be able to find my way back. They gave me their business card with a phone number, just in case!

∼

When Scott had somewhat revived, Stephen got right to business, asking directly about his shoulder twitch. "Scott, how long has this been going on?" I had seen Stephen notice it with a wrinkled brow when we had first walked in. I waited to see how Scott would respond. Resigned, but a bit surly that he had to admit the presence of this anomaly, he stated, "Almost thirty years." Scott was surprised to see Stephen waiting patiently for the rest of the story, so Scott told him. I was thrilled that Scott would start opening up to him; none of us like talking about the bad aspects of ourselves.

Scott started by telling how he decided on a degree at the University of Utah. "Because I was smart in math, people told me to go into chemical engineering, as that's where the money was. I didn't even know what chemical engineering was, but I followed what they said."[255] He then told of his first job in San Jose, where he planned to spend his adult life, only to come back to Utah after two months. (His new job was in a cavernous warehouse-looking facility. Trying to be friendly, he'd asked the man next to him how long he'd worked there. The employee had proudly responded, "Twenty-five years." Scott had rolled his eyes as he thought, "Great, in twenty-five years I will have moved from *this* desk to *that* one, not to mention they've assigned me mechanical engineering work and I was hired as a chemical engineer. And they just stuck us new guys at a desk with no help, and we don't really know what we're doing!") He told about that locked-in-a-closet-and-emerging-three-years-later-with-your-degree feeling while getting his Ph.D. He told about his first job as an assistant professor at BYU, how the department chair had assigned him tasks that none of the veterans in the department wanted, and how he had put his heart and soul into them, not realizing they were of virtually no importance to his main job. He talked of writing articles and papers and even part of a book, only to have them published under the dean's name. He finished with his loss of tenure and the contracted work he had done since. Through all of it, there was a theme that he felt he had not had a choice in his vocation, that he had merely been driven from one area to another.

Stephen commented every now and then at how difficult this had been for Scott his whole adult life. "And yet you stuck with it, Scott, so you could provide for your family. I admire you for that. That took a tremendous amount of persistence and determination."

Gratitude and amazement were written all over Scott's face. To have his difficulties appreciated instead of being thrown back in his face (as happened with that first therapist we had gone to see) felt glorious and relieving.

---

[255] At least Scott was led into a field of study that would always be needed, as stated by Dr. Wiser: "Petroleum reserves are finite and cannot endure indefinitely against the reality of increasing world consumption. Furthermore, it is a reality that reserves in the United States are being consumed more rapidly than discoveries of new domestic reserves are made." Wendell H. Wiser, *Energy Resources* (New York: Springer, 2000), 359.

When Scott finished, Stephen looked from the twitching shoulder to the tumor right below it. "There may be a connection and there may not. But the cancer is a rare form that started in smooth muscle and it's directly below the shoulder. We need to get the spasms stopped, Scott."

Scott was pleasantly agreeable then, seeing that Stephen's evaluation exactly matched Reg's, Holly's, and Becky's. (As an interesting side note, *every* integrative worker that we met was alarmed by Scott's shoulder tic, but *not one* Western healthcare worker mentioned the twitching or even seemed to notice it, let alone draw possible dots from it to the cancer that was directly below it.)

By the afternoon, Scott was looking and feeling much better. Nutritional IVs had again done the trick! Stephen felt Scott was well enough to ask for his case history, and Scott listed his usual health concerns as contained in the folders he had created at home. Here at New Hope, though, a medical history was only half of what they considered a case history. Stephen asked about career, family, and emotional responses, but Scott had a hard time answering. He was annoyed with questions about how he felt on certain subjects. How did *feeling* a certain way have anything to do with his cancer? Scott, the engineer, wasn't following Stephen's psychological line of reasoning any better than he had Director Pam's. And Scott, the perfectionist, didn't want all these aimless questions; he just wanted to get rid of the cancer, quickly and efficiently.

"Actually, feelings are very important, Scott," Stephen ended kindly. Then, taking a breath, he added brightly, "Tomorrow we'll start working on some exciting things!"

At the end of the day, a taxi dropped us off at our beautiful hotel. The Hotel Lucerna consisted of a new high-rise unit and an older two-story unit, separated by a pristine turquoise pool. We were in the high-rise, and when we got up to our seventh-floor room, I looked in vain for the thermostat. The rain that had drizzled all day was part of a cold front, and it was chillier than normal in Tijuana. I ran down to the desk. It turns out that there was no heat in the high-rise, thus no thermostat! (Coming from Utah, said to be the most seasonally challenged state in the nation, I was totally nonplussed.) Baffled as to what to say, I asked to be changed to a heated room. Those rooms, I was told, were only in the older part of the hotel, the two-story section across the pool from us.

"All right, could you please put us in the older part of the hotel?"

"Not tonight. We can get you into one of those rooms tomorrow."

I asked, "What do I do now? I have a sick husband who is freezing."

The man at the desk replied that they offered space heaters in the meantime.

"Great. Could you get me one of those, please?"

No, they couldn't. All the space heaters had already been taken. We were on our own for the night!

I bundled up Scott (and myself) and got us as warm as I could. His comments were of perplexed worry, of discomfort in being cold, and of going to such a small clinic. Then, from under the covers, he grumbled, "Why have we come here? This is barbaric."

CHAPTER 32

NEW HOPE:
HIS DAD'S BIRTHDAY

MARCH

The next morning, Scott was able to walk on his own to the clinic, which was an enormous improvement over yesterday. He walked slowly, head down, and leaned heavily on my hand, but it gave us time to talk (well, gave me time to talk to him) and to look at the beautiful flowers that were draped all around the Hotel Lucerna like a lei. Yesterday's rain had brought out their beauty. The rectangular pool had a rock waterfall off to one side, dripping with red, white, pink, and yellow blossoms. Although we didn't speak much Spanish, the employees knew enough English to help us get by. Every person who worked there was extremely kind and solicitous. I also noticed that every employee treated his or her job as the most important job at the hotel, whether it be maid, pool cleaner, custodian, clerk, or bellhop. There was something right about the management of this hotel!

At the clinic, Scott was a pitiable sight: thin neck, thin bare chest, and that horrible tumor poking out his right side. Dr. Jorge gave him more IVs "to beef him up," always talking with him, making him comfortable, and working with him to let him know what procedures were being done and why. Stephen met with him to give him a specific list of supplements he had made up overnight. I suspected that many of the supplements were basically the same as ones we had already bought, but we had put ourselves in a new place, so we had to play the new game. I hoped, at the least, that Scott would quit throwing up long enough to swallow them.

After Scott had rested, received enzymes, and been nourished through the IVs, the doctors said they needed an MRI. My heart sank. He was so ill; how could we move him again? Down three flights of stairs, across the lawn to the testing building called the Rayo, wait on hard chairs, and then back across the lawn and up three flights again. And the money! The cost of an MRI in the States was about $1,000. Here, there was no insurance; everything was out of pocket. Well, if they needed it, they needed it. Reluctantly, I gave my permission. Seeing my concern, Dr. Jorge quickly amended, "Oh, by the way, here in Mexico, it's $170!" The MRI was the *same* as we would receive in the States, just less money. It turns out that, years ago, Mexican doctors threw out the salespeople who wanted to bring insurance to the country, so procedures here were still done at cost. My question is: If a $170 MRI costs $1,000 in the States, who is getting the extra $830?

The MRI was necessary for the positioning of the big medical event of the day: the clinic's *tour de force*, the bioelectric therapy (BET) or Galvano machine.[256] This machine was the reason these doctors chose not to use chemotherapy or black salve for Scott's sarcoma. Some machines similar to this are now used in the United States for breast cancer, but they weren't allowed in the U.S. at the time for any kind of cancer. The BET machine, administered by the surgeon, was a combination of German and Chinese techniques.

---

[256] The bioelectric therapy (BET) or electro cancer therapy (ECT) machine was based on the groundbreaking research of Dr. Nordenstrom and Dr. Pekar.

Dr. Jorge possibly felt comfortable with this machine because he had received medical training in China for three years after he had received his medical degree from the International Medical School in Tijuana, the only medical university outside of the United States that licenses doctors to practice *in* the United States. In China, he was so good that the Chinese practitioners wanted him to stay, but he'd been drawn back to his family and his home country of Mexico.

The BET machine worked via two long, thin, gold acupuncture-like pins, one acid and one alkaline. They were poked through the skin at either end of the tumor, in the "beefiest" parts of it. (The tumor, having grown back after surgery, now measured thirteen centimeters by twelve centimeters—bigger than before—and was erratic in shape. The MRI showed the precise size and location of the tumor.) Electromagnetic waves ran from pin to pin. The electrical current killed cells most strongly at the heads, a little less strongly in the field between the heads, and weakest in the corona field that surrounded the path of the main electrical current.

Dr. Jorge had Scott lie down on his left side and covered him gently with a bright red blanket. Then, after donning surgical gloves and a mask, the doctor carefully inserted the long gold pins into that horrible protruding tumor and then, just as carefully, attached the wires from the machine to the pins. I could tell that Scott was breathing in a controlled, measured fashion to distract himself from the pain caused by the insertion of the long pins. Dr. Jorge kept a running dialogue of what he was doing, both distracting Scott and, at the same time, gauging how much Scott could stand. Finally, Dr. Jorge trilled happily, "We have blastoff!"

Dr. Jorge trilled happily, "We have blastoff!"

Scott stoically put up with the stinging that the treatment initially caused, but then, this is what he'd come for! I think another reason he put up with the pain caused by the needles is because Scott strongly responded to male authority. Duty and authority were important concepts in the fifties and sixties, when we grew up—in society, in our families, and in our church. (And, of course, we know that he stopped his use of green tea because he respected the authority of his church leaders.) Because of Scott's internal desire to conform to leaders, he was willing to do whatever his New Hope doctors wanted him to do. I was very grateful for that, because when he was back at the hotel with me, he didn't have any compunction to comply. He was stubborn and intractable—what my mother would have called "a pill." He got angry a lot, almost as if I were the cause of his difficulties. Now I realize that he was full of fears as well as agony, and those fears came out as anger. Nevertheless, life was definitely more pleasant at the clinic.

Scott's afternoon was filled with a private appointment with Stephen. I know some of what was said because Stephen later gave me my own session. "You are here too," he had told me, "and you need to learn this so you can help Scott."

Stephen said, "Remember yesterday I said that we'd learn some exciting things? We are! We're going to talk about changing thought patterns, because we need to identify and change what allowed the cancer to grab hold in the first place." (It sounded like OHI!) "Remember, unless one changes thoughts and behavior, the cancer *will recur.*"

> "Unless one changes thoughts and behavior,
> the cancer will recur."

∾

I was invited into their next session. Stephen asked Scott if he could substitute as a muscle tester for Scott, since Scott was so weak. My husband agreed. Stephen spent a minute muscle testing himself, then looked up and asked, "Scott, what happened to you at about age thirteen?"

Scott's eyebrows shot up, and he turned to look at me. Then he looked directly at Stephen. For a moment there was complete silence. Finally, taking a breath to pull himself together, Scott told him the story his mom had related to us. Stephen nodded his head, acknowledging the truth of it as it was told.

"It sounds like a boy who wanted more of a relationship with his father."

Scott agreed. Stephen waited patiently while Scott continued his thoughts.

"My dad was gone for two years of my early life. When I was one, he went on a two-year church mission to Hawaii. There was just my mother and me." Moving his thoughts to the present, he said, "I've thought about this war that I see on TV, and the children whose parent goes to war; when the parent comes home, the kids don't even know them."

"Do you think there was an issue of bonding with your dad?"

"I've wondered about that. Don't get me wrong; I loved my dad." Scott related memories about Blair that brought a smile to his face: the dad who jumped like an Olympian to grab the end of little Scott's balloon string as it started sailing away; the dad who inadvertently lit a pine tree on fire when he built a campfire too close to the tree; the dad who coached a city team so the small, slim boy could have a chance at baseball; the dad who took the family boating and played the ukulele with abandon.

Stephen said thoughtfully, "He sounds like a fun guy."

Scott answered, "He was, except when he took back my twenty-five-cent allowance! I just wish I'd had a little more of him. I wish he'd gone to priest-hood meetings with me on Sunday mornings—I walked to church, a mile down and a mile back, by myself every Sunday at 8:30 a.m., starting at age twelve. I wish he had come to my Eagle Court of Honor instead of just my grandpa being there. I wish that he had gone to church on Sundays instead of choosing that day to go boating. And I wish that he had not divorced my mom."

Stephen pictured that slim boy stretched out on the grass. "That thirteen-year-old felt it particularly hard. Did you know that your cells have been vibrating that hurt over and over and over? It's time to let that go; no use keeping it. It's not doing you any good."

Scott was thoughtful that afternoon as we walked slowly back to the hotel. Then he said, "Do you know what today is?"

March 5. It was his dad's birthday.

A cell cannot be in growth and protection
mode at the same time.

One of Stephen's Teachings at New Hope:
Cancer Is a Cell's Protection against Fear

What do you think of? Where are your thoughts? If there is fear, part of the body holds on to the vibrations in the cells and constantly passes on fear vibrations.[257] Cells naturally move outwardly in growth and replication but are forced to retract or conserve their energy when repairing or feeling attacked. A cell cannot be in growth and protection mode at the same time. Chronic protection leads to a disruption of the tissue and its function. When bad experiences occur, fear is solidified. The body, then, feels that it needs protection. Cancer is that protection. With further fear, the protection increases. In the case of your shoulder, Scott, for thirty years it's been ready to wield a sword to go into battle against the fear. Finally, the fight against life has gone down to the life-giving structure—the diaphragm: the breath organism.[258]

---

[257] In meditation, people are taught to take the split second between breaths to direct the conscious into new paths.

[258] Private session with Stephen Linsteadt.

CHAPTER 33

NEW HOPE: WRITHING

MARCH

After two days of cold, the weather had finally turned agreeable. The hotel had changed us, though, to the older, two-story unit that had heat, and Scott was slowly walking to and from the clinic every day. "A turtle could go faster," he lamented.

"You're doing fine," I praised. "At least you're walking!"

Every day he received three IVs (two vitamins and one amino acid), enzymes, the BET/Galvano machine, and more concept training while sitting or lying on his left side, which didn't have the tumor protruding. I read or embroidered over by the windows in the clean, spare BET room, now with a thermal blanket over my lap, getting up often when Scott needed my help. The surgeon played wonderful music in the surgical room—Sarah Brightman one day, Vivaldi's *Four Seasons* another. He and I had interesting conversations about art, music, and religion when he had a free minute. He admired

Michelangelo's *David* statue, and I said I'd seen it in Italy and also admired it. He had seen the inside of the beautiful Latter-day Saint San Diego California Temple, which juts out prominently above the 5 freeway in California, aptly calling it the "House of Heaven."[259] Scott joked occasionally with the doctors, but otherwise he said little. It seemed that he was saving what energy he had for his treatments. Beyond that, he was pale, cold, and depleted. He was still throwing up—nothing new there—while he tried to get off OxyContin. Stephen had again told him, "The drug is not only addictive; it works along the same pathway that you need to have open for healing. The pathway can't do both things."[260]

> "The drug is not only addictive; it works along the same pathway that you need to have open for healing. The pathway can't do both things."

Scott's mom called my cell phone from her house in Temecula, worried like crazy. I told her the surgeon said that Scott wasn't making enough red blood cells and that 60 percent of his right lung was filled with fluid. "They're working to get a lot of that fluid to leave his body. They seem to know what they're doing." I told her they had started the BET and reminded her what it was supposed to do. "Instead of surgery, it uses an electrical current to go in and destroy the tumor. It's nice because it's quite specific and only kills the cells near the current." After I finished, she sounded calmer.

For this day's session, Stephen talked about how being connected with God and with each other leads to a flow in life that allows a person to submit to life's experiences and not be fearful. He was trying to show Scott that "letting go" is not the same thing as "giving in," and "allowing" is not a sign of failure. "When we feel ourselves working with God and with nature," he said,

---

[259] "San Diego California Temple," www.ldschurchtemples.com/sandiego/.

[260] In 2007, the maker of OxyContin and three of its executives were fined for misleading the public about the painkiller's risk of addiction. In 2002, the drug caused 146 deaths and contributed to another 318. Patient Kenny Keith said, "The withdrawals were worse than the pain I was having." *Deseret News*, July 21, 2007, A3.

"we become greater than ourselves, not less than." He gave examples from nature: a leaf blown by wind, a ripple of water, and a grove of banyan trees that is actually one tree because of being connected underground.

All of us are extensions of God. Our energy comes from God. A leaf is stirred by God's hand. God's energy made the leaf; God's energy made the wind, and God's energy is still in the motions, and causing the motions that stirs the leaf. If we accept that, we don't have fear. We allow. We release. We let. We also recognize that a ripple seen on top of the water doesn't stand alone. Ripples join together and become part of each other—they are all connected to the water underneath.

Likewise, a banyan grove looks like a whole bunch of separate trees, but, in actuality, it is one tree with a common root. We, too, are part of a whole, although it seems we are separate. The whole of creation is tied together. Being submissive means being part of that banyan tree, being part of a larger energy than we personally possess. If we think we are a separate banyan tree, that is ego. We will actually fail if we try to do things separately.[261]

Needless to say, this little bit about the banyan tree is only the iceberg tip of what we were taught. For me, the vocalist, I had already come to terms with many of these ideas of connectedness through my singing and teaching career, and *still* the concepts were a lot to digest. For instance, I had felt connectedness and God's power radiating through me when my singing was greater than my natural abilities. And I had felt submissiveness in the fact that you work, you study, you practice, and you prepare, and even though you're never really as good as you would like to be, somehow you're good enough to touch people's hearts with your music. And strangely, the act of singing, which can seem so strong and powerful to a listener, can, at the same time, make the singer feel totally exposed. Singers often feel naked in front of an audience (and have dreams about it)! A perceptive listener can actually tell much about the singer's character as well as the topics of the songs, just as a

---

[261] Private session with Stephen Linsteadt.

personal trainer can look at someone entering a gym and sense immediately much about their muscles, their eating habits, and their overall level of health.

Even though I'd had many experiences of feeling connected to something greater than myself through music, an extraordinary thing occurred when Stephen taught this banyan concept: I started feeling *joined* to Scott in an uncanny way, almost as if our molecules, our very cells, were actually melded together. The feeling didn't last long, but while it did, it was a lovely, exciting feeling.

But to my anguished husband, what Stephen said seemed arcane or confusing. Scott didn't talk about the concepts when we were together or even seem electrified by them. Maybe he was just too tired and hurting to process anything new. Maybe he was too hollowed out by this horrible parasitic thing growing inside him to think at all! Or maybe the concept of "being part of" just didn't ring a bell at that time. After all, his whole life he had done things by himself: research, writing reports, rebuilding engines, learning instruments, and learning languages. His psyche may have objected: "Self-imposed diligence has worked well for me; why change?"

$\approx$

Friday started and ended very differently. The morning started with a cab ride because Scott was too tired to walk. It ended in his walking home from the clinic, body erect, and without holding my hand for support! His back didn't hurt, and he was quite energetic. He'd had more BET and IVs and was weaning himself off OxyContin—no easy task. He'd had another session in Resonance Repatterning and responded well to the doctors. Overall, he'd had a good week. It looked like they had stabilized his condition with the nutritional IVs, and they'd started to kill the cancer cells, which would ultimately reduce the tumor.

Dr. Jorge was pleased with their "dance" so far, and Stephen had told Scott, "I'll kick your butt Monday if you can't talk yourself into thinking, 'I don't have cancer.'"

When the surgeon had indicated he was happy with the BET, I enthused, "Why don't we do it twice a day, then?"

He had laughed merrily, and that's when I knew that I'd again said something naive.

"Every time we use it, it kills cancer cells. Those cells are toxic. How many of those toxic cells do you want running around in your husband's body before they are eliminated?"

Okay. Point made. We left the clinic and had fish tacos from a food stand.

∾

Saturday was a half day of treatment. Dr. Jorge's three sons came to the clinic with him. They were all as polite, handsome, and considerate as he was. They wanted to follow in their father's footsteps as a physician and even shared a joke with me. "A Brief History of Medicine" goes like this:

I have an earache. What should I do?

2000 BC: Here, eat this root.

1000 AD: That root is heathen; say this prayer.

1850 AD: That prayer is superstitious; drink this potion.

1940 AD: That potion is snake oil; swallow this pill.

1985 AD: That pill is ineffective; take this antibiotic.

2000 AD: That antibiotic is artificial; here, eat this root.

There was some truth in the joke, and we laughed. Some aspects of medicine are cyclical, though, such as the use of herbs or magnets. Chemotherapy, as I mentioned earlier, was viewed as quackery in the 1920s and now is widely accepted. As Scott was hooked up to the BET machine, Dr. Jorge again mentioned that the Galvano/BET machine and their other methods worked *in concert* with the body, as opposed to chemotherapy, which works *against* the body by administering poison. "No method has a guaranteed outcome, but our modalities give the body a chance to work with itself."

Scott didn't look as well on this Saturday, though. He threw up twice and never ate lunch or dinner. His appendages were swollen with edema. The surgeon told me that the swelling was an expected reaction: as the cancer cells were killed with the BET, the dead, toxic cells went out through the lymph system, causing swelling on the way. After they were eliminated from his system, his appendages would go back to normal. Indeed, the next day the edema was down.

The doctor also told him, "You are also still in shock from being told that you have cancer. Any of us would be in shock." Shock causes reactions in the body, and they're not good ones.

Mom B and Lorin gave us a welcome surprise visit. They brought letters from Sara and Katie that had been mailed to Grandma's house. Sara said that Katie was painting her room, and it was going to be a luscious Asian look in red, gold, and black. (The deal was always that I bought the paint and the kids did the work.) Other news from home was that Sara's husband, Allen, along with two friends who knew construction, were framing the family room in our basement—finally! (Again, I'd buy the lumber and they'd do the work.) Scott had wanted to build the room with the twins, but by the time he'd been ready to start, he'd gotten that job in Ogden that required so much extra travel time he couldn't fit in a construction project. I wasn't sure he'd be thrilled that someone else was taking over his project, so I didn't say anything to him.

When Mom B and Lorin had gone and night had come, Scott's pain, nausea, and general discomfort increased. He and I were up and down all night.

Sunday was a lazy day. I woke late, Scott hardly got out of bed at all, and Mom B and Lorin came again. Dr. Jorge came with one of his sons at 11:00 a.m., after their church. We were very relieved to see him. One of the consequences of working with a small clinic is that they may not have anyone covering for them when they take a needed break once a week. After OHI, we were relieved to have doctors on hand, but we weren't prepared to have a day and a half without them! After they left, I sat on the edge of Scott's bed while his mom fed him and Lorin dozed in a chair.

She asked him, "Are you in a lot of pain?"

Scott was stoic, but his eyes had an underlying look of fear. He answered, "Yes."

I ventured, "Do you want to live?"

"Yes, I want to live!" he answered vehemently. "But I've got to get out of this pain."

"Yes, I want to live! But I've got to get out of this pain."

I thought of what the doctors had said when we first came to New Hope— that the pain would go away when the tumor imploded. I wished that huge sarcoma would hurry and respond to the treatment, but at least I was relieved that Scott said he wanted to live!

Napping and playing four rounds of Rack-O alleviated his distress for a while. Then, while he napped, I napped too. While I was sleeping, a remarkable thing happened.

I had been praying earnestly—as far-fetched as it sounds—to take some of his pain onto myself that maybe he could stand the rest of the pain until the tumor imploded. I wished for it fervently. As I mentioned, I felt very tied to my husband, almost as if he and I were one being. Suddenly, I noticed something horrible inside me, burning and writhing all around my middle and right side. It roiled inside me—thin, searching tentacles coiling and twisting, probing for places to invade. It circled over and under, around and through, like a tangled mass of telephone wires from old Ma Bell. It snaked inside my chest with a painful, ever-present vileness. With an emerging awareness, it occurred to me that this was Scott's cancer! It wasn't a sharp pain like a knife, and it wasn't a dull pain like a hammer, but *pain it was*. It was anguish and pure torment made doubly so because it shouldn't be there and you couldn't get rid of it. No matter how hard you twisted, contorted, or swiveled around, you couldn't get it out of your body!

As repulsive as it was, I wanted this anguish to stay and to remain at this horrible, excruciating level because I hoped it would help Scott, that maybe I could share his burden. After a time, though, the feeling slowly started dissipating. By the time it had ebbed away completely, I was awake. With profound disappointment, I realized I hadn't taken any of his hurt at all—it had only been a dream. What an amazing gift to me, though, to feel, for just a moment, something of the horror he was going through.

I thought of a story I had read long ago in *Reader's Digest*. An older woman kept calling out, "Snakes! Snakes!" Her family thought she was crazy; there were no snakes in her room. After she died, an autopsy was done. Her torso was filled with coiling strands of cancer. "Snakes" indeed.

Sunday ended in the sounds of the city—an Andean flute outside, planes flying low overhead, the Spanish language, and stadium noise: a soccer game? a bullfight? lacrosse? You could hear a fountain, mourning doves, traffic along the Boulevard of Heroes, and a car alarm going off. And, yes, there was the sound of Scott's nausea resulting in that night's supplements and dinner leaving him. Who could blame him for refusing to eat more?

CHAPTER 34

THE "DANCE" CONTINUES AT NEW HOPE

MARCH

Monday morning started with Dr. Jorge energetically saying to Scott, "Are you up for a new and different round of crusaders against your cells?"

Scott answered a solid "Yes." He was told that every three days he would receive a cobra venom suppository.

"These are extremely alkaline and suffocate the cancer cells." Good. Bring it on! That strategy was added to the other ones: BET, enzymes, and IVs.

Scott was pleasant again now that he was back in the clinic. I wanted to put my hands on my hips and say, "Hey! Be nice to me like you are to the doctors!" but I just sat back and listened. They began an interesting discussion on, of all things, the Salem witch trial (in which one of my ancestors, by the way, was hanged as a witch) and somehow ended with a discourse on the immune system.

Dr. Jorge was convinced that "we are getting away from nature too much. Too many people think that a completely sterile environment is the best way, the safest way. That is not how the body was designed. We are designed to be part of the earth, and if something goes awry, the body's immune system is designed to fix it. The immune system is a wondrous thing!"

> *"We are designed to be part of the earth, and if something goes awry, the body's immune system is designed to fix it."*

In the afternoon, Stephen tried to teach Scott how to change his circumstances—that is, his cancer—instantaneously. Deepak Chopra said that this dramatic shift in awareness is called "spontaneous remission" by doctors, but by scientists it is called "quantum." The word denotes a discrete jump from one level of functioning to a higher level—the quantum leap. "Suddenly [a patient] feels, 'I am not limited to my body. All that exists around me is part of myself.' At that moment, such patients apparently jump to a new level of consciousness that prohibits the existence of cancer."[262] It had to do with awareness, or as Bob Proctor said at a seminar, "What's going on on the inside *shows* (or manifests) on the outside."[263]

Using the analogy of a baseball stadium, Stephen tried to show Scott how he could attain the miracle he wanted, even in this dire moment.

Let's imagine an atom as if it were the size of a baseball stadium. The proton/neutron combination is in the middle, about the size of a baseball. The electrons are the size of gnats flying around the bleachers. Now, we want to move this cancer, which is nothing more than a "baseball" and a bunch of "gnats." Moving the baseball is no big deal, but most people try to move the stadium. That's hard. What we must do is identify the fear under the cancer that created it, and then

---

[262] Chopra, *Quantum Healing*, 15.

[263] Bob Proctor, *Lead the Field Seminar* (Irvine, CA: Nikken, 2000).

forgive. When we do, that allows "the baseball" to move or leave. Often our desire is to control outside events, but that moves us away from our inner peace and gives rise to negative thoughts and feelings. If our tissues and organs perceive a need for protection due to our negative thoughts, they will compromise their growth behavior.[264]

I wish I had room in this book to further explore these concepts. They are very exciting and are just beginning to be understood. Stephen taught about sitting enthroned at our heart-chamber, which is filled with white light from a Higher Source. He taught that the fabric of the body (the body's matrix[265]) should be even and coherent, free from hurt, anger, toxins, or free radicals that get it out of whack—similar to Dr. Bradley Nelson's "Six Things" that shouldn't be in bodies. And he used the image of scalar waves and the eternal Möbius coil to allow breath to enter and to configure a person to truth.

When Stephen gave me my own session on these concepts, I had a dramatic shift in awareness. I felt like I was poised on the edge of a "precipice of uncharted territory"[266] and if I just jumped a wide chasm to the other side, all my own negativities would be changed. All my negativities would be healed. All I had to do was jump! But in that crucial split second when I needed mentally to commit to action, I refused to do it. I was too scared to leave the solid ground under me. Still, having stood on the precipice and seen the other side was something.

Scott sat through sessions patiently and talked with Stephen readily, but he didn't talk about them with me afterward. I didn't mind. He was getting what he needed at the clinic, and anything beyond that was a bonus.

∿

[264] Stephen Linsteadt and Maria Elena Boekemeyer, *The Heart of Health* (California: Natural Healing House Press, 2003), vii–6; private session with Stephen Linsteadt.

[265] Ursula Dowd's Biopulsar machine visually shows an un/even matrix in the body, youtube.com/watch?v=2HdrM918LBs.

[266] Phrase from Josh Cummings's blog, August 16, 2016.

That evening when Mom B and Lorin came back, they brought visitors: Scott's brother, Chip, and his family. Gathered around Scott's bed, we laughed and joked. We talked animatedly about those funny old grainy home movies from the 1960s, and how both his dad and his grandpa, tilting their heads while squinting intently at the camera, would say, "Can you see the red light? Can you see the red light? All right, it's on. Walk forward and wave!" Chip's family's energy lightened us, and Scott and I were grateful for their support.

All of a sudden, however, the mood grew somber when Scott told Chip, "When I die, I want you to take charge of the family movies." When, not if. The room was suddenly charged with electricity. Everyone made the usual comments—"Oh, you're not going to die, Scott" and "You're doing so much better"—but everyone was fighting back tears. I had something in the back of my mind, though, that none of them had. It was what the Spirit had told me:

"Scott will make a choice; once chosen, it will be irrevocable."

Nevertheless, it was baffling. He was saying two different things—telling me he wanted to live and then telling them he expected to die. Did he even know himself? Just yesterday he had said he wanted to live! One plus one makes two, doesn't it?

All too soon, Scott grew tired and his family had to leave. One by one, they leaned over the bed and hugged him. On the way out, their teen son, confined to a wheelchair every day of his life because of cerebral palsy, murmured to his parents, "I'm *way* better than he is."

∼

On Tuesday, I walked Scott over to the Rayo, the building across the grass, to have lab work done. His lung fluid levels were still high, and the tumor was not considerably smaller yet. I could tell our doctors were exerting a great deal of patience doing their "dance" with a stage IV cancer patient. Part of the dance was judging how much the body could take as they waited for natural processes, like elimination, to take place.

Back again in the clinic, I chatted with the surgeon while Scott was in another room.

"Mozart today, huh?"

"Would you prefer something else?"

"Oh no, it's wonderful. I enjoyed the Vivaldi the other day."

"Yes, I like having music that provides inspiration."

The surgeon was also an artist. He smiled conspiratorially and tilted his head. "Did you know that the left side of your face is more interesting than the right side?"

I laughed. "I know. I'm in theater; I look in the mirror all the time." (That's how I knew that my right eyelashes were often stunted, and the right side of the face was less open and malleable than the left.) I told him my biggest mistake in mirror gazing: "You know how driver's license pictures always look like mug shots? I decided that my next driver's license picture would be beautiful. I practiced looking 'noble' in the mirror, so I would know what to do when they took my picture. But I practiced looking straight ahead—at eye level—and I didn't know that their camera now looked up from chest level. The result was a 'nose shot.' I had wanted to look regal, but the license picture only looked conceited!"

He laughed heartily. Then he humbly ducked his head slightly and said, "You know, once I thought that the work we do here in the clinic would earn me the Nobel Prize."

> "You know, once I thought that the [integrated]
> work we do here in the clinic would
> earn me the Nobel Prize."

It was said so simply, so unadorned, but what a phenomenal thing to say! What company he would be in: Roentgen, the Curies, Pavlov, Einstein! It made me realize for the first time how unique the techniques were that they were doing here at this clinic. How different his concept was of building up the immune system, nourishing the body, creating more alkalinity, and balancing emotions while *simultaneously* attacking the cancer! And how difficult it was to administer the different elements in their "dance," all the while monitoring the person's body. I had no notion of how rare their concepts were until this moment.

My newfound knowledge split cancer choices as keenly as a knife cleaves warm bread. The Western chemotherapy method of "attack" didn't address much else but attack. And since the attack came against the entire body, it depleted the immune system—the *very* system the body needed to recuperate! I felt that this clinic's method of using several treatments simultaneously— their five-pronged approach—was more refined and detailed than the Western medical model. In addition, the clinic's treatment was integrated and designed specifically for one person. At this clinic, where they combined Western *and* Eastern methods, they created treatment that was sometimes localized, definitely multidisciplinary, and always working to build up the body. It's no wonder that a man with Dr. Jorge's humble dream and a man with Stephen's desires for change had come together in this clinic!

"Do you know why MD Anderson has started a program of immune support and of including nutritional and emotional support?" Dr. Jorge went on. "Because *we* did. People went to them and said, 'Why can't we have something like this in the States?'"

I smiled. The multidisciplinary aspect was the very reason I had looked into MD Anderson in the first place. I hadn't known it had roots here.

Stephen, overhearing, entered from another room. "Insanity. At least here you're dealing with people who are not insane, the definition of insanity being doing the same thing over and over but expecting different results. What results with chemotherapy did they promise you? At least we *don't* do what doesn't work." Without rancor, he stated, "I do not have a doctor's degree in Western medicine, and so I am not recognized. What we do here is safe and effective, but I have to stay here because if I practiced in the States, I'd be *required* to do chemo—something that fills the whole body with chemicals it is not designed to receive—and if I didn't, I'd be blackballed." He finished,

"Integrative medicine is the key to the future. That's what we're trying to promote."

"It's crazy," I complained. "Why don't they have methods like what you do in the States?"

Dr. Jorge answered, with a wistful voice, "It's money. Dr. Pekar, who invented BET, said that a lot of money was to be made in medicine, yet with the method he developed, there wasn't much money to be made. Doctors in the States haven't been allowed to use the simple, less expensive therapies. Like Stephen said, they have been blackballed." Indeed, the site on BET quotes Dr. Pekar: "Doctors studied so many things at school that my method appears too simple to them."[267]

∾

Later, back in our hotel room, Scott suddenly yelled, "It hurts!" Again, it was like he expected me to do something, and I couldn't do any more than what the doctors were doing. At the clinic he mustered up patience, even the occasional joke, but his humor stayed there. Here there was no humor and no softening of responses. Even though the adage is "It's the disease talking, not the person," it was still difficult to handle.

Mom B and Lorin gave a surprise visit, bringing concern, love, the TENS unit to take away some pain,[268] more mail from Sara, and even some from the twins in Hungary and Romania! At the end of telling how the missionary work was going, one twin wrote, "I just want my dad back—even the corny jokes."

---

[267] Rudolph Pekar, Healing Cancer Naturally, www.healingcancernaturally.com/greatesthits4.html.
[268] Transcutaneous electrical nerve stimulation. See Chapter 9.

Late in the evening, Scott took some Endocet and had a bath that really relaxed him. The doctor mandated the bath; otherwise, he wouldn't have taken it. Thank goodness for his feeling of duty to male authority! I thought, "If he can keep going, these two doctors just might be able to pull him through!"

∼

The night was better for him, but now a horrible Wednesday lay ahead. He threw up at 4:00 a.m. and again at 9:00 a.m. Insides raging, back and sides hurting, he dragged himself to the clinic at 9:30 a.m. I looked at his bare back, all misshapen. With horror, I said quietly to the surgeon, "This is not the husband I know." His statuesque, David-like physique had changed. His neck was thin, his back was square and blocky instead of tapered, and of course that horrible tumor was poking out of his right side like a trouble-seeking ferret poking its nose out into the world.

Sadly Dr. Jorge said, "You know the pictures of third-world children— bony arms and huge stomachs?"

I nodded.

"That's what's happening to him. The cancer's eating him and changing his body."

While Scott was having his regular treatments, Stephen did a session of Resonance Repatterning with me. "Nothing in the universe is neutral. Everything either energizes us or de-energizes us."[269] Stephen helped me to see only the positive in everything that happens. The concept is that there are no failures; setbacks are opportunities for change and deep personal growth. I smiled; it was like an extension of OHI and Director Pam. Stephen muscle tested me to see where to start, then asked me, of all things, what I didn't like about myself.

Hmm, lack of flexibility, too great a tendency to yell when frustrated,

---

[269] Chloe Wordsworth, seminar with Stephen Linsteadt.

making assumptions, and lack of organization for starters. We got into a discussion on the lack of self-esteem, and I said I had read that people who were spanked as a child got the idea that they were bad.

"Why did your mom spank you?" Stephen asked.

After a moment of thought, I looked up and said, "Because *she* had low self-esteem."

He asked me if I knew why, and I told him her pivotal story—her "age-thirteen" story. Her story was that when she, Carmen, was nine, her seven-year-old, golden-curled brother drowned. She found out from a neighbor kid who ran by, yelling, "You better run home! Your brother's deader than a doornail!" Little Rex was the youngest of the children and the darling of the family. Her mother was inconsolable. Nine-year-old Carmen climbed up on her mother's lap to comfort her, and her mama, in her grief, pushed little Carmen off her lap. Ever since that time, my mother had felt deep down (unconsciously) that she wasn't loved, maybe wasn't capable of being loved. It was one of the important things my mother processed with my dad and others of us in the last year before she died. Stephen muscle tested himself for me as I spoke, and he felt the truth in what I was saying. In addition, he found from the muscle testing that a generational lack of self-esteem went back from mother to daughter, mother to daughter, for eight generations!

We continued talking about things I did when I was little where I was told I was naughty. I was the energetic fourth and last child of a mother who was sick my whole life. Therefore, *much* of what I did was considered naughty! Every time Stephen purposely said that word, I inwardly squirmed. I was startled at the little-kid feelings that surfaced and at how vulnerable and uncomfortable I felt! Then I thought of other attributes I didn't like in myself, such as procrastination or not finishing things.

Stephen said, "How can you finish things when you are bad and naughty?"

His constant use of those words was painfully purposeful, but they helped to cut through the childhood memories to allow more mature, reasoned ones to take their place.

Then he pretended to give me a magic wand and asked me, "What would you want if you had one?"

"Lots of things!" I smiled. My list included singing in some major venues, writing, traveling, rafting, being with the family, and doing genealogical research.

Stephen said that I was a Yellow in one color coding system.[270] Yellows are carefree, fun-loving, spontaneous, optimistic, and creative. "But you've had to be a Blue in your role of being a caring, nurturing wife and mother, and then you've tried to be a bit Red through your home business and holding your own in your marriage," he said. "You've been sacrificing yourself," he said. "Why would you do that?" Answering his own question, he continued: "Because being 'you' isn't good enough, because you are 'bad and naughty.'"

I then confessed that selfishness was another inadequacy. Understandingly, he smiled. "Aren't we all selfish?"

Where else but here at New Hope would Scott and I be learning such amazing things about ourselves in a medical setting? Scott would not have learned any of these things had he stayed in the States and had chemotherapy. No, he wasn't out of the woods by any shot, but this way his energy and thoughts could be going toward something that would create lasting change. If he'd had chemo, like my sister had, fighting through the drug would have been his battle. But because his battle plan was different, the things Scott was learning were different. For one thing, he was facing uncomfortable feelings from the past instead of keeping them buried. He was actually facing "the key question in…all diseases," as therapist Tom Laughlin put it: "What is the Self trying to get me as a patient to learn about myself?"[271]

~

In the afternoon, Scott sat with me at the hotel by the turquoise pool for the first time. To sit outside was an improvement for him. It was pleasant to

---

[270] See Chapter 28.

[271] Tom Laughlin, quoted in Siegel, *Peace, Love and Healing*, 45.

just enjoy the beauty of the hotel and the warm Mexican climate. Then, when we walked up to our room, we had a surprise: Mom B and Lorin had moved in next door! That was a superb display of support. Ah, if support alone were all he needed!

The big event of the day was a bad one: we ran out of Endocet! And, of course, Endocet was the substitute that had helped him get off OxyContin. Undeterred, I went to the *pharmacia*, just two blocks away. To my bafflement they said, "No, we don't have Endocet in this country. Bring back a prescription for something else." When I came back empty-handed Scott stormed, "You're playing with my life!" I felt bad. I'd been assured there were pharmacies in Tijuana. How could I know that a pharmacy wouldn't have the medication he needed?

I called the surgeon. Percocet would be a good choice, but because Percocet wasn't available in Tijuana either, the prescription was a substitute for that. Scott felt that the Perc substitute had no effect. On the positive side, though, he didn't ask for OxyContin anymore.

In the late evening, Scott went to bed, watching news of the war in Iraq as he often did. I didn't think watching a war zone constantly could be very good for someone so seriously ill. As he watched, he kept shifting positions as if somewhere amid the excruciating agony there were pockets of comfort to be had.

Finally, he railed, "I can't imagine anything worse than this pain I'm in!"

With hindsight, I wish that I had first acknowledged the incredible pain and fright he was living with—insistent pain that never went away, pain that was part of his every waking moment, pain that fed into a terrible fear for his future. What I did instead was try to offer a different perspective.

I quietly said, "I can."

He looked up, surprised out of his self-pity for a moment. "How?"

Looking at the television, I said, "Being shot far away in Iraq; bleeding to death on the dirt, away from your family, away from everything you know and love; being young and knowing you'll never make it home to live another year."

"Yeah," he conceded, dropping his anger like a shoe to the floor. "That would be worse."

I sat by him and stroked his head. I thought, "You are not yet 'as Job' whose friends turned away from him and whose wife advised, 'Curse God and die.'[272] Oh, Scott, I hope you can look back on this as a precious learning experience. I hope you keep up the resolution to live; at least let those of us who have that resolution sustain the will to live for you when you feel too tired to go on."

At 1:00 a.m., he took his hurt into the bathtub, and the warm water alleviated some of his pain. After that, though, in the wee hours of the night, we were up every half hour.

∼

The previous day had one bright spot besides sitting by the pool: Elizabeth Smart was found! The fourteen-year-old had been dragged at night out of her Salt Lake City bed and kept up the mountain near her home and then in California with a crazy man and his wife for nine months. But even the elation we felt over the fellow Utahn was not enough to escape the fact that Scott was wearing down. His color was pale, and even after being at the clinic the full day on Thursday, he was weak and dizzy when we left.

The next day, we sat by the pool again after his clinic work. I was happy he was strong enough to sit outside, where he could soak up the warm Mexican sun and be energized by looking at the sparkling turquoise pool. I was looking at the array of flowers when Scott's hand reached up into the air.

I couldn't figure out what he was doing until he said, "There was a rose, growing, growing up a vine, in the middle."

I reached over and gently pulled his arm down. "Scott, you're hallucinating." I watched as recognition came back into his eyes and he smiled sheepishly at me.

Once back in our hotel room, he did it again. He started reaching up for the "Winnebago cabinet," muttering, "The insurance statement, you just

---

[272] Job 2:9, KJV.

had it. The guy that was just here, does he like his dulcimer?" It was spooky.

In the clinic earlier that day, Dr. Jorge had told Scott, "Faith, Scott. Faith is the most necessary thing right now." How astounding that was to me, to hear a fully certified physician say that faith was more needful than all his training, degrees, and expertise put together.

> *"Faith, Scott. Faith is the most necessary thing right now.*
> *Scott, you make a decision."*

Stephen also had said, "Scott, you make a decision. The body is a bag of fluid; it works with will. Otherwise, the doctors are working on a big hot dog on the table."

Scott had me pray. My prayer was meaningful and emotional. I was happy when he said, "Amen," but then he added, "Thank you, Bishop."

I blinked and pointed out to him that I wasn't the bishop.

He smiled, "But the bishop was giving us something."

I smiled back. "Well, at least you're polite while you're hallucinating."

He had a two-bath night but finally managed to sleep three hours hunched over pillows on a chair. And as for me? Well, every time he was up, I was up. Rest was infrequent that night.

~

Friday morning, Scott had me call a cab even though the clinic was such a short distance from the Lucerna Hotel. Stephen had a Resonance Repatterning session with both of us. Toward the end, Scott started dropping off to sleep, pointing to a problem on the ceiling and muttering, "The tile up there isn't done well." Stephen looked at me quizzically and I nodded as if to say, "Yep, that's what's been happening lately." Neither doctor was happy about the hallucinations.

Out in the hall, Stephen said to me, "He needs to decide if he wants to fight for his life or take narcotics and be comfortable until death. It's his decision, Elaine."

On the way home, Scott complained about not having enough energy. The complaint itself seemed an improvement over nausea and pain protests. I couldn't help but notice how weak he was, though, and throughout the night I got up again with him constantly.

Then on Saturday morning, the surgeon noticed how exhausted I was and offered, "We have a free bed right now. You go lie down on that."

I laid myself flat and gratefully wrapped up in warm white blankets. As soon as I did, I heard Scott, from the BET room, berating me for resting. "She should be in here with me," he declared forcefully.

Dr. Jorge caught him immediately. "Are we blaming again, Scott?" Then gently he added, "Leave her alone. She is up all night with you, and she needs sleep too. She will be back after she has rested."

I appreciated his going to bat for me. As I drifted off, I heard their discussion. Scott had calmed down and was being guided into being patient, optimistic, and kind. I prayed that Scott was exercising his faith as the two doctors had suggested.

When I awoke, I got up and went back to helping Scott, after which I had an appointment on Resonance Repatterning with Stephen. He said that the method's founder had said that any problem in the present has roots in unconscious patterns we resonate with. At the end of the session, he shined a yellow light into my eyes. He said merely that it was to "balance" me. It was similar to what had been done through "toning" at OHI, but here it was done through light. The light was changing the frequencies inside my body so that my vibrations were more whole.

I was intrigued that of all the colors he had used, yellow was apparently an important color to my psyche. Years ago, Scott and I had attended a "hardiness" class designed to help couples be hardier in adjusting to life situations rather than reacting to them.[273] The teacher had asked us all to "empty our minds" and see what image came up for us on that blank slate. At first, I thought

---

[273] Dr. Salvatore R. Maddie and Dr. Deborah Khoshaba, Hardiness Institute, 1984.

nothing had happened. Then I realized that a simple image had come to my mind: a large acute triangle held by my kneeling figure at one lower corner, Scott's kneeling figure at the opposite corner, with the top corner held by no one I could see. (I decided later that must have been an unseen God.) The triangle was filled simply with the color lemon yellow.

After the clinic closed, Lorin and I went shopping for food and a couple of things that Scott needed. We got lost. What should have taken us fifteen minutes took an hour. I knew I was bad with directions, but the two of us together were even worse! The evening was pleasant, though, and the four of us had enough energy to play four rounds of Rack-O, with Scott, of course, winning most of them.

CHAPTER 35

NEW DECISIONS AT NEW HOPE

MARCH

When we had first driven into Tijuana, it was my hope that Scott would get stronger, hurt less, and start healing. My fantasy was that he and I would stroll leisurely through the border markets, I'd buy myself the perfect black leather jacket while he bought something fun for himself, and we'd go to church on Sunday, even though we wouldn't understand a single word. When Sunday came, Scott wasn't hurting less, the stroll wasn't going to happen, and church was definitely out of the question. Scott's body was too worn down and pale.

As soon as showers were over, at about 9:00 a.m., Mom B and Lorin came next door to our hotel room. Scott was having a hard time breathing again, with all the fluid in his lung. Not only that, he felt, inexplicably, like he was bleeding internally. Mom B became frantic and cried out, "We've got to stop this thing!" In loud, agitated voices, both she and Lorin vented: "He needs to be seen immediately!" The room was a whirl of emotion. Like living things, loudness, anger, and fear surged and swirled, filling the room with their glaring insistence.

I tried to pull the emotional level down, saying we should call Dr. Jorge and wait until he came. An altercation ensued, and now I was the one with the loud, agitated voice. I thought, "*Just* as Scott gets close to optimism and positive thinking, something always happens!"

To lower emotions, they suggested I call one of our Provo surgeons. That meant going clear over to the other part of the hotel and up to the sixth floor, but getting away at that moment seemed desirable, so I did.

"But hurry!" Mom B called.

I ran past the pool and pushed the button for the elevator. It seemed to take forever. Finally arriving and stepping out onto the sixth floor, I crossed directly to the window where I could get cell phone reception. It took ages to get one of our doctors on the phone. Urgently, I told him Scott's current symptoms and then listened to his advice. Afterward, I took a quick minute to call home for the first time in two days, even though something in the back of my mind was telling me I shouldn't stay and chat. But the kids were cheery and happy, with lots to tell me, and it felt so good just to feel normal for a minute. The prompting to go back stayed in my mind, though, so after too short a time, I told them I had to go.

I waited again for the elevator to take me down, then sped back past the pool and sprinted up the stairs to our second-floor room. To my utter astonishment, no one was there. My eyes scanned the room in confusion. I called out loud, but the only answer was utter emptiness. I raced next door and pounded on Mom B and Lorin's door. Nothing. No answer. I knew before I'd knocked that they wouldn't be there. I went back into my room and sat on the edge of the bed. Scott was gone, and I was alone. I have never felt so lost or forsaken. I was nine years old again. All the neighborhood children were gathered in my friend Shawna's backyard doing something inane like catching bees in jars. I hadn't wanted to play their game, so I had gone to her front yard instead and just walked around and around her lamppost by myself, singing in plaintive tones, "I wonder, I wonder" the melancholy tune from Disney's new *Sleeping Beauty*. Now I thought, "This could be the most important decision my husband has ever made, and I'm not with him!"

> *"This could be the most important decision*
> *my husband has ever made,*
> *and I'm not with him!"*

~

"Think! Think!" I said to myself after the numbing shock of Scott's being gone had subsided a bit. I remembered something about their wanting a test done. Tests—the Rayo! I headed across the grass. The building was locked. I jiggled the doors, as if that would make them magically open. I shook my head in disbelief. "Why is it locked? This building has never been locked. Oh, it's Sunday." Then I realized this was the wrong kind of building for what Scott needed, anyway.

I turned another direction, remembering that a group of medical buildings lay to the west, past the lawns and the trees. Then I stopped; I didn't know where I was going, and I'd probably get lost. At that point, all I could do was go back to the hotel room and wait. "Come on," I reasoned. "He's with Mom and Lorin; he isn't lost. Surely, they'll call, won't they?" I finally found a hurried note saying they would call as soon as they could.

"Soon" was a miserable hour and a half of pacing the room, sitting down, then up pacing again. I wasn't good for anything while I waited. Finally, Lorin called. "Get a cab," he said, "and come to the Carmen Hospital."

The hospital across town was a small, dark affair. Nothing like the beautiful vaulted-ceilinged, glass-windowed Utah Valley Regional Medical Center that even featured a grand piano in its marble-floored entryway. When I was guided to Scott, Mom B and Lorin apologized twice for leaving me. "We didn't know where you were."

"I was on the sixth floor phoning. Remember?" They were the ones who had sent me.

Just before he fell asleep, Scott interjected, "Is there a sixth floor?"

In this case, Mom B and Lorin's panic paid off. Scott's sense of what he needed was right on; he did need blood! He received a transfusion of two pints of blood as soon as he came. By the time I arrived, he was starting to feel better.

His improvement didn't assuage Mom B and Lorin, though. Their fright and worry for Scott grew and fed off other things. They were repelled by the smallness and the developing-worldness of the hospital. They commented on the hospital as if it were not clean, had no supplies, and had subpar personnel. But it was clean, it did have basic supplies, and the doctors and nurses attended to him with everything he needed. It was just small, old, and rather dimly lit. Mom B and Lorin hovered over him, fretting and complaining, their voices verging toward hysteria. At one point, their panic overflowed and Lorin yelled, "This boy shouldn't be here. He should be home! I'm going to call the airlines and get him home!"

I had had enough of the hysteria. The attitude wasn't what Becky used and it wasn't what our two Tijuana doctors used. I retorted, "Lorin, go make the call and see what you can do!" But I knew he'd never find an airline that would take someone as sick as Scott was right then. He stomped out of the room, leaving us in silence. Mom B looked at me sheepishly and whispered, "I'm sorry." We both looked over at Scott, who was blessedly asleep during that exchange.

Dr. Jorge finally came at 2:30 p.m. He looked from Mom B to Lorin to Scott, immediately taking in the emotionally charged atmosphere. When he heard Lorin say that Scott needed to go back home, the doctor said, "No, no, don't be hasty." He knew that the "dance" he and Stephen were working on was dangerous and that it could go either way according to Scott's wishes. But he also knew that no one in the States would be able to do that dance.

> *Dr. Jorge knew that the "dance" he
> and Stephen were working on was dangerous and
> that it could go either way according to Scott's wishes.
> But he also knew that no one in the States
> would be able to do that dance.*

The day wore on. Scott stabilized, emotions ebbed, and no, Lorin couldn't find an airline. It was suggested that someone stay with Scott through the night. I let them know I would be the one to stay, although Mom B was certainly willing to stay with him again. "No, you've been with him all day," I said. The staff assured me that there was a place I could sleep next to him. It turns out that the "couch" they provided was a small cracked red leather love seat from the sixties with metal armrests. I twisted and turned every way I could to be comfortable on that short thing, but nothing worked. Meanwhile, Scott groaned and needed reassurance often. I talked softly with him, at times getting up for him, and at other times encouraging him to rest and be quiet. It was a relief to see a new day finally approach.

~

Monday, March 17 was St. Patrick's Day. Scott, the former leader of our Celtic family band, wouldn't be performing, wearing green, or even thinking of pinching anyone. Today, Scott would be getting his lung drained by a Tijuana lung specialist, Dr. Ramirez. Lorin and Mom B were there in our hospital room bright and early at 7:00 a.m. to take us. As we drove down the Boulevard of Heroes, Lorin grunted sweetly, "Scott should have his own statue, after all his suffering."

Statue on the Boulevard of Heroes, Tijuana, Mexico

Dr. Ramirez's office consisted of a couple of tiny rooms a few streets away. It was too small to fit all of us. Scott stripped to the waist, and once again I was sad to see his once beautiful, Adonis-like form distorted. Dr. Ramirez inserted a long needle into Scott's back, and a machine started drawing out the fluid. The needle insertion was painful, as one always was to him, but then the drawing action didn't hurt so much. Dr. Jorge stayed with us while Dr. Ramirez performed the removal. Our surgeon explained that Scott's type of sarcoma made hard pods and then moved on to make new lumps, which, in turn, hardened. The result of the hardening was that the diaphragm couldn't move. The default of the diaphragm not moving was that the lung filled with fluid.

We watched as a thick yellowy liquid filled a mason jar. It was fascinating in a gruesome way. After a long time, the liquid started turning pink because of the addition of blood. "When it starts being mostly blood coming out, we know that we have gotten as much fluid as we can. Then we stop," Dr. Ramirez commented. The amount of fluid that was drained was staggering—almost a gallon! No wonder Scott couldn't breathe!

～

When he felt somewhat better, we stopped by the Rayo to get a CT scan. The tumor had originally been nine centimeters by four centimeters when it had first been discovered in early December. A month and a half later, Dr. David had scraped it out, which allowed Scott to breathe better. But Dr. Jorge said that surgery, just like pruning bushes in your yard, encourages fast growth. In this case, it was the growth of new capillaries.[274] The second CT scan had read twelve centimeters by thirteen centimeters, and now this one said thirteen centimeters by fifteen centimeters (roughly five and a quarter inches by six inches). The doctors at the clinic shook their heads. Stephen said reasonably, though, "This is just what we anticipate; it won't start getting smaller for another week."

But pain and panic had beaten him; Scott would not be remaining for another week. As I look back, he was always conflicted. It seems that he followed whoever exerted the strongest influence at the time. For two weeks he had responded well to these doctors, and we'd learned some remarkable things. He'd been mystified by some things—like the idea of moving the baseball

---

[274] Dr. Pekar, inventor of the BET machine, said, "During operations, the veins are cut which allows cancer cells to swarm. The electric current seals the blood vessels so no metastases are formed." Healing Cancer Naturally, www.healingcancernaturally.com.

instead of the stadium, or people's interconnectedness like the banyan tree—but under the tutelage of these two men, he had gotten stronger physically. He had even gotten off OxyContin—no small thing! But he was worn down. He was worn down by unfamiliar events, strange surroundings, people's worry, and mostly and always by physical pain—never-ending, omnipresent, day-and-night physical pain. The idea of going home won out.

I was sickened. There was no one back in the States who could help him. No one to support him in his "dance." No one to monitor him the way these doctors could and to encourage him in his fight; no one to help him live. I had been excited for what was ahead in week number three—more Resonance Repatterning and more discussions that would help him to "flow" instead of control, to accept rather than to blame. The tumor was projected to start shrinking too.

The doctors were sad too, but leaving was Scott's decision, and their philosophy was truly to support their patients' decisions. They hitched up their optimism like an ant hiking a load onto its back and energetically showed us how to continue this fight at home. They fostered confidence in us and sent supplies—the remaining cobra venom suppositories for the even days, enzyme injections for the odd days as well as thalidomide and the food supplements. The only things we wouldn't have were the BET and IVs. I knew the instructions and promised to fulfill them. I would rather have used all these modalities here, but at least we could continue "the dance."

"Please call us with any problem," they said. Kissing my cheek and giving Scott a tender hug, they let us go.

Mom B and Lorin drove us back to our car, which had been left at OHI. The two of them thought Scott would be happy to be going back to civilization and back to normality.

He replied sadly, "No, *this* was our hope. There's no real hope back in the States."

Mom B kindly offered to help me drive back to Utah, but I knew that she'd been gone a lot on our behalf. Lorin needed his wife, and Scott needed his. I'd be fine, I said, and I was. If I listened to an audiobook to keep my mind active, I could drive for hours. Our *Lord of the Rings* (LOTR) CDs were in the car, and narrator Rob Inglis's rich, expressive voice would easily keep me awake for the ten-hour drive.[275] As we pulled away, Scott reclined his passenger seat almost as far as it would go and tried to get comfortable.

Before LOTR, though, I turned on an audio presentation given to us by Cherie before we had left Lemon Grove. This was the first chance I'd had to listen to it. It dealt with a special alkalinizing product and started with a story about a physician who had what she considered a miraculous experience. The doctor had seen a spot on her own chest X-ray. Recognizing it as cancer, she had said, "I knew I was looking at my own death." She took this special alkalinizing product for a week, and when she had another X-ray, the spot was gone!

In an instant, the stunning realization of the size of this tumor we'd been battling hit me. She had gotten rid of her cancer in one week—but hers was a spot! Scott's tumor had been nine centimeters by four centimeters—the size of half my fist—the first time we'd even learned of it! All at once, driving on a desolate sagebrush-lined highway, I saw in my mind's eye what we'd been facing all along. It seemed again that all the unusual efforts we'd done so strenuously in December—all the cleansing, juicing, shakes, hot/cold showers, lymph brushing, and avoiding oils and sugars—had only been a start, a beginning, a primer, like a Dick-and-Jane reader against so formidable a foe. Disheartened, I shook my head as I changed CDs.

~

Meanwhile, Scott gyrated constantly in the passenger seat. He literally turned around in complete circles trying to get comfortable. It was like he kept wishing that twisting the outside of his body could uncoil the writhing on the inside. We were both happy to stop in the pleasant shade of an oasis-like

---

[275] J. R. R. Tolkien, *The Lord of the Rings*, www.RecordedBooks.com, recorded in 1990.

restaurant in Mesquite, Nevada. Then we continued on past the rugged, steep-cliffed Virgin River Gorge in the corner of Arizona and on into the stunning red rock of Utah.

As we left behind the warmer climes of southern Utah, it started raining lightly. Darkness came on as we reached a higher elevation around Beaver, and the rain turned to snow. Where the road narrows and climbs in those passes, it can get scary. I already had a bad picture in my head associated with this stretch of highway, and that was in the summer, not even in the snow. Our old Winnebago had overheated on just this section after climbing interminably up the road. The children and I had sat off to the side of the highway for hours while Scott had gone back to a city to get a tow for us.

In both directions in these passes, there were always lots of accidents and stalled vehicles, obviously more in the winter. Scott looked at the snow now driving against the windshield, an endless barrage of white darts. He stopped his pretzeling long enough to encourage me. He always used to joke that he was a better driver asleep than I was wide-awake. (Not true, by the way; I'm just quoting him.) This time he said, "Just keep concentrating on the road; you'll be fine." I appreciated his sincere confidence and did just that. We both breathed a huge sigh of relief when we arrived in our wet driveway!

CHAPTER 36

THE SEVENTH FLOOR

MARCH

The first thing we needed to do to continue "the dance" was to drain Scott's lung again. The very next morning, I took Scott to the hospital, where they sent us to the seventh floor. His procedure was accompanied by a large dose of morphine. Because of the morphine, he was probably unaware of the mood that pervaded this floor. The seventh floor was silent, somber, and dark. The third floor, where he'd had surgery, had been energetic, ebullient, and happy. This cheerless floor smothered everyone with despondency. Same hospital, different floors. The message was clear: people get better from surgery; people die from cancer. Yet Scott had asked me to help him *live*. I did not like the seventh floor.

> The message was clear: people get better from surgery;
> people die from cancer. I did not like the seventh floor.

They kept him overnight, and on the way to the hospital the next morning, I reflected on the blessing I had received from the stake president's counselor. The blessing said that I would be able to work with the people who were working with Scott. I would *need* that now, when it was apparent that their goals were so different from ours.

The white-smocked nurses, doctors, dieticians, and insurance representatives who wandered in and out of Scott's room knew nothing of our goals. They babbled on and on about swing-out benefits, deductibles, medication, hospital stay, and so on. The unspoken word that loomed behind their phrases was "death." The word I wanted to see reflected in their eyes was "hope," and the phrases I wanted to hear were holistic ones like our Tijuana doctors had used, words that told Scott that he could change, that he had choices, and what his future could hold.

> *The word I wanted to see in their eyes was "hope."*

Dr. Bernie Siegel tells a story of a woman who brought her dying mother the most beautiful winter nightgown she could find. The mother had her daughter take it back and exchange it for a fabulous purse that she wouldn't be able to use until summer. The daughter got the message: despite what the doctors said, her mother intended on living. And she did, well past the summer.[276]

On the seventh floor I saw no hopefulness, no brightness, no thoughts of the future. I endured a stream of hospital workers telling me things that didn't seem to relate to us. The worst appointment was the one with four residents who represented our primary care physician because he worked out of his office and didn't come to the hospital. I was on my own on this occasion; Scott was over in the bed, in morphine-land. Dressed in their flowing white armor and carrying shields of clipboards, the four trooped into the room, looming over me and inundating me with numbers, statistics, medication, the portal

---

[276] Siegel, Peace, Love and Healing, 18.

vein, the liver. They were so proper and official, flipping through papers and knowledge as they talked to one another but not really to me. I was like an inanimate puppet, expected to respond only when they pulled my strings.

From my perspective, they felt like the enemy. I looked up at them through slit eyes, as if viewing through arrow slits in a fortress wall. When their presence became too intimidating, I averted my gaze and looked at the floor. They seemed more intent on impressing each other or telling each other their findings than seeing if I understood or agreed with their conclusions or had anything to say at all. The only thing they said that my brain really registered was that they wanted to get him on some sort of codeine, completely ignorant of the fact that we had just worked for a month to get him off OxyContin! (Not to mention the fact that OxyContin was very likely the substance in his system that had kept him vomiting this whole time and therefore not ingesting his nutritional supplements!)

Then I silently remembered the blessing given to me: to work with people who had different points of view. With a little prayer, I finally pulled myself together. I looked up at them and told them energetically what we'd been doing and what we were trying to do. Now it was their turn for their eyes to glaze over and not acknowledge me. They stood like concrete, a four-piece white statue with pencils poised but too frozen to write.

Later, to his great credit, one of the doctors came back. He was a D.C., a doctor of chiropractic, and he sat down on a chair next to me rather than looming over me. He didn't talk; he asked—curious at what Scott and I had done and were doing. I told him, and his head shook in wonderment at the different modalities we'd used and the places we'd gone. Finally, he apologized for the callous way I had been treated as well as for the hospital and for current medical practices in general. "I'm sorry we don't have more to offer your husband. It won't help you, but I want you to know that I hope someday we will have more to offer." Glancing briefly at my swollen, sleeping Scott, he left with a sad smile. His kindness and willingness to listen did much to smooth over the earlier troublesome visit.

Our children were happy to have us back home again. They brought normalcy to Scott's and my world, which had been turned topsy-turvy. During visiting hours, Ben told us of trying to arrange his career in California; Lindsey told us about her last semester at BYU; Sara entertained us with exploits of her English students at an alternative high school where the principal didn't require students to attend; and Allen simply gave me a huge hug, saying, "I know this is hard." When I indicated how exasperating the day had been, Katie told me, "Mom, you're okay. Calm down." Allen quietly told me how the framing was going in the basement—quietly because he knew the right time hadn't yet come to tell Scott about that project. And little Davis just smiled.

Scott was still spacey but awake enough to visit. We were talking about the fish tacos Scott and I had eaten ("You mean they were good?" "Yes!" "And you didn't get sick?" "We were fine.") when Scott looked at Allen and earnestly asked, "Allen, do you like pearls?" The kids turned to me quizzically. I scrunched up my face and admitted sheepishly, "It's hallucinations." They looked warily back at their dad. It was kind of funny in a pathetic way.

I was so happy for their company! I wanted to get off this horrible seventh floor. I was just waiting for the procedures to be done so I could take Scott home and keep working with him. He kept saying he wanted to live, and I was thrilled that our Tijuana doctors had sent home all those therapies to continue toward that end.

As the evening wore on and the children went home, Scott continued to be happily oblivious in his morphine. Meanwhile, I kept trying to be a nice person through the insistent barrage of official papers, questions, and appointments. ("Breathe, Elaine, breathe!") Finally, at the end of a solid day of the hospital system and after an hour-long call that wasn't going well with my mobile phone provider, I completely lost it. Dr. Jorge had said to call if I needed anything, and if ever I needed a calm voice of reassurance, it was now.

It was 11:00 p.m. my time when I called. After listening to my frantic little-girl complaints, he said, "You must keep doing what you are doing. I wish I were there." Then he said in both chastisement and admonishment, "Don't hold grudges; the doctors don't know any better." His voice held a sad but kind tone. Both of us silently wished that Western medicine would incorporate his fivefold dance.

> *Both of us silently wished*
> *that Western medicine would incorporate*
> *Dr. Jorge's fivefold dance.*

CHAPTER 37

A BIT OF HEAVEN

MARCH

The hospital had set up an appointment with hospice, or end-of-life care in the home. Hospice is a wonderful addition to healthcare that started in about the mid-1970s. My mom and dad both used hospice in their last months, and we loved their hospice facilities and caregivers. But hospice was not for Scott, not at this time. He hadn't said he was ready to "buy the farm." I had trouble making the hospice staff understand that he hadn't come home to die; he had come home to *work*. Actually, I had more than "trouble" with them. Since their viewpoint was to help people die with dignity, they simply could not comprehend our point of view. Of course, I knew he might die; that was a distinct possibility. But not yet.

Then one of the workers said the magic word: "bed." I was told, "You don't have to use all the services hospice provides, but if you sign him up, they will bring a hospital bed that will be a lot easier for him." I signed up, still adamant about my caveat of not talking about death.

They brought a real crank-up hospital bed. We moved one of the couches in the family room against the fireplace and put the bed in its place by the window. Scott was thrilled with it. Now he could lie flatter than he could in the recliner without having to be as flat as in a regular bed. Hospice also included oxygen with a long tube, medication, a walker, and appointments with their hygienist, their chaplain, and their on-call doctor.

Scott liked the hygienist; she came every other day and sponge-bathed him, cooing gentle words of support along with her soothing touch. The chaplain, though, insisted on keeping to her script that included telling us about death and beseeching me not to stay in denial. I told her I wasn't in denial, that I knew Scott could die and definitely looked like he was ready to, but that was simply not where we were right now. She. Couldn't. Get it. I did not have her return. A hospice nurse added to the conflict by continually making condescending and pointed jabs within my hearing, such as "You need to get used to the idea that..." and "you need to understand..." and "hmm...an eventual decline."

Finally, I couldn't take it anymore. I called and said, "Come take back your bed."

The receptionist was apologetic. "Oh, has your husband died? I'm sorry; we weren't informed."

"No, he is still very much alive. But you have reneged on our agreement."

"How did we do that?"

"You said your workers would not talk of death, but they do it all the time. I don't want hospice anymore."

"Wait, wait," the receptionist said. "Wait until the doctor comes to see you."

The next day, Dr. Jane came. She was professional and pleasant, and apologized for the hospice workers. She was also willing to work with me on our position. She thoroughly examined Scott, noting that his lung did not need redraining right now and that his thickened abdomen was the result of the tumor and organs replacing spaces. Of chemotherapy she said, "Chemo is the ultimate toxic experience. It's horrible to live with and only worth the treatment if the outcome is good. I've worked with leiomyosarcoma before," (that was surprising) "and the cancer doesn't respond well to chemo." She shook her head, reiterating, "Chemo is really not viable for leiomyosarcoma." She told me out of Scott's hearing range that she thought he had a few weeks to two months to live. Dr. Jane was the reason we stayed with hospice. Anytime there was a difficulty thereafter, she smoothed it over. She was always kind and open. I found out later that our Intermountain Healthcare would have provided us a hospital bed without any chaplain or talk-of-death strings attached.

> *"Chemo is the ultimate toxic experience. It's horrible to live with and only worth the treatment if the outcome is good."*

∾

Out of the blue one night, we had a marvelous surprise—Jacob, Jenise (eight months pregnant), and their little daughter, Courtney, arrived from California! The rest of the family came over and sat around Scott in the family room. Jacob gently put his toddler on the floor and then leaned over to give his dad a hug.

"Hi, Dad. How are you?" His voice was sweet and concerned.

Scott smiled up at him while we pointed out, "He's still kind of out of it. Morphine."

"Oh," Jacob nodded, registering our comment. Then, slapping his hands on his thighs as he sat down, he asked, "Well, Dad, what do you think of the basement?"

Eyes wide, the rest of us looked at him in disbelief. The cat was out of the bag now!

"What?" Scott asked. Jacob looked in consternation from me to Sara to Allen. Even in his spacey condition, Scott could tell he was missing something. He looked at me.

"Um, the kids have a surprise for you," I told Scott. "They've started framing the basement family room!" I hoped my bright, pleasant announcement would end that conversation right there. The rest of us went on immediately to other topics, but a moment later a wobbly Scott got up quietly. He didn't request any help. I had no idea if he was going to go to the bathroom or to get a drink or what. Suddenly he was by the basement door. He opened it and started down, with the long white oxygen tube dragging in his wake.

"Quick! After him!" I called. The banister had been taken down and the equation in my head was: unstable Scott + no banister = possible disaster! Jacob, Ben, and Allen ran after him, with the girls and me following. Scott made it safely to the lower landing and craned his head all around. I cringed inside, waiting for Mr. Control to voice his displeasure that they were doing this without him. Instead, his eyes were soft, and he said with real pleasure, "Good job, boys, good job."

"Good job to you too, Scott. You're learning to let go!"

I smiled with relief and thought, "Good job to you too, Scott. You're learning to let go!" That was a real milestone in his progress—for him to genuinely congratulate others who were doing something he had previously planned on doing. Way to go, husband! It's what all of us had been wanting him to do!

We had three more days of family togetherness. Eighteen-month-old Courtney played with ten-month-old Davis, tilting her curled head as she tried to see if he would roll a ball back to her. She also tried desperately to find his lost binky, which was evidently more important to her than it was to him. We sent and received emails from Elders Aaron and Matt, and we received some from my brother and his wife, who were serving a medical mission in Bolivia at the time. We played board games and card games every night, with Scott winning a good share of them. Several more people joined us Sunday after church, including Jenise's parents from California, Scott's brother, Quinn, from Illinois, and Takuji, his friend from Japan. Later, after spaghetti for all (even Scott), we played Scum (or President) until 10:30 p.m. Scott should have let Ben and Lindsey win as "president" for bringing over warm brownies!

It was wonderful to see Scott so energized by the family's attentions, although every now and then he would demand something cantankerously, and I would sheepishly remind my surprised children that it was "the disease, not the man" acting out. Sometimes the patient wasn't very patient! Otherwise, the weekend was pleasant and happy.

~

On Monday, the children and I held a council. Everyone wanted an assessment of where their dad's health was now and a chance to voice thoughts. I recorded:

The negative: Red blood cell count is slightly low. His stomach is hard and enlarged (what used to be a thirty-one-inch waist was now almost thirty-nine inches). The partially collapsed right lung often fills with fluid, which must be drained. Breathing is difficult. Edema is very bad in legs and feet, making a svelte racquetball player look like a football player. The fluid seeps through his calves and shins instead of leaving the lymph system through sweat and urine.

The positive: He is receiving potent supplements, cobra venom suppositories, and enzymes per our Mexican doctors' instructions. He has done some good energy work in the form of releasing negative emotions and feelings that he has held on to for many years. He figured out an age-thirteen mystery with his mother's help and has started working on forgiving his father. He says he wants to live, although he has started yelling lately in his fear about breathing.

Jacob clarified what he'd heard. "So, doctors advised against radiation, and he's not having chemotherapy?"

I nodded and said, "Yes. Apparently, the cancer in the liver is too close to the lung for radiation. And you know the literature says that chemo's not very effective with Dad's kind of cancer. The hospice doctor agrees with that."

Jacob mused, "No, I didn't know that. But for some reason, I don't think chemo is the answer for him either."

Ben quietly said, "Dad's been praying for a miracle. Miracles like in the scriptures."

Sara had been looking distant, as if she was having her own private, pensive conversation. Now she came back to the group and offered, "Lately I've been thinking about 1 Corinthians 13:13: *And now abideth faith, hope, charity, these three; but the greatest of these is charity.*[277] We've had *faith* and *hope* in concepts like 'supplements are the way' or 'detoxifying is the way' or 'cobra venom is the way.' We've tried those, and we're still using those, and that's good. But what we haven't tried enough is charity—*love*. That's what we're left with. Love's energy is *tremendous*; it's the most important thing there is. I feel that there's something more to do with love—that love's energy will work whatever Dad needs."

My mind shot back to what Rebekah and Chris had both said when they'd been practicing with us in December, how they'd felt it would be through *love* that this thing would be eliminated.

Love as a curative seemed amorphous, though, and even a little mystical. It left Ben and Jacob momentarily stumped. Sara sensed the confusion, so she steered the conversation in an entirely different direction, offering an example: "Do you guys remember that Japanese researcher who took photos of water crystals?"

"Emoto," I contributed his last name.

"Yeah, he's the one. Anyway, when some muddy spring water was prayed over, it took on a perfect, symmetrical snowflake shape, compared with the cloudy, distorted shape that it was before the prayer.[278] That's what I'm talking about—just like prayer, *love* is an energy. And the energy of love changes things."

> *"Love is an energy. And the energy of love changes things."*

We got out Emoto's book and looked at the two photos Sara was referring to. Ben said, "Wow, these really are different." Jacob asked, "So just praying changed this?" Sara answered, "Yes."

---

[277] KJV.

[278] Emoto, *Hidden Messages*, 32.

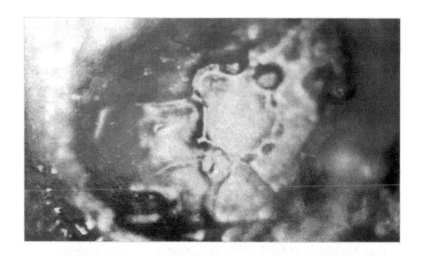

"Lake water before and after a Buddhist healing prayer" taken by Masaru Emoto

Ben added, "1 John 4:16: 'God is love.' Everything Jesus did when he was on Earth, he did out of love."[279]

Everyone nodded, and Jacob added, "Everything He *still* does for us, He does out of love."

A profound statement that I heard later distills the thoughts my children had then:

> Faith means that we trust not only in God's wisdom but that we trust also in His love. It means trusting that God loves us perfectly, that everything He does—every blessing He gives and every blessing He, for a time, withholds—is for our eternal happiness.[280]

At the conclusion of the family discussion, it seemed there was little we could actually do except send our love and prayers with greater intention toward Scott—and that was something positive we *all* could do. In addition, we decided to fast again on his behalf in a couple of days, after Jacob and Jenise had returned home.

Elaine's Thoughts on
Energy as Visualized in Water

Brown silt and debris are physical things that make water muddy, and we can see that visually. Masaru Emoto showed that *other* things change water, and, thanks to him, we can also see those visually. His photographs show that music, prayer, words, and thoughts also change water. This has enormous repercussions for us as living beings because "throughout our lives," said Emoto, "we exist mostly as water."[281] Seventy to seventy-five percent of our being is water, and the brain is composed of at least 80 percent water. The things we put into or allow into our body—chemicals, hormones,

---

[279] KJV.

[280] Dieter F. Uchtdorf, *Ensign*, November 2016, 17.

[281] Emoto, *Hidden Messages*, xv.

coffee, candy, angst, happiness, stress, or joy—all have different energies, different wavelengths associated with them. Those vibrations—those wavelengths—are carried throughout our bodies via water. "Water flows through our bodies similarly to the way it moves within the Earth, enlivening and sustaining everything it touches."[282] Emoto's photos demonstrate how "the condition of the mind has a direct impact on the condition of the body. When you are living a full and enjoyable life, you feel better physically, and when your life is filled with struggles and sorrow, your body knows it."[283] Our thoughts, emotions, and physicality are linked, and water seems to be the tool that pulls everything together.

∾

Scott's lung had been drained. Hospice had provided services and a bed, and I was convincing them to stop being so negative. Scott felt the support of family and friends in his continued desire for a miracle. Now we stood at a point of just needing to work. Work to keep giving him the supplements and treatments we'd brought back from Mexico. Work to keep him comfortable, clean, and relatively happy. Work to give him enough medication to dull his pain, but not so much that he lost his will. Especially work to give him hope that he could make it through this.

But I was so tired. I had left Scott in Jacob's capable care on our son's last night here. At 1:00 a.m., though, after just two hours, Scott had asked for me. Another night of no sleep. I didn't know how I could continue. I wrote in my journal, "I can't make wise choices, I can't think or eat, I have a headache from not enough sleep. Scott is irritable, just from illness, and then so am I. He is working so hard just to exist. I appreciate that he usually remembers to tell me 'Thank you' for getting drinks and little things I do for him, but I am so tired!"

---

[282] Pangman and Evans, *Dancing with Water*, Cover.
[283] Emoto, *Hidden Messages*, xvi.

I didn't understand then how emotions themselves can wear out a person. I only know I felt like the princess in the Hans Christian Andersen fairy tale *The Wild Swans*, whose task was to madly, fervently, continuously knit shirts of stinging nettle for each of her eleven brothers, who had been changed into swans. Even while she was being carted to the stake to be burned as a witch for going into the cemetery to gather the stinging plants, she frantically kept knitting. Later I read author Sang Whang's acknowledgment of this, with which I heartily concur: "Mental stress can be more devastating than physical stress because there is no rest period. One can continue on with mental stress until it can acidify the person."[284]

> Mental stress can be more devastating than physical stress because there is no rest period.

My next-door neighbor offered to bring me something from the store. I readily said, "Fresh vegetables! Organic if you can." (Organic so there wouldn't be chemicals and pesticides for Scott's body to have to process and eliminate.) But after she brought them, I stood dumbly in the center of the kitchen—carrots drooping limply in one hand and cucumbers in the other. Somewhere in the far, far distant recesses of my mind was the tiniest flicker that you could combine them together in some way, but I honestly couldn't remember how. The word salad? My brain never even registered it. I stuck all the vegetables in the refrigerator crisper where, unfortunately, they probably rotted.

During the day, Scott slept in fits and starts, and I used those times to run upstairs to the computer or to make phone calls. Otherwise, I was helping him on the main floor. At night, he didn't sleep much, yet he wanted me to stay up with him. I found out later from our neighborhood hospice nurse that people who are severely ill are unconsciously afraid that if they sleep, they will never wake up again, so they resist going to sleep at night.

How life had changed! Instead of the workaday garage smell of carburetor

---

[284] Whang, *Reverse Aging*, 45.

fluid that permeated Scott's clothes when he was rebuilding engines, the house had an antiseptic scent. Instead of his beaming, energetic eyes intent on memorizing chords or words, or inventing something new, his too-large eyes looked tormented. Instead of his strong, sculpted hands picking up a banjo or guitar, they were arched over the handle of a walker. Once, shuffling slowly around the room, bent over his walker, he commented, "I'm an old man." And you know what? He looked like an old man. He looked like he had aged ten years for every month he had been ill with this cancer.

As Scott's illness continued, it morphed into demandingness. One day Scott asked me to get him a drink. I brightly said, "Sure!" and got up. I had taken two steps when he ordered brusquely, "Open the door. It's too hot in here." I stopped in mid-step, unsure of which to do. If I went to the door, he'd get mad at me for not getting the drink, and if I got his drink, he'd get mad at me for not opening the door. He couldn't think reasonably, and I couldn't win.

In the midst of dealing with his horrible pain, he also felt his independence being taken away, like an elderly person who can no longer drive. In frustration, he would occasionally cry out something like "Let me hold the apple juice! I'm more important than spilling." *Of course* he was more important, but *I* was the one who had to clean up the mess. My back hurt and my spirits were low. I wondered, "Is this my choice—to give him more Ativan so he won't struggle so much, but then have him drugged until he dies?" This was just as I feared in coming back to America.

It finally occurred to me that one of three things would happen: Scott would die, he would get well, or I would die. One of those three was inevitable.

The bishop came over at 8:00 p.m. to see how we were doing. He saw through my smiling and positive "We're doing fine." He offered to come back at 10:00 p.m. to spell me.

"You can't do that!" I objected. "You won't get any sleep. You'll be tired for work tomorrow."

"I want to," he countered. I objected again, and he countered again. He won. He came over at 10:15 p.m., told me he and Scott would be fine, and sent me upstairs. That night I got a blessed eight hours of sleep and woke in the morning ready to go again!

After that, the bishop started making changes to help us. He arranged for men in our ward to come over every other night to stay with Scott so I could get some rest. I felt enormously blessed, and the men who came felt blessed that they could help. A while later, the women in the ward, aptly called the Relief Society, were organized in shifts to come juice wheatgrass and vegetables for Scott. Other kind neighbors were there every time I turned around. Some brought dinner for all of us ("You and Katie have to eat, too, not just your husband"). Others brought health books, apricot kernels, and calcium, and one family came over to clean our bathrooms. They didn't call first; they just came!

Ken Stika, who'd built our hammered dulcimer, built a low stand for it so Scott could play while sitting down. Scott's family came often to visit or to clean, and the youngest brother, Marty, and his wife helped him to doctors' appointments. In the midst of trial, our friends and family were a little bit of Heaven.

In fact, I felt Heaven smiling down on us. It was crazy; here was a man who was in desperate straits with his exhausted wife and stressed family, yet I felt like we were enfolded in a heavenly cocoon! Feeling the Lord's Spirit felt secure and positive. I would think, "How can I mope and go buy a headstone when I feel like God is smiling on us? I have to behave as I feel directed, not according to what is 'visual' or 'obvious' or 'known' or 'real' to others." Still, watching Scott was hard. I didn't know if he would live or die, but I knew that God was content with what was occurring. I felt at peace.

~

As the week progressed, Scott slept entire days. He was now on MS Contin —were they prescribing so much that it was overwhelming his system? Other days, he became agitated and felt like he was going to drown because of that fluid-filled right lung. His stomach felt tight and ungiving, and his breathing was shallow. His insides gnawed and hurt, and the horrible feeling never went away. Often, he rocked back and forth, groaning, "Ah. Ah. Ah." As I continued his treatments from Mexico, I felt like a whip-driver at Rocky Ridge.

I first became aware of the story of Rocky Ridge when I originated the character of Angela Hopewell in the musical *The Trail of Dreams*. Angela was considered the angel of death by the captain of a pioneer wagon train because she was always present when one of the travelers he was responsible for died from their hardships. In the end, he came to see that she wasn't killing people. Instead, *she* was the one who was there to ease their way into the life beyond this when their mortal days had ended.[285]

The real incident behind the Rocky Ridge experience occurred to a handcart company captained by James Willie in 1856. Headed from Nauvoo, Illinois, to Salt Lake City, Utah, a distance of more than twelve hundred miles, the company came to a standstill in Wyoming, stopped by an early October snowstorm. At this point in their journey, "men, women, and children, worn down by drawing hand carts through snow and mud (were) fainting by the wayside; children (were) crying, their limbs stiffened by cold, their feet bleeding and some of them bare to snow and frost."[286] One of the stranded pioneers later told friends, "I followed my sister Jenetta. It was easy. She left bloody prints of her toes and heels in the snow behind her."[287]

Rescuers from the Utah Territory finally arrived and found the best way to shield them a bit from the wind's fiercest assault was to get the stranded handcart pioneers to the other side of a rock-filled ridge fifteen miles away. The way the rescuers got them through the two feet of snow covering the craggy mountainside was to drive the people like cattle—cracking whips over their heads so they wouldn't lie down and die. It took them twenty-seven hours to go the fifteen miles!

---

[285] James Arrington, Marvin Payne, and Steven Kapp Perry, *The Trail of Dreams* (Orem, UT, 1997). See scera.org/events/the-trail-of-dreams/.

[286] George Grant, quoted by LeRoy Reuben Hafen, *Handcarts to Zion: The Story of a Unique Western Migration, 1856–1860* (Lincoln, NE: University of Nebraska Press, 1992), 228.

[287] Arrington, Payne, and Perry, *Trail of Dreams*, 100.

"Ever Onward" by Joseph Brickey, printed by permission.

My journal recorded, "I challenge him, encourage him, even push him because he says he wants to live. But it's difficult to fight the establishment we're in. Ever since we returned to America, the medical system has taken one look at him and proclaimed him dead. They drug him, and then when his body responds and heads downward, they point to that as if it proves that he is ready to die! They've never given him a chance. I'm swimming upstream, alone in a big river, to see if he can be reclaimed."

> *"Ever since we returned to America, the medical system has taken one look at him and proclaimed him dead. They drug him, and then when his body responds and heads downward through inactivity, they point to that as if it proves that he is ready to die!"*

~

Soon after the bishop had instituted more help for me, Ben, our oldest son, came into the house and sat down beside me. Despite having been at our family council when Jacob had been in town, Ben was filled with worry. His face was earnest, his body as taut as a bowstring. He leaned toward me, his voice tense with desperate urgency, and pled, "Mother, you've got to *do* something!" What I suspect he meant was, "Why are you not starting chemotherapy?"—chemo, the go-to remedy, the cure-all, the entity that people think they know and therefore perceive as reliable. On the other hand, maybe he didn't know what he meant, and he was just plain scared.

With an anguished look on my face, I answered, "We have!"—flinging my arm out to the counter where supplement bottles stood like soldiers. "*Those* are what we have been doing."

My eyes followed my arm as it pointed to the battalion arrayed on the counter, and in a blink I saw this part of Scott's treatment in a new light. There stood oxygen from Reg; cesium, C-Buff, aloe, Graviola, Artemix, and N-Tense from Nurse Lorna; chelated minerals, antioxidants, and other things from Stephen—*all half full*. These powerful nutrients, these allies, were meant to nourish Scott's body, alkalinize it, and help it to create the right environment to fight off the cancer. But he'd been vomiting the entire time since his surgery, and only *one day* out of the last sixty had he been able to complete his full allotment! Even worse, according to our New Hope doctors, OxyContin—which he took because it had been prescribed after his surgery—was the major cause of that nausea.

So, really, what net effect had the synergy of all these substances created for him? I shook my head sadly, thinking, "Apparently not much." As Ben and I continued talking, I couldn't help but think that everything we had thought about or tried had turned into a dead end, even though each of these modalities had cured other people. Juicing, cesium, CSCT, green tea, black salve, Essiac tea, ozone—Scott's usage of them had been curtailed over and over, so he had never received the total efficacy of any of them. It was like being in a maze where you thought there was a way out, but instead you kept bumping into blockades. An image came to my mind of J. R. R. Tolkien's small, insignificant hobbits, whose path in the Old Forest kept shifting, changing, and closing off until they were led by default down to the river, only to be captured by Old Man Willow.[288] Where were we being led? Was death the only default?

---

[288] J. R. R. Tolkien, *The Fellowship of the Ring* (New York: Ballantine Books, 1965), 162.

CHAPTER 38

RECLAIMING SCOTT

MARCH

After an intense week of being home, my brain finally cleared enough to think. Who could give Scott a chance? Who would understand the modalities that we had brought back from Mexico? If anyone were to take charge of the reclaiming of Scott, it would be Becky. I called her, and she immediately muscle tested herself on his behalf to see where he was in his desire to live.

Her response was, "I don't think it's necessary for Scott to die."

My eyebrows quirked at such an unusual response. Still, she agreed to come again.

The first thing she tackled was getting the extra fluid out of his body. Currently his thin legs were as large as a Tongan football player's, and it was unsettling to see fluid seep out his shins, calves, and feet, like his legs themselves were weeping. He was using compression sleeves like he had used in the hospital, and it looked like they were doing a wonderful job of pressing the edema out of his legs. The task, however, had to be redone every day.

Becky explained, "That's because the sleeves aren't getting the excess fluid *out* of his body; they're just pushing it to other parts of his body, so it keeps coming back. We want to get the body to expel the excess."

I had no idea how she was going to do this, but I noticed her phrasing was the same as our doctors in Mexico, that is, getting the body to work with its own processes.

She did it through parsley juice because parsley juice is a diuretic. We gathered some parsley from neighbors, bought more at the store, and juiced it. It didn't taste bad; it tasted "green" and a bit salty. Scott obediently swallowed dropperful after dropperful of the juice. The very next day it was apparent that his legs were not as huge, and they were weeping less. Wow! Such a simple and natural remedy!

This was a different side to Becky; this was the cancer-healing side. Everything she'd told us before had been words suffused with hope. Now I saw action. She brought oils and had me help her rub them all over Scott's front, back, arms, and legs. These were essential oils—powerful antioxidants that absorbed through the skin to strengthen the body's immune system and raise the energy level of the body. Around and around, rubbing, rubbing—it was good for him, and it felt good to him.

Becky had us get back to juicing vegetables for him as well as giving him wheatgrass juice implants. "We want as many nutrients as possible to go into his body so it has something to fight with," she said. "Wheatgrass implants get nutrients into the body about the fastest way possible."[289] She also took away the canned shakes the hospital had suggested—the sort elderly people are given—because there was way too much sugar in them. Cancer feeds on sugar, and there's really not much nutrition in them anyway.

On Sunday, Scott's sister, Lani, came to be with him so I could attend church. They laughed about their childhood escapades, such as her getting into her oldest brother's locked and forbidden bedroom by unscrewing his

---

[289] An implant, again, is kind of like a backward enema.

doorknob! Scott thanked her for the luscious strawberry pie she'd made just for him for his birthday the previous year. Mostly, he just appreciated her being there.

On Monday, Becky came again, bringing her protégé, Rachel, with her. The three of us ministered to him by rubbing oils and giving tinctures and drinks designed to open the lungs, relax him, and pull out toxins.

Becky took me aside and admonished me, "Only let people who are happy and fun be around Scott. None of this moping." Her words helped me to feel hopeful instead of worried, as I had been last week.

A bit loony from medication, Scott repeated her words: "Only people who are happy." He then asked for people who were not there. Hallucinations again. It was scary to me, but Becky just laughed merrily. She had worked with so many seriously ill people that it didn't faze her. She didn't want any medication in him, though, and she did want lots of "green drinks" and a "brew" she made. "Come on, Scott!" she encouraged. "You can *do* this!"

> *"Only let people who are happy and fun be around Scott.*
> *None of this moping."*

Earlier that day, Dr. Deirdre had called from the Huntsman Institute. A new clinical trial was available, but Scott was too tired to drive up to Salt Lake. He had waved off the phone call with his hand. "Tell her no." She asked him to come up anyway, just to check body functions, so he relented and went up one more time.

Ben came with us to help get his dad into and out of the car. He could see that his dad's legs were significantly smaller, and that stimulated many questions about what Becky was doing and more about what had been done in Mexico. I was happy to be able to talk with Ben all the way up and back—why we had chosen the route of holistic modalities, the limitations of the Western medical system, and what could still be expected at this stage, such as the tumor imploding, the pain going away, and his dad feeling a whole lot better.

Inside the Huntsman Institute, Dr. Deirdre said that Scott was moving so slowly because the liver wasn't functioning properly, but all her other tests came back normal, except for protein. That was good news! That would give him a better shot at living, if that's what he chose.

∾

The day was hard for Scott, but the evening was much better—he got to talk to both of his missionary sons on the phone! Hungary was eight hours ahead of us and Romania was nine, so we waited until evening, which would be morning for the twins. I truly felt Scott would choose to live because he had told me he wanted to live, and I knew from the Spirit that he had a choice. Nevertheless, he *looked* like he was headed the other way. Seeing how weak he was, a couple of leaders at our church had had the marvelous idea to have him talk to our twins, Elder Matt and Elder Aaron, on the phone—just in case the unthinkable happened.

"If I don't make it, I'll still see you at the Second Coming!"

Both young men told their dad that they knew he could make it and that they wanted him to come pick them up in Romania and Hungary upon the completion of their missions. Scott and his boys held back tears while words of love, of forgiveness, and of commitment to the Lord flowed back and forth.

Scott reminded them, "Remember that 'when the mighty storm beats upon you with hail and whirlwind shafts, you can rely on Christ.'"[290]

"I know, Dad, I know," each said.

Finally, he told each of them again, "If I don't make it, I'll still see you at the Second Coming!" My spirit soared when he said that because it wasn't just a sweet sentiment—it was true! The Apostle Paul described it vividly in what is surely one of the most triumphant verses in the Holy Bible:

---

[290] Helaman 5:12, Book of Mormon.

For the Lord himself shall descend from heaven with a shout, with the voice of the archangel, and with the trump of God: and the dead in Christ shall rise first. Then we which are alive and remain shall be caught up together with them in the clouds, to meet the Lord in the air: and so shall we ever be with the Lord![291]

I was so grateful he could talk to the twins! Scott was too. He had loved his mission to Japan—loved the people, loved the work, loved his companions, and loved Christ's Gospel. Having children involved in missionary work was precious to him. As he prepared for bed late that night, he reveled giddily, "I got to talk to *both* of my missionary boys today!"

~

This night was going to be one of my all-nighters with Scott. That afternoon, Becky came by and changed what she had said just two days earlier. Drawing me aside, she said pensively, "Elaine, he might not want to live. Will you be all right with that?" This from cheery Becky, Becky the optimist, Becky who doesn't like hospice because they talk of death.

I replied, "Of course, if that's his decision." But it made me again feel a little hopeless.

By the time Rachel came later that evening to do energy work on Scott, I was forlorn and weary. As I let her in the door, she walked by me and scanned her hand down my body, about two inches away from it. Even though visually her hand seemed to go straight down, I could feel the numerous times it dipped in and out, as if her palm were tracing a pitted surface.

"Well, you're full of holes!" she exclaimed cheerily.

"Tell me about it," I replied wryly.

"When I'm through with Scott, I'll do you."

> *"Well, you're full of holes!" she exclaimed cheerily.*

---

[291] 1 Thessalonians 4:16–17, KJV.

I don't know what I would have done without the cheer she brought! She greeted Scott and proceeded to give him her full attention. Gaunt-eyed, sunken-chested, he looked up and brightened. He truly loved having Rachel come. She went first to his feet, as she always did, directing negative energy to come out through his heels. Then she worked on other areas, sometimes working "hands on" and sometimes "hands off." I could visibly see him relax and look more peaceful, so I knew that what she was doing was beneficial for him. She finished with a real massage to his shoulders that soothed his body and troubled spirit. The process took her about forty minutes.

Then it was my turn. Rachel had me lie down on the couch with just my shoes off. She told me to relax and close my eyes. She "smoothed" down my whole body, and again I felt how bumpy the ride was for her hands.

She laughed. "We'd better do something about these 'black holes'!"

She placed her hands under my heels and directed negative energy to come out into her hands, which she then shook off. At her direction, energy started running pell-mell out of my feet, giving me a physical feeling as of gravel being sprayed out behind the wheels of a semi.

She complimented me, saying, "You're really letting it go."

"I can feel it!" I smiled. After a time, the physical feeling of gravel spraying crept up to my ankle, then up to my calves, then up as far as my thigh on my right leg. This took maybe ten minutes.

Rachel then moved to a different area. All of a sudden, I felt my throat being choked! I couldn't breathe! "Why would she *do* that?" I thought and flung my eyes open. To my surprise, she was nowhere near my throat; her hands were perched over my heart. Closing my eyes again, I recalled Karol Truman's *Feelings* book and how she said emotions register or reside in us in certain locations. I would have to think about this: was I holding something negative in my heart that manifested itself in the throat? Dr. Brad Nelson's term for this blockage would be a "heart-wall."

Kelly Call, my therapeutic massage therapist, would later come to mind. He assigned specific emotions to specific body locations based on over thirty years of listening to people as he worked on them. His mantra was "motion creates emotion" because as he moved tissue, an emotion that had been locked in that specific location was often released. He said, "When tears come to someone's eyes, I know I'm doing a good job." Tears are often released when an emotion is released. (His chart of these locations—the Ematosoma—is freely given for our use in the Appendix.)

The Heart-Wall

Dr. Bradley Nelson on the heart-wall:

"One of the biggest breakthroughs that I have ever made is regarding what I have come to call the heart-wall. Sometimes, trapped emotions can cluster around the heart. The heart is the core of your being.[292] New research reveals that the heart is actually a second brain that has memory and thinks. When you fall in love, you use your heart-brain. When someone really hurts you, you may feel like you have been hit in the chest; this sensation is where words like 'heartache' and 'heartbreak' actually come from. Sometimes, emotions trapped in this [heart] area will form into a 'heart-wall' which blocks our love from getting out to other people, as well as blocking others' love from getting into you. A heart-wall will prevent you from being able to live a full and complete life."[293]

> *Sometimes, emotions trapped in this [heart] area*
> *will form into a "heart-wall," which blocks our love from getting*
> *out to other people, as well as blocking others'*
> *love from getting into you.*

---

[292] "It is at the heart that the center of the vascular Mobius coil is found. The electrical activity of the heart muscle sets up its electromagnetic field, the strongest field of the body." Linsteadt and Boekemeyer, *The Heart of Health*, 5.

[293] Dr. Bradley Nelson, *The Body Code* e-book introduction.

Never touching me, Rachel's hands then went to the top of my head, and again I could feel that "gravel spraying" straight out from my crown at breakneck speed like people running in all directions out the double doors of a burning building. She finally smoothed down my body again, her hand still about two inches away from me. This time the scanning was not bumpy. She asked if I felt lighter, and I did! I felt as if I were enveloped in sumptuous layers of puffy gauze. Her process had taken about thirty minutes. I stood up feeling rejuvenated, refreshed, and new. I was ready for another long night with Scott. I smiled inside to imagine how, with such beneficial work and with such tender care, Scott could start getting better.

CHAPTER 39

MISSING PIECES
FOR A MIRACLE

APRIL

A new marvel from Heaven came at the end of our extended family fast for Scott. We had each felt a secure, deep faith that Scott *could* be healed. Two who felt particularly peaceful were our daughter, Sara, and Scott's sister, Lani.

Sara said again, "I think the miracle will come because of love."

Lani said, "I just feel God is watching over this whole experience."

Even Scott continued to say, "I think I signed up for this," indicating that Heavenly Father knew and approved of Scott's journey.

My journal recorded simply, "I feel Heaven smiling."

The family gathered to break our special fast, and *just* as we had said "Amen," the phone rang. Answering it, I was surprised to hear the voice of a friend from across the country. The voice was Norma's, a woman from New Jersey I'd met through our mutual wellness businesses and who talked with me regularly but infrequently—maybe once a year. Her reason for calling today piqued my interest.

"I was thinking today about your husband, Scott, for some reason, and then I thought of a Jewish friend I know, Sam, who does energy work. Would you have any need for that?"

I was stunned. Norma was not aware that Scott had cancer.

"Yes," I thought, "we would like more people doing energy work on Scott." I told Norma that Scott had cancer and that we did use energy workers. But this would be unusual: Sam lived in New York! "How does it work, with Sam being so far away?"

"I don't know how he does it," she admitted, "but he does it for a living, and he's helped many people." Thoughtfully, she added, "I just thought it was odd that your husband's name and Sam's popped into my mind together today."

I didn't think it was odd; we'd been fasting. We'd been praying for the miracle that Scott wanted, and out of nowhere she had considered my husband and her friend together in the same thought!

> *I didn't think it was odd; we'd been fasting.*
> *Out of nowhere she had considered my husband and*
> *her friend together in the same thought!*

Norma continued, "I don't know if you can use Sam's help, but I felt guided to call. By the way, he won't answer the phone—something about the phone's waves or something disrupting his abilities. He'll have his daughter, Pearl, answer the phone."

I thanked her profusely and got Sam's number. I jubilantly told my children that there was a new source of help for Dad that had been sent in response to their prayers.

I was already a bit familiar with "long-distance" energy work, meaning work that was done away from the person's immediate presence, because Becky had related an incident concerning an eighteen-year-old girl, Danielle. (Danielle's mother, Amy, later corroborated the story.) Danielle was in intensive care after a serious car wreck, so Amy had asked Becky and some other healers to do energy work for her daughter. Danielle was in an induced coma at the time. After a period of having energy work done for her, Danielle appeared to Becky and to each of the other energy workers in dreams. She said to each in her bright, cheery voice, "Don't do any more work on me. Pray for me to die instead. I have found that I have much more work over here than I do on Earth. Besides, I *hate* to be in pain!" When Becky had reluctantly relayed this information to Amy, the mother immediately recognized Danielle's sparkling voice in the way Becky relayed it. The mother then smiled. "And she *is* a wimp. She can't stand pain!" Danielle died a few days later, as she had wished.

Later, I had found out that Becky had been doing energy work for Scott from her house, forty miles away.[294] One night in particular after our return from Mexico, she had worried and fretted whether what she had told us—"It isn't necessary for Scott to die"—was true. At 2:00 a.m., she had stayed up praying and sending out energy work until she was satisfied that, indeed, death for him was not a certain outcome. I was touched and reassured that Becky would do that for Scott.

∿

Since Sam was two hours ahead of us, I waited until the next day to call him. Sure enough, his daughter, Pearl, answered the phone. She reiterated what Norma had told me, then politely said, "I will relay to him anything you want to say."

Pearl was good at her job. Anything I said or asked, she relayed in my exact tone of voice to her dad. It was fascinating. It was truly as if he were hearing me personally!

I could hear him in the background relaying his questions to Pearl. Sam had only two simple questions to discern whether he could be of benefit to

---

[294] A fellow singing teacher is another person who works on her family's health through a long-distance source; her family lives in Utah and her homeopathist lives in Colorado. Using bioenergetic testing on a computer, her practitioner has been "stunningly accurate." Michele Scott in discussion with the author.

us or not: Scott's full name and our address. After hearing the answers, there was a pause as he muscle tested himself, or whatever he did, and found that he could, indeed, help Scott. He said he would do six sessions, one every other day and each an hour in length. We could expect to see some result (e.g., the tumor starting to implode) in about ten days to two weeks. He asked me to mail a floor plan of our house when I mailed the check.

Pearl ended, "When my father does the first treatment, we will call you."

It was as surreal as it was straightforward. I had a good feeling about the call, but I was really going on faith because Norma had called us out of the blue at the time we were fasting. In addition, I had three serene déjà vu experiences, which to me indicated that Heaven was happy. These were positive signs all around. Surely something good would come of this association with Sam!

A while later, Sam had Pearl call us. Again, I could hear his instructions from the background. He said he was going to give the first treatment but that we wouldn't notice anything at all until at least the second one. Then he said, "Your upstairs office has a great deal of electromagnetic energy. It is not helping."

I knew that. What he said was similar to things we'd learned about dangerous EMFs (electromagnetic frequencies) and AC current in American buildings, such as "Considerable evidence suggests this [alternating] current may interfere with the subtle electric currents within the human body and may disrupt biological processes"[295] and "Unnatural EM [electromagnetic] fields create chaos and confusion at the cellular level."[296] In Scott's upstairs office, we had a computer, printer, scanner, land phone, cell phone, charger, radio, camera, hub, and mouse—a lot of electromagnetic waves running through one room! The office is where the internet and the phone were connected, though, so I didn't see that I could change it.

---

[295] Pangman and Evans, *Dancing with Water*, 99.

[296] Ibid., 236. (Instead of AC, the human body is designed to receive energies from the earth and sun—magnetism, negative ions, the far infrared portion of the sun's spectrum, energized, structured water, minerals, and other nutrients in food. Anything outside of this [such as processed food, pollution, or 5G] creates a burden on the body that the body has to sort through in order to function. No wonder there are so many chronic illnesses nowadays!)

"Well, keep him away from it," Sam finished.

~

Finally, we were back on track!

Finally, we were back on track! We were doing New Hope's fivefold program the best we could here in the States. We had modalities to **attack** and **alkalinize,** juices and wheatgrass implants to **nourish** and **build immunity,** and **balancing** energy work being done by Becky, Rachel, and Sam. I felt calmer, but it seemed like there was *still* something else that Scott needed to do—a final puzzle piece for his rejuvenation.

That puzzle piece came in the form of the Rife Machine. If the Rife did as purported and gave him the miracle he wanted, though, it wouldn't be the machine that was the miracle-giver—it would be Heavenly Father for sending these treatment methods for Scott to use. Every day we tried our best to do what we felt God wanted us to do and to use the things He sent us. Now here was one more therapy choice sent our way. Becky knew of a chiropractor in Salt Lake City who used the Rife machine. Scott had faith in Becky, so, as weak as he was, he let me drive him, once again, an hour to Salt Lake.

Every day we tried our best to do what we felt God wanted us to do.

Scott said our morning prayer out loud while I drove. He asked Heavenly Father for a miracle of healing. As he did, a sentence zipped horizontally through my mind like a line on a typewriter: *"You will have your miracle."* Hot tears sprang to my eyes at this unexpected confirmation of his prayer. I knew the Lord *always* fulfills His promises. A fluttery happiness simmered under me as I continued driving toward Scott's appointment, and I arrived at the chiropractor's with excited expectation.

Scott was made comfortable on a recliner, and then the machine was turned on for close to an hour. While he was in the room with the machine, the chiropractor clued me in on the American inventor, Royal Rife. In the 1930s Rife had developed a resonance machine with a sophisticated microscope composed of nearly six thousand parts. (This was beyond the abilities of electron microscopes even as late as 1998!) Rife worked daily with sixteen incurable terminal cancer patients. After three months, fourteen of the patients were declared clinically cured by a staff of five MDs.

> [Yet,] when word of Rife's breakthrough got out, the conventional medical authorities closed ranks and began to discredit him. The American Cancer Society refused to acknowledge his clinical study, the AMA threatened to revoke the licenses of doctors using the device, and the FDA outlawed it.[297]

Rife was what is called an *early adopter*. In the business world, that phrase indicates someone who recognizes a new trend or paradigm before anyone else. The road to success is not easy for early adopters. Hans Selye, the Nobel nominee (whose concept is illustrated in Chapter 13) wrote, "Sometimes I feel lonesome, uncertain on my new trail, for where I go, no one has been before, and there is no one with whom to share the things I see."[298]

The most poignant example that comes to my mind of an early adopter was portrayed in a play about the nineteenth-century Hungarian doctor Ignaz Semmelweis. Semmelweis recognized, seemingly before anyone else, that germs from one person could infect another person. More specifically, the germs from the *doctor's* hands—*their* hands—were infecting healthy young mothers in the birthing section who would then become ill and die. I can still see the horror on the actor's face as he looked at his hands, uplifted in a stark red spotlight, when the realization fell on him that it was *his* hands that had killed women. The real Semmelweis tried desperately to tell the other doctors to disinfect their hands—what an easy solution! However, he was ridiculed until he went insane and was placed in a mental institution, where he died at age forty-seven.

---

[297] "Royal Rife," Wikipedia, en.wikipedia.org/wiki/Royal_Rife.
[298] Prayer of Hans Selye, *From Dream to Discovery*, 41; *The Stress of My Life*, 2nd ed., 230–231.

Royal Rife didn't end up in an asylum, but he was ridiculed and ruined. The doctors who had initially examined the patients from his 1934 experiment lost foundation grants and hospital privileges, until they denied even knowing Rife.[299] During the Depression, commercial production of his frequency instruments ceased completely. But in the twentieth and early twenty-first centuries, different technicians had found his blueprints and built their own versions of his machine, with some versions working better than others.

The session with the Rife machine relaxed Scott, and what I had heard about the machine sounded reliable. On the way home, I started wondering where we could find one. They were about $3,000 or more, so I was looking to borrow one. Back home, I found a woman in our high school area who had one, but she wasn't lending hers. She had cancer herself and was using it every day. (After quite a time, by the way, her cancer was eliminated.) She directed us to an older lady who had previously used one, and it turned out that we knew that lady's son. Since his mother was through using the machine, he and his mom let us borrow it. It had a *lot* of glass pieces, so our friend brought it over, set it up himself, and showed us how to use it.

Every day thereafter, we turned the machine to the proper frequency and let its happy little blue light flicker out into the room as it did its work. I felt calm when the Rife machine was on. I knew it was helping Scott, and if it had any effect at all on other people, it was a positive one. Unlike the wavelengths in our upstairs office, the Rife machine created wavelengths that were healthy for the body. There was even some similarity in the Rife and the CSCT machines in that they disrupted cancer cells while not harming healthy cells. Another nice aspect of it was that Scott didn't have to move or drive or do anything special to be treated. He could even be asleep and it would still work! I felt humble and grateful to have it in our home.

---

[299] Barry Lynes, *The Cancer Cure That Worked* (California: BioMed Publishing Group, 1987), 1.

> With its little blue light broadcasting, the house felt
> so peaceful. I smiled, feeling peaceful too.

The next day, Scott fell, and our neighbor Pete came to pick him up. After Pete and I got him settled again, Pete noticed the Rife machine. He was astounded at the complex apparatus, with its glass pieces and little blue broadcasting light. Pete mentioned that the house felt so peaceful. I smiled, feeling peaceful too. I thought often about that new statement that had come into my mind: "*You will have your miracle.*" I felt that Scott had chosen life and that now—through Becky, Rachel, Sam, New Hope, and Rife—we would help him achieve that miracle. Things *did* seem peaceful. They seemed right.

That night, I was up every hour with Scott, but we had a nice time. After viewing the horrible Iraq War on the news ("Do we have to watch that, Scott?"), we watched the hilarious *What About Bob?* with Bill Murray, then turned on CNN and the Jessica Lynch rescue. At 3:00 a.m. we watched *Dirty Rotten Scoundrels*, after which both of us managed to sleep a bit between 5:00 and 8:00 a.m.

The morning started all over with Rife, juicing, oils, massage, wheatgrass, cobra venom, and phoning. I was grateful for all these modalities we had right here in our home to help reclaim him! And in about fourteen hours I would be grateful for something else—for one of the neighborhood men to come and stay with him through the night!

CHAPTER 40

KNOB'S DOWN!

APRIL

I t's impossible for a house to stay quiet when there are children around, even when a member of the household is desperately ill. Katie was going to Junior Prom! Tuesday afternoon, she and Sara had gone to Salt Lake City, shopping for the perfect dress, and they had found it. They walked through our front door holding a clear plastic bag with a voluminous, long pink ball gown, and Sara crowed triumphantly, "It's exactly what she wanted!"

Katie exulted, "The exact color, the exact style!"

They took it out of the bag.

"It's gorgeous!" I exclaimed, and then added suspiciously, "How much did it cost?"

Sara answered deviously, "Well, look at it this way. I didn't go to prom, so I gave her my share." Sara failed to mention that her junior prom was ten years ago! In other words, this dress cost twice what I had planned to pay.

I held up the frothy pink concoction. "Where are the sleeves?" I wondered out loud, knowing that Katie wouldn't wear a strapless gown.

"Oh, there aren't any, but it's also too long. You're going to have to cut off the bottom anyway, so we figured you can use that for the sleeves," said Katie.

"Of course," I responded, seeing a sewing project ahead of me, in addition to tending their sick father.

"Oh," Katie said brightly as they bounced out of the family room, "it's nonrefundable."

"Of course," I growled, smiling at Scott, who raised his eyebrows in mock consternation.

The next day, Wednesday, Katie was chosen as prom queen. When she told her dad that she and her king would be announced to the school in an assembly Friday morning, he said weakly, "Well, I'll *have* to stick around for that!" Added to the spiritual confirmation that we would have a miracle, his goal sounded great to my ears!

More happiness came in the form of glowing emails from both Elders Aaron and Matthew. Aaron, always quick to the point in half-page letters, said, "I've been teaching people that the blessings of the Gospel depend on our faithfulness. We learn the primary steps to get us on the right track—faith, repentance, baptism by immersion, and the gift of the Holy Ghost—but those don't do us any good unless we follow the road that we've found."

Elder Matt relayed an insightful true story from a Romanian lady who had first learned about Jesus Christ as a grown woman at the end of the Cold War in 1989. She had come to rely wholeheartedly on the Savior, and the knowledge that He loved her filled her with overwhelming joy.

I was cleaning, and I saw a spiderweb one day. A spider was crawling around on all its threads. There were lots and lots of threads that had been spun all around, but there was one strand that went up through the middle to the top. It seemed like all the other threads were supported by it. Sure enough, when I cut the one center thread, the whole web collapsed. Christ is like that middle thread; He is our focus. He is the person around whom everything we do is centered.

Scott and I were so proud of our twins! They were doing such good in Hungary and Romania. The youth and the younger adults raised under Communism hadn't had a chance to learn about Christ, let alone how He redeemed us and loves us. The missionaries got to share that good news with them!

The greatest happiness of all came that evening when Rachel came for Scott's nightly rubdown. She hadn't been over for two days, and, like an aunt who notices the growth of a child whom she hasn't seen for a while, Rachel noticed something that the rest of us had missed.

"The knob's down!" she cried in surprise, and we all gathered around. Sure enough, the grapefruit-sized tumor on his side had imploded to a smaller, flattened-grapefruit shape! Even Vicky from hospice walked over to view the protrusion. When she saw the smaller size, she became a believer in Becky's methods and the other things we were doing, although her eyes betrayed confusion that someone in Scott's fragile state could actually improve. I calculated the amount of time that the New Hope doctors had said it would take for their modalities to work and also the amount of time that Sam said would pass before we noticed anything. The times coincided and made sense with what we were seeing.

> *"The knob's down!"*
> *Sure enough, the grapefruit-sized*
> *tumor had imploded.*

Scott was energized immediately. With as much conviction as a partially drugged man can have, he exclaimed, "Okay! Now what do we do?" It wasn't a question. It was a command to action. We immediately did another wheat-grass implant to add nourishment to his depleted body.

By the time Becky came the next morning, the list of improvements was vast: Scott's lower back was not so swollen and puffy; the protruding tumor knob was down considerably; his legs had less edema; his colon and urinary tract were working; his voice was stronger; there was no cancer-death smell as

I washed him; and the pain was not unbearable in his chest and side, although he now noticed pain in his legs.

Our backdoor neighbor came to stay with Scott and got to see both Rachel and Becky work. Seeing energy work done firsthand was an eye-opener for him. He listened to Becky remark that she didn't like Scott's color; it was too yellow. He commented that Becky didn't seem afraid of anything and that she displayed a different kind of assuredness than what he'd seen medical personnel display. I, too, was impressed with her knowledge and was constantly amazed that she knew what to do, even with someone as bad off as Scott was.

> *Becky didn't seem afraid of anything.*
> *She displayed a different kind of assuredness than*
> *what he'd seen medical personnel display.*

"I get the incurables," she told me once, similar to what Stephen had said at New Hope. "I just have a lot of experience with them." She worked on all of them with faith and love, with expertise and patience, with hope and prayer.

I felt a sudden need to surround Scott with more energy workers. I called Holly, but she was not available now that her soldier husband was going to Iraq. Not knowing whom to call, but figuring Heavenly Father did, I sent up a prayer to Heaven requesting energy workers. Becky and Rachel had gone for the night, and Scott was set with our neighbor. I gave Scott the Ativan he required and then headed up to bed with hope in my heart.

~

When I came down on Thursday, the morning of April 9, it felt that seven and a half hours of sleep had only been four. Then, to my utter dismay, I found that Scott had been given more Ativan than his nighttime dose.

I normally shy away from confrontation, but this time, with eyebrows furrowed in consternation, I asked the man who'd stayed with him, "Why did you give him more?"

He said, "It seemed he needed it, and it was here."

My heart dropped. Scott had too much in his system! Becky had been trying to keep just the amount needed to relax him, but not so much that he would lose lucidity. He needed to be able to control his thoughts so he could fight. Now he would be too drugged and sluggish to think properly.

What does one do? You just keep trying your best. It was frustrating, though, because the addition of so much Ativan seemed to negate all the good from the day before. Our life here, which finally felt like it might be getting on an even keel, now felt out of control again. Moment by moment, life seemed to bounce between ups and downs, between goods and bads, between hard things and happy things. For instance, Mom B, who had been staying at Lani's (that was bad, in Scott's estimation), came to help (that was good). Scott fell again (bad), but our neighbor Pete came to pick him up once more (good). The Rife machine broadcast its perky blue light through the room (good), but Scott was unresponsive most of the day because of the drug (bad)—and just yesterday he'd told Katie he would see her be the prom queen (good)!

Katie came home after school, telling us she'd made the madrigal singing group, and that was very good. In part, it offset the hardest and the worst experience that happened just before she got home. I had reminded Scott's mom that Becky had asked only happy people to be around him. If she were to stay, I needed her to be positive. Mom B understandably worried a lot and exuded a great deal of fear and pity. Scott would become anxious and unsettled, even sometimes acting like a little kid again. When I reminded her, I was hoping that she would put on a smile as she had before and say, "That's right. I've been fretful."

This time, she said forlornly, "Well, maybe I'm in the way."

I was at a loss for words. She certainly was not in the way, but I needed her to be cheery and hopeful instead of desolate. Scott couldn't be pulled in two emotional directions. So many good things were working together for him right now. I wanted to continue to buoy him up so he could be strong again.

She got up quietly and went over to his bed where he lay sleeping. She touched his arm and stroked his hair. Then she walked aimlessly in a circuit all around the house, her fingers falling lightly on anything in their path, and without saying another word, she walked out the front door and drove away. Letting her leave was one of the hardest things I have ever done.

In the midst of all this, a thought came to me with absolute clarity. I suddenly *knew* what the Spirit had meant so many months ago by the phrases,

"Scott will make a choice; once chosen, it will be irrevocable."

It wasn't a choice over treatment plans, like I had assumed all along; it was the choice to *live* or *die*. Oh, Scott, choose to live!

The happiest event of the day came at 6:53 p.m. when Jacob and Jenise's first son was born by C-section in California. Dark-haired and almost eight pounds, he was named Brandon Blair after Scott's first name and Scott's father's name. Scott was awake enough by then to appreciate that wonderful gift and to be happy that both mother and baby were healthy and fine.

That night, I asked Ben to come stay with his dad. It was my night to be with him, but I just had a feeling that Ben needed to have that opportunity. Scott couldn't settle down, however, so I phoned Verna, the hospice nurse in our neighborhood who worked for a different company. Since she was only two minutes away and our agency's nighttime hospice nurse was forty minutes away, Verna had encouraged us to call her anytime we wanted.

She came over immediately, and even though it was 11:00 p.m., she was dressed in her uniform. "Patients trust me more and feel more comfortable when I wear it," she smiled. She was a wonder to watch, talking gently with Scott, asking him how he felt, and monitoring him. I told her frankly that I was concerned with his receiving too much Ativan. She countered that he needed a certain amount to calm him down. It took her two hours, administering bits at a time, while Ben and I looked on. Finally, pronouncing him calm, she went home to sleep. Ben settled on the couch next to Scott, and I went upstairs to a grateful slumber.

CHAPTER 41

MORNING REVELATIONS, NIGHTTIME REIKI

APRIL 10

At 7:00 a.m. a wonderful dream woke me up. Scott was downstairs, sitting up in his hospital bed, shaking daze out of his eyes like a dog shaking water droplets off its fur. His body looked normal again, not bird-eaten, and his attitude was of triumph and relief, as if he had just finished a marathon. His broad smile conveyed a happy amazement, like "Wow! I made it through that!"

"Could it be?" I thought, sitting bolt upright. We'd been looking for a miracle, praying for a miracle, and I'd had that statement come to me: "*You will have your miracle.*" Maybe there was a miracle waiting for me downstairs!

I threw on a robe and flew downstairs to find Scott. What I saw was not the miracle of my vision. My husband looked worse than ever—head thrown back, breathing raspy and hard, features strained. I've seen death—my father, my mother, my sister, three aunts, Scott's grandmother—they all looked like that just before they passed on. He looked like death.

I ran into the other room, knelt, and prayed the fastest prayer of my life. There were three parts to the answer. First was an outpouring of peace. Second was the sense that everything was under control and would be all right. Third were the words "He doesn't *have* to die." All right, I thought, getting up, if he doesn't have to die, what can I do for him now?

> There were three parts to the answer.
> First was an outpouring of peace. Second was the sense that everything was under control and would be all right.
> Third were the words "He doesn't have to die."

I helped Scott to sit up, got him dressed, and then called Sam. Yesterday I had sent up a plea to Heaven, requesting energy workers in general. Today I had a question of ethics for our long-distance energy worker.

To my utter surprise, it was Sam, himself, who answered the phone. He told me that Pearl was gone right then; he'd seen my name on the caller ID and had felt this was an emergency. He made an exception to not talking on the telephone for us! Hearing the urgency in my voice, he asked what he could do.

"Sam," I asked, "is it ethical to request energy work to give someone hope? You know it's always been my role to help my husband's body to stay put together should he decide to live, and to give him hope to help him want to live. He's pretty bad off right now. Should I be asking for hope on his behalf?"

Sam was quiet for a minute. When he answered, it was not a reply to my query. I was astonished when he began, "Scott feels cheated by a man." Sam asked me to figure out who it was.

I ventured, "Is it one of the professors who denied him tenure at the university?"

"No, it's not any of them." I was relieved to hear that. Those professors are good men and still our friends. I didn't want to think that Scott held a grudge against them.

Sam continued, "This was three or three and a half years ago. He has great bitterness toward a man over money. The man is young. Can you think of someone who hurt him?"

I knew immediately. I told him the name, and Sam said, "Yes, that's the one. You go tell Scott, 'It won't do any good to keep these feelings toward him. Don't let him ruin your life. Your feelings toward him are only blocking your continued progress.' Scott has many things ahead to do in life, much to give. Tell him to give up those feelings toward that man and let them go to the Lord."

> "You go tell Scott, 'It won't do any good to keep
> these feelings toward anyone. Don't let him ruin your life.
> Your feelings toward him are only blocking your continued progress.'
> Scott has many things ahead to do in life, much to give.
> Tell him to give those up and let them go to the Lord."

I went to Scott's side immediately, feeling strange to say this in front of Vicky, the hospice nurse, who had come and was sitting in the corner quietly (as I found out later, waiting for him to die, in spite of what she'd seen of his recent improvement). Knowing that Scott's need was greater than my embarrassment, I relayed loudly in his ear what Sam had said. Instantly he started to be agitated and to gyrate his head and body around. I was pleased. I could see that Scott, in some marvelous way that I don't understand, was working through this issue—breaking free from negative bonds deep within him.

When I came back to Sam on the phone, I could hear a deep concern for us in his voice. He talked to me about being positive and said he would pray for us. That was very tender to me. Both of us, though of different faiths, believed in the power of prayer and of God's goodness.

The next thing I did was to call Scott's mom back. The thought crossed my mind that Scott had his agency, and he *might* die today. If he died and his mother wasn't there, that would be a travesty. I told her that he did not look good at all and asked her to come. It took forty-five minutes from their house in Sandy, Utah, and she came with Scott's sister in forty.

After an hour of agitating, Scott was calm again. Having dressed myself now, I held his hand and stroked his chest. I talked softly to him and gave him permission to die. I reminded him that I loved him and not to worry. What I hoped he'd do was to breathe a sigh of relief in knowing—absolutely knowing—that he was loved and then choose to stay here on Earth with me.

The bishop and the Relief Society president wandered in and out of the house throughout the day. The Relief Society president was one of our neighborhood medical professionals; in fact, she was the dean of the school of nursing at BYU. When we had returned from Mexico, I had told her all that we had done, and she'd replied, "You've gone to the ends of the earth!" Still, I figured that she, like nurse Vicky, thought that I was in denial about Scott's condition. She didn't know, though, as I did through the messages of the Spirit, that his outcome would be *his* choice and that a miracle *would* be granted.

Dr. Dan came over in the evening. Ben left only once to go to the gym and to pick up Lindsey and Katie. Sara stayed except for one disconsolate walk around the nearby temple.

After a while, I received a phone call from Gael, one of our musician friends who, with her husband, had performed at our Celtic Christmas concert. Gael and Scott had a strong connection; she was one of the few hammered-dulcimer players we knew. People who have to tune sixty-two strings maintain a strong bond! In fact, Gael had taught Scott his one and only hammered dulcimer lesson before he started learning by videotape.[300]

"Elaine," Gael's voice started tentatively, "does anyone there need any Reiki?"[301] I had no idea until that moment that Gael knew Reiki. I only knew

---

[300] Most acoustic instruments can be learned through Homespun: www.Homespun.com.

[301] Reiki is a healing technique based on the principle that the therapist can channel energy into the patient by means of touch to activate the natural healing processes of the patient's body and restore physical and emotional well-being. *Oxford Dictionary.*

her as a musician and as an artist. "Yes! Come over! Scott's in very bad shape." That was news to her; she didn't know that Scott had cancer.

Later, she told me her whole story. Yesterday she had received an impression to call us. She opened the telephone book to "Brewster," but as she started to dial, she stopped. People who have special healing gifts are so often scoffed at. She rationalized, "So, I'm just supposed to call and ask, 'Anyone there need Reiki?' They probably don't even know what Reiki is!" And so, she hadn't called. She'd just walked away, leaving the phone book open. In the morning, she had walked past the telephone book and "Brewster" had jumped off the page at her. Looking skyward, she'd said cryptically, "All right, you don't have to shout!" That's when she had called us.

Gael came at 5:00 p.m. The house was silent and still by then. Vicky, having waited all day for him to die, had gone. The bishop and the Relief Society president were home eating dinner. Mom B and Lani had been sent by Becky to obtain an oil called "Rescue," and then Becky had had to leave.

The first thing Gael did was to help Scott breathe better. She leaned him forward, slapping his back over and over in certain places, her shiny, dark hair falling over her shoulders. She challenged him, "Scott, I just got back from Ireland, and if you want to see the photos, you're going to have to get well enough to see them!" (I found out later that a feeling had prompted her that she was needed at home, and she'd cut her Ireland trip short by three days.)

Scott grunted and half-smiled a response. Gael kept prodding him and teasing him, telling about the music she had played and had listened to in Ireland, until, forty-five minutes later, he breathed more easily. I thought of the hospice nurse, who had just sat silently for days waiting for him to die; couldn't she have helped him to breathe instead?

Gael laid him back again, and we watched her guide her hands gently over different areas of his body, always about two to three inches above his body.

"See how strong he is!" she exclaimed, this time holding her hand a good seven inches above his left side. "There is a lot of energy here. And notice," she winked, "I'm not working on the cancer side."

I *had* noticed.

"He's working on other issues over here." I had shared with her the problem about money with the man, which Sam had discovered, and Gael said, "Oh, he got rid of that as soon as he heard it from Sam. No, this is something else that he's working on." Turning back to him, she cajoled, "Come on, Scott. You don't need to keep this. Give it up!" She was referring to spiritual and emotional quandaries that were vibrating deep within him, negative concepts (even generational ones) that had been in him for years. Interestingly, it was exactly what Stephen had said to him at New Hope: "Give it up; you don't need to keep this."

> *"Come on, Scott.*
> *You don't need to keep this. Give it up!"*

Rachel arrived about 6:00 p.m., starting off, as always, by cupping her hands under his heels. It was gratifying and a little unusual to have two energy workers working on him at the same time, but they were at different places on his body. It seemed that Rachel had a quizzical look on her face, but I figured that maybe I couldn't see her properly since her blond hair was hanging in front of her face. Or maybe she was praying, since her head was bowed.

After a while, Rachel rather suddenly left his feet and sat by his side, holding his hand. She told him what a wonderful man he was and how she'd loved working with him and on his behalf. She had learned so much, she told him, and said she knew how much he loved his family. I smiled wistfully at the family portrait on the wall, wishing that she could have seen him when he was healthy and handsome, not bird-pecked thin with those haunted eyes. Nevertheless, she respected and loved him. That was special.

At 7:00 p.m., Rachel left to go home to her children. The bishop returned with Dr. Dan, and Mom B and Lani were back from the store. The attention turned again to Gael.

She gave hope to Scott by telling him, "Scott, you've already done everything hard—you didn't get tenure; raising children is a challenge; worrying about a job took a lot of effort; and feeling like you didn't have enough money was difficult. Everything hard is behind you. From here on out, it'll be smooth sailing."

As she finished, she swept her hand back and forth above his entire side in long, smooth, even motions. Then, with finality, she pronounced, "There. There's nothing negative in your body. You can come back to live a wonderful life, because now you know how to do it. Or you can go on to your Heavenly Father and be able to stand before Him and say, 'I'm clean. I'm ready. What do you want me to do?'"

> "There. There's nothing negative in your body.
> You can come back to live a wonderful life, because now
> you know how to do it. Or you can go on to your Heavenly Father
> and be able to stand before Him and say, 'I'm clean.
> I'm ready. What do you want me to do?'"

She let her healing hand drop. The room was quiet. Within the last hour, there had been two and two and two and two people surrounding Scott. It wasn't done on purpose, but it seemed that those groups of two represented different facets of Scott's life. Two energy workers represented new things he'd learned and his willingness to change and to embrace truth, wherever it may be found. Two from his nuclear family represented the great love he had for me and for his children, and the efforts he'd put forth all his adult life to provide a good life for us. Two from his family of origin represented the deep love of his family, his roots, his heritage, and his upbringing. And two members of his ward's highest priesthood authorities represented his love for the Savior, his desire to be obedient, and his desire to serve. The room felt sacred and peaceful, like a temple. The telephone rang, and I answered it. After a moment, Gael fortunately came and brought me back to the circle around his bed.

Dr. Dan had explained to the group, and now explained to me, how Scott was now breathing anaerobically, where the body had changed and gets no oxygen. I was so conditioned to searching for new supplements and treatments to help him that I automatically began thinking of a new oxygen supplement I had just heard about that day.

Somehow Dr. Dan noticed the gears moving in my head. He leaned his tall frame down and looked at me kindly, saying, "That means he's going, Elaine."

"Oh. Oh," I thought. "Oxygen won't do him any good. Nothing will do him any good. He's going to die."

At 8:00, the doctor had Gael remove the oxygen tube from his nose, since it wasn't needed. At 8:02, we all watched his chest rise and fall, never to rise again.

I stared, stunned, at that still chest, not even aware that I was holding my breath. I felt like someone had pulled the rug out from under me. I'd known all along that he had a choice, but recently the Spirit said that a miracle would be granted. Since Scott had continually said that he wanted to live, I assumed that meant he would live. When Rachel had noticed the day before that his tumor was imploding, he'd even been excited as he'd directed us to keep helping him. And I'd been given feelings of peace and serenity from Heaven just this morning. So how did this happen? Of course, I knew it was possible, but I'd never believed for a minute that he wouldn't make it.

We all knelt around his hospital bed, and the bishop offered to say a prayer. I felt my chest drawing in—my upper body in a stiff fetal protective mode, I guess—and I felt like a tiny speck lost on the vastness of the nearby mountain. The bishop's beautiful prayer thanked the Lord for the life of this good man and thanked Scott for all he did to help everyone around him and for loving his family so much. After the prayer, a vague picture of me adrift on an endless ocean played in the distant recesses of my mind. As I opened my eyes, I thought simply, "I'm a widow." I didn't like that word.

⁓

Two exceptional things happened the day after Scott died. The first was the reception that Katie received as the junior prom queen. Word had spread like wildfire in the huge high school auditorium that her dad had died just the night before. Standing on the stage in all her sparkly pink glory, with her hand on the arm of her king, she smiled as wave upon wave of applause poured over the two of them. I was so happy for her, even as tears of sadness coursed down my cheeks. Then, with a sudden little ping, I realized that there was now nothing to hinder Scott's being there to see her. I'm sure he was there, just as he had said he would be!

I'm sure he was there, just as he had said he would be!

The second amazing thing was what Rachel said. She called and asked to come over. Of course, I welcomed her. Without much small talk, Rachel got right to her purpose in coming. Holding her hands nervously in her lap, she tentatively said, "You know, yesterday when I came, I didn't feel any energy down by his feet. I was puzzled, because Gael kept saying how strong he was on his side."

"Yes, I thought you looked baffled," I said. "But then I thought maybe you were praying."

"Well, I always pray for a client, but in this case, I was really trying to figure this out. Then I looked up and I saw Scott standing by his body."

She waited a moment to see how I'd respond to that. As she saw my eyes brighten, not doubting her for a minute, she plunged on.

"He was peaceful, radiant, and glowing. And he looked like his picture; he didn't look cancer-ridden or tired or worn anymore. He looked at me and smiled and said, 'I'm going to go.'"

"He was peaceful, radiant, and glowing.
He smiled at me and said, 'I'm going to go.'"

Her statement electrified me. Rachel didn't realize it, but she had just completed part of Scott's story. I had not mentioned to a soul what the Spirit had told me:

"Scott will make a choice; once chosen, it will be irrevocable."

Now, using *his* words, she had confirmed that he had, indeed, made his own choice! My soul soared! God had, for some reason, safeguarded that ultimate choice so that *no one* besides Scott could make it! I was thrilled for my husband! The man who so often felt that the path he was on was not of his own making had himself finally chosen!

CHAPTER 42

CHOICE, HEALING, AND MIRACLES

APRIL

A person processes a lot of things following the death of a loved one, especially when that loved one had a choice, like Scott had. In the midst of preparing for his funeral (during which his children sang a touching rendition of Dan Fogelberg's "Leader of the Band"),[302] I wondered about those two statements from the Spirit. "*Scott will make a choice; once chosen it will be irrevocable,*" and "*You will have your miracle.*" What the Spirit said to me and what actually happened didn't seem to jive. I still had questions.

First of all, choosing: when did Scott choose? If he was going to make a decision, he had to be given options. When on earth did that happen? I now think that the spiritual learning or heavenly instruction took place during times I thought he was asleep, for it was always upon awakening that

---

[302] Dan Fogelberg, "Leader of the Band," *The Innocent Age*, Full Moon / Epic, 1981.

he stated, with wide eyes, "I think I signed up for this." (It makes sense that when the brain is in a deep meditative state, like Theta, or in a relaxed state, like Alpha, one may be more open to the subtle influences of the spirit world or the heavenly realm.)

So, what about that last statement, "*You will have your miracle*," and what about that wonderful word "healing," which was so prevalent in all the blessings given to Scott? Dying was neither what I considered healing nor a miracle! About a week after his funeral, it hit me with such clarity, I wondered why I hadn't seen it before—the healing was *spiritual*, not physical, and *that's* what the miracle was! That is what Heavenly Father wanted from Scott, and that's what Scott did when he released everything negative from himself. That's what he did when he forgave everyone, including himself—the hardest person of all to forgive.

That is what Heavenly Father wants from each of us. Neal Maxwell's fundamental statement holds even more significance now:

The submission of one's will is really the only uniquely personal thing we have to place on God's altar.[303]

In light of that, perhaps C. S. Lewis would allow us to add one thing to his beautiful analogy of God's "building a castle" as opposed to a "decent little cottage:"[304] in order to complete the job, God needs *our* compliance in the form of our permission, in the form of our letting go, in the form of our submission. And just like Sara had sensed, it's done through loving and trusting Jesus.

> *To complete the job, God needs our help in the form of our permission, in the form of our letting go, in the form of our submission.*

---

[303] Neal A. Maxwell, *Ensign*, November 1995, 24.

[304] See the Introduction.

Did the alternative therapies work in Scott's case? Apparently so, as the tumor was getting smaller and his pain was lessening. Interestingly, Scott chose to move on to the world beyond this Earth life just as his cancer was abating and he had a chance of staying here. That indicates completion, because you don't move on, if you're given a choice, unless you're finished. At least finished enough to call it good. I imagine that he'd made his famous pros and cons list and, like Danielle, the eighteen-year-old girl in a coma, had found that he had "much more work over [there] than on Earth."[305] When Rachel saw him "peaceful and glowing," he exuded not only a radiance, but a confidence of someone at ease with himself. He stood tall and straight and smiled at her. His heart had changed. His mind and body were finally on the same page to the point that he could feel comfortable being in a place where he would stand before the Lord.

> *His heart had changed.*
> *His mind and body were finally on the same page*
> *to the point that he could feel comfortable being in a*
> *place where he would stand before the Lord.*

Those thoughts brought me to the curious statement made by Sam: "Scott, [you have] many things ahead to do in life, much to give... Your [bad] feelings are only blocking your continued progress."[306]

Progress. Much to give. Many things ahead. What curious things to say about someone who was not going to be on the earth anymore. Dr. George Ritchie, the first to write his own near-death experience (NDE) about his glimpses of Heaven, had a conversation with a psychiatric patient, which sheds some light on this conundrum. His irate patient had just found out he'd been given four months to live.

---

[305] See Danielle's story in Chapter 39.
[306] See Sam's comment in Chapter 41.

Patient: "What a joke, huh doc? All this digging around in the past so I can do better in the future—only now I'm not going to have a future!"

Dr. Ritchie: "On the contrary. These things are more urgent now than they've ever been. Your future depends more than you can guess on how swiftly you get on with this business of relationships...I have no idea what the next life will be like. Whatever I saw was only—from the doorway, so to speak. But it was enough to convince me totally of two things from that moment on. One, that our consciousness does not cease with physical death—that it becomes, in fact, keener and more aware than ever. And second, that how we spend our time on earth, the kind of relationships we build, is vastly, infinitely more important than we can know."[307]

> How we spend our time on earth,
> the kind of relationships we build, is vastly, infinitely
> more important than we can know.

Since his death, I have felt Scott's presence often and, in actuality, his hand once, so I can testify that his consciousness, soul, or spirit does still exist.[308] He seems contented, and it seems that the best parts of him are what shine through to me—the parts of him that love dearly and want to give service. Choosing to see himself honestly—to give up grudges, bitterness, anger, and a need to control—is just what he needed to be changed from a little cottage into a glowing palace.

~

We humans really want our loved ones to stay here on Earth where we can see them, watch over them, and be with them. Like one little boy is reported to have said, "I know that Heavenly Father loves me, but right now I want

---

[307] George G. Ritchie, *Return from Tomorrow* (Carmel, NY: Guideposts, 1978), 14–16.

[308] "I kept getting in and out of my physical body...but while I did, I was still in a body...If I had to put it into words, I would say that it was transparent, a spiritual as opposed to a material being." Raymond Moody, Jr. *Life After Life* (Carmel, NY: Guideposts, 1975), 36.

someone with skin." It is simply not in the plan of God to have all His children here on Earth at one time. So, to make up for losses, Heavenly Father sent Jesus so that *all* of us can live again. An old folk song tells of the longing we all have to live forever:

> My soul doth long to go where I may fully know the glory of my Savior;
> And as I pass along, I'll sing the Christian song: I'm going to live forever.[309]

We will *all* be resurrected; that is a given. Jesus died and was resurrected so that *all* people, every one of us, will rise from the dead. I already knew that, but now it struck me with more meaning than ever before. The question really is *How will we live*? That is what God is concerned about. What's truly exciting is that *we* get to decide. The *how* of our lives is totally up to us! To forgive and to love, to be kind and to have integrity with ourselves because we are in alignment with God—that is *our* choice and our main work on this Earth.

> *The question really is* How will we live?
> *That is what God is concerned about.*
> *And what's truly exciting is that* we get to decide.
> *The* how *of our lives is totally up to us!*

I would say that for Scott to be able to relish his family more wholeheartedly than he'd ever done before, to forgive everyone in his life, and to allow all negativity to leave him in a mere four months' time were remarkable acts of healing and of letting go. As for the Spirit's saying *"You will have your miracle"*—I believe we did.

---

[309] "Pilgrim Song," American folk hymn.

EPILOGUE

Immediately following Scott's funeral, I saw two extended family members who were distinctly uncomfortable around each other and rarely spoke to one another. As these two women passed each other in the church foyer, I braced myself for what might happen. Instead, I saw one put her hand gently on the other's shoulder, and they both smiled and spoke kindly to each other. I thought of Sara's prediction that change would come through love. It looked like Scott's example of love and forgiveness was already rubbing off on the rest of us.

I grinned inside and thought, "Healing. The miracle's already begun!"

ACKNOWLEDGMENTS

I want to thank my first editor, Eric Schetselaar, who has championed the topics in this book and spent countless hours working on this project. I also want to thank Kacy Wren and Bailey Hayes from Scribe Media, as well as the entire Scribe staff. I so appreciate many colleagues who read my manuscript or conversed with me, giving me their time and their incredibly valuable insights—Holly Beard, Mandy Oscarson, Linda Solen, Dr. Ken Solen, Susan Sample, Kathy Newton, Tana Page, Jean Marshall, Stevens Nelson, MJ Pangman, Emily Ellsworth, and Karol Truman. I'm grateful to the inspired authors and leaders from whom I've learned and who have graciously allowed me to use quotes and photographs from their work. Lastly, I'm grateful to my wonderful children, who are such a support to me, and to my friends, who were catalysts as they listened to small segments of Scott's story with amazed expressions on their faces, saying, "You should write a book."

APPENDICES

APPENDIX A

ADDITIONAL INFORMATION

1. POTASSIUM BROTH RECIPE
(CHAPTER 4)

- Twenty-five percent potato peelings
- Twenty-five percent carrot peelings and whole chopped beets
- Twenty-five percent whole chopped celery and dark greens
- Twenty-five percent chopped whole onions and garlic

Add hot peppers to taste. Add enough distilled water to just cover vegetables and simmer on very low temperature for one to four hours. Strain and drink only the broth. Make enough for two days; refrigerate leftover broth.

(Use only organic vegetables! You do not want to consume any toxic, immune-suppressive insecticides, pesticides, or inorganic chemical fertilizers while you are on a detoxing program.)[310]

---

[310] Schulze, *American Botanical Pharmacy*.

2. STORIES OF RAIDS
(CHAPTER 5)

"Shortly before Thanksgiving 2000, Neal and I were awakened by a frantic phone call. It was Allen on the line. To our shock, he told us that an FDA SWAT team dressed in flak jackets and carrying weapons had raided his offices. They burst in late in the afternoon, brandishing their guns and claiming to have a warrant that allowed them to confiscate all his records. Over his protests they then proceeded to seize his computers and all his files. Terrified and bewildered by the Gestapo-like raid, Allen wasn't sure what to do, so he had called us. We were stunned. It wasn't as if they were dealing with a drug dealer or some dangerous criminal. Things like this, I thought, didn't happen in America! At least that's what I thought. What I found out was even more shocking than the FDA raid on Allen. As it turned out, the FDA has its own SWAT teams! Not only that, but they have been used with increasing frequency."[311]

"Another raid was on Dr. Jonathan Wright's clinic in a Seattle suburb. He was a holistic healer with a steady stream of loyal patients. Suddenly, a squad of flak-jacketed, gun-wielding police officers and FDA representatives kicked open the door and burst in screaming, 'Freeze!' Dr. Wright and his employees looked on helplessly as the FDA agents and police seized file cabinets full of records, medical equipment and the 'dangerous drugs' that had justified the raid. As it turned out, what they were after were vitamins and other nontoxic supplements...And who is sending out the flak guys? There were no complaints on file from Dr. Wright's patients or reports of any problems associated with his practice. The answer is simple: Wright refused to be intimidated by the FDA."[312]

---

[311] Deoul, *Cancer Cover-Up*, 100.
[312] Ibid., 124–126.

3. HEAVEN'S GOLDEN LIGHT
(CHAPTER 29)

Many people have seen a golden light that emanated from Heaven. Some of the following statements are from near-death experiences (NDEs), some from visions, and some just seen.

"The yellow light that appeared was dazzling."[313]

—Betty Malz

"After my husband died and I was recording the last song for our Celtic CD, the same amber yellow light that was present at my mother's funeral suddenly appeared in the tiny recording room. In the warmth of its comforting light I was given to know that I would complete my song in no more than two takes."

—The author, on finishing the recording of the CD *Castle Kelly*

"There was . . . a warm golden light, very bright."[314]

—Heber Q. Hale

"Spacious stretches of flowers, grasses, and shrubbery, all of a golden hue."[315]

—Heber Q. Hale

"The whole thing was permeated with the most gorgeous light— a living, golden yellow glow."[316]

—Raymond A. Moody, Jr., M.D.

---

[313] Malz, *My Glimpse of Eternity* (Carmel, NY: Guideposts, 1978), 87.
[314] Jean Scott, quoted in Lee Nelson, *Beyond the Veil* (Utah: Cedar Fort), 107.
[315] Ibid., 58.
[316] Moody, *Life After Life*, 57.

"There was a gold-looking light, everywhere. Beautiful.
I couldn't find a source anywhere.
It was just all around."[317]

—Raymond A. Moody, Jr., M.D

4. THE HARRY HOXSEY STORY
(CHAPTER 30)

In 1840, Harry's grandfather, a horse breeder, had developed a natural remedy for the tumors horses sometimes developed on their forelegs. Harry's father, Dr. John Hoxsey, a veterinarian, had continued to use the remedy on animals and occasionally to treat cancer in humans. Because of his success in treating human cancers, the elder Hoxsey eventually had so many human patients that he had to turn his animal practice over to an assistant. When John Hoxsey died, he entrusted his son, eighteen-year-old Harry, with the formulas for his tumor remedy.

A banker diagnosed with terminal cancer came to see Harry. Harry wanted to become a doctor and resisted treating the man because he didn't have a license. The banker prevailed, and Harry treated him successfully. Later, local physicians in his area complained to the state medical board that he was practicing medicine without a license. This charge precluded his acceptance to any medical school in the country. Not being able to become a doctor, Harry, nevertheless, set up a clinic.

Dr. Malcolm Harris, a prominent AMA (American Medical Association) figure, offered to allow him to test his remedy on a terminal cancer patient with a huge tumor on his shoulder. His doctors had told the patient there was no hope for a cure. Under the watchful eyes of AMA officials, Hoxsey initiated a series of treatments. In short order, the huge tumor began to dry up and loosen. After several treatments, and to the amazement of the doctors

---

[317] Ibid., 153.

watching, Hoxsey was able to detach the tumor with forceps, leaving only a scar underneath.

After witnessing this amazing demonstration of his remedy, Dr. Harris made a proposal. He offered to set up a large-scale clinical trial of the Hoxsey therapy. All that Hoxsey had to do was sign a contract that required that Hoxsey sign over all rights to the remedy to Harris and his associates. He would be entitled only to a 10 percent royalty on fees they would establish for patients seeking treatment. When Harry's father had entrusted the formula to him, he made the young man promise that no patient would ever be denied treatment due to lack of funds or because of race or religion. The treatment wasn't for profit, but for the good of humanity. When Harry referred to signing the contract, Harris threatened him, vowing, "Try to set up anywhere in the country and you'll end up in jail." And for thirty years Harris and his successors tried to do just that.[318]

---

[318] Deoul, *Cancer Cover-Up*, 101–103.

AN EXERCISE IN MODALITIES: A REAL-LIFE EXPERIMENT IN INTEGRATION

Sometimes we think we can remedy a problem by
just doing one thing—go to the doctor or go to the chiropractor
or use herbs or take a special drink or rest.
Often a combination of modalities is needed.
This is an example from my life of
needing to use several modalities.
The last is a modality that is often overlooked.

—The author

I woke up one morning with an ache in my right arm. "Wow," I thought, "I must have slept on it wrong." I couldn't lift my arm without getting a "ping" in a muscle that caused me to cry out and drop my arm quickly. So here are the methods I used:

Leave it to nature: First, I figured it would go away within a day or two—surely a week at the most—so I just tried not to irritate it further. No lifting the blow-dryer. No circling my arm at the gym. To my surprise, the pain did not go away.

Physical therapy: My gym was owned by a physical therapist, so next I asked him. He told me not to do lateral arm exercises and not to overdo the weights. That was good to hear, but the pain in my arm when I tried to raise it at an oblique angle already told me not to do that. Nothing changed, and my arm still hurt.

Personal trainer: There are a bunch of personal trainers at the gym too, so I asked one of them. His reply was to do exercise with the arm straight (no lateral movement) and to strengthen muscles to prevent anything further from occurring. I did that, but my arm still hurt.

Nutrition: Meanwhile, I was undergoing a nutritional program. As I lost weight, joints were eased and climbing stairs was easier. Diet, however, didn't help my arm.

Doctor: Two months later, when it still wasn't improving, I finally saw a doctor. He indicated, rather sadly, that he did *not* want to give me a steroid shot, although that is what his colleagues would do. He recommended an anti-inflammatory over-the-counter drug. He gave me those two choices: a shot or a drug. I didn't want either of them, and I left without any improvement.

Stretching/dance: On the theory that the hurting "ping" was the result of tightening, I stretched gently as often as I could. The stretching exercises came from a former ballet dancer who was now a coach on aging gracefully. As I allowed my arm to go the opposite direction of the hurt, I started feeling slight improvement. Finally.

Chiropractor: At three months, I saw a chiropractor. He said my hips were out of alignment and I had a very stiff neck, so he adjusted the hips and worked a little on my neck. He told me that what he had done with the spine and neck might very well help lessen the pain in my arm. It did. I could now start to make complete circles with both arms, albeit small, tentative ones.

The chiropractor recommended a structural or therapeutic massage therapist.

Therapeutic massage therapist: I went to structural massage therapist Kelly Call, who said the body is like a bunch of rubber bands pulled to and from different locations, and they all interact. It took three one-and-a-half-hour sessions of following tensions in those rubber band muscles before he finally located a debilitating stiffness on the right side of my body—not in my arm, but down on my right side. Curiously, the tension was in the exact location where my husband's cancer had been. He said that the rigidity he felt there was a "heart-wall" response, that is, a physical barrier set up to protect the heart (remember Dr. Brad Nelson). Sound therapist Olivea Dewhurst-Maddock calls it "armoring." "Parts of your body that seem to be stiff, tense, and tough [are] often the residue of painful (usually forgotten) experiences, *frozen into muscular resistance.*"[319]

Kelly removed most of the stiffness or the muscular resistance (I'd say about 90 percent), and I again could swing, lift, and circle my arm. Yay! He and I talk about a lot of pertinent topics during my sessions. That's how I found out about his ematosoma—his identification of body locations that hold on to specific emotions. These emotions may turn into ailments. It was in the last session that I realized my problem wasn't a sudden event. It wasn't waking up one morning and telling a friend, "Whoa, I've got a knot in my arm today." This had been building and accumulating for quite some time!

Literature / the arts: The next day I was listening to the audio version of the book *Delirium* by Lauren Oliver.[320] At the end of the book, Sarah Drew's incredibly emotive voice described the sacrifice of a young man for his girlfriend. I could clearly picture his looking at the departing girl "with eyes as bright as the sun," and tears came suddenly to my own eyes. I cried and cried. I wasn't even sure why I was crying, but afterward, I found my arm wasn't stiff, sore, achy, or nonresponsive anymore. Most of that remaining 10

---

[319] Olivia Dewhurst-Maddock, *The Book of Sound Therapy: Heal Yourself with Music and Voice* (London: Gaia Books, 1993), 47.

[320] Lauren Oliver, *Delirium* (New York: HarperCollins, 2016).

percent was released, and I could lift my right arm at an oblique angle again, almost as good as new.

The conclusion that I drew is, as complex beings, we need a combination of modalities to maintain our health. It is well for each of us to become as conversant as possible with many different health modes, including the arts.

—The author

CHARTS AND DIAGRAMS

HOLLY'S CHART OF FIVE CATEGORIES SHOWING HOW SCOTT FELT (CHAPTER 19)

SELF-FULFILLING PROPHECIES	NEGATIVE BROADCAST MESSAGES	ACCOMPANYING EMOTIONS	FAULTY CORE BENEFITS	POSITIVE AFFIRMATIONS
Life will always be a tough struggle.	Put it on *my* shoulders.	Unresolved anger	Too much furiosity got me into trouble.	I am releasing toxic distortions.
I will never be able to call the shots.	I have enough on my shoulders. Go away!	Lack of affection	I don't want to hear what's going on.	I release feelings of despair and loneliness.
I will always be depressed and have ill will toward others.	You disgust me.	Boiling	Because of life's conflicts, I am burdened.	I am calm, quiet, and relaxed.

(Read about this chart in Chapter 19, "The Mind Influences Behavior.")

APPENDIX D

MODALITIES INVESTIGATED BY SCOTT BREWSTER
FOR THE TREATMENT OF CANCER

THERAPY	PROCESS
Affirmations	Positive statements that encourage the subconscious to entrain to a higher level of energy.
Aloe	Aloe is rubbed onto and absorbed into the body through the skin; taken as a supplement or as a drink.
Alternative Therapy	Many forms of therapy and processes are used. Each process is individual to its type of therapy.
Arts	Reading, attending, or listening to something that heightens enjoyment, provides insights and inspiration, and improves mood.
BET	Two thin needles are inserted, one on each side of a tumor; an electrical current is passed between needles.
Biofeedback	Patient is hooked up to a machine that monitors body functions such as heart rate, breathing rate, oxygen consumption, and anxious energy release. By mentally "tuning in" to their own physiology, the patient learns to affect these functions by either slowing them down or speeding them up.
Black Salve	A dime-size amount of topical ointment is rubbed onto the skin. After that, a drawing salve is applied to the skin until the cancer emerges and sloughs off.
Castor Oil Pack	Cloth seeped in castor oil is laid over the affected area for an hour. A hot-water bottle laid on top provides warmth.

Cesium	Liquid is held in the mouth to be absorbed sublingually. After a time, the rest of the dose is swallowed. Also, certain supplements are required.
Chemotherapy	A poisonous substance is internalized into the bloodstream through an IV that is to attack the cancer cells.
Chi Machine	Patient lies on a flat surface (e.g., floor) and puts heels in depressions on the machine. The machine then swishes the spine to and fro in a "goldfish" swimming motion.
Chiropractic	Chiropractic includes many techniques, from manipulation (adjustment) to energy work.
Cleansing	Fasting: eating only certain food; foot baths or special detoxification pads placed on the soles of feet.
Cobra Venom	Suppository is inserted every few days or every other day for a period of ten treatments.
Colonic	A large amount of water-based cleansing solution is forced up into the large intestine, after which the solution and fecal matter are flushed out, leaving the intestines free of old and hardened debris.
Colostrum	Swallowed.
Counseling	Talking to a licensed practitioner about life issues.
CSCT	A powerful magnetic arm sweeps over the patient's body to diagnose where cancer cells are. On a different setting (frequency) it kills the cells.
Emotion Code	Talking to and being muscle tested by a person trained in the Emotion Code, which was created by Dr. Bradley Nelson.
Enema	A small amount of softening solution is inserted into the rectum and held there for a brief period while it softens hardened stool, enabling easier elimination.
Energy Technologies	Devices that increase an individual's energy are placed on or near the body.
Energy Work	Gifted and skilled individuals "tune in" to a person's frequencies and change those frequencies through many methods.
Enzymes	Supplements and injections.
Essential Oils	Can be rubbed into the skin or internalized by infusion.
Essiac Tea	Taken through supplement tablets or as a tea.
Faith	Prayer, scripture reading, meditation, church attendance, contemplation, and pondering.

Far Infrared	Quilts, thermals, or joint wraps are placed on the body.
Far Infrared Sauna	Patient sits in a cubicle heated to about 110 degrees for twenty to thirty minutes. Far infrared heats the person, not the area, so the room is dry (no steam). Profuse sweating will occur, which releases toxins.
Flaxseed Oil	One method is to grind seeds in a small coffee grinder, then add to shakes or toss on top of salads.
Garlic Pack	Cloth seeped in mashed garlic and oil is laid over affected area.
Green Tea	Swallowed.
Herbs	Taken as a tea or in supplement, tablet, or capsule form.
Holistic	Many energy processes are available: energy work, spiritual work, sleep, energy technologies, diet, etc.
Hot/Cold Shower	Alternate hot and cold shower water on the affected area (or the whole body) to shock the body's system.
Humor	Laughter, jokes, puns, comical books or scenarios, pets, clean comedies— anything that lightens our mood or feeling.
Huntsman Cancer Institute	Treatment options include surgery, radiation, chemo, hormonal, and immunotherapies, as well as clinical trials.
Integrative Healing	A combination of Eastern and Western healing modalities. The best of both worlds would include the concept of balancing the body as one whole entity—using natural means whenever possible—and then resorting to surgery and drugs only if needed. Change is happening, but to revamp our Western system, change would need to occur in medical schools.
Iridology	The practitioner looks into a picture of the eye(s) of the patient, focusing on the irises. This allows diagnosis of certain body parts that have past or current issues. Homeopathics are prescribed to heal or relieve the issues.
Juicing	A special juicing machine is required to break down plants, vegetables, and fruits into a juice, which is then drunk.
Love	Caring, understanding, and listening; spending time with another person.
Magnets	Placed over affected area or placed at a chakra point related to affected area.
Massage	All types of massage apply a certain amount of cyclical or consistent pressure to affected parts of the body.
MD Anderson	Treatments include such things as genetic testing, cancer treatments, screenings, tobacco outreach, and generic counseling.

Meditation	This is done by quietly and deeply thinking, pondering and focusing on life's experience. It is usually done in private and often with eyes closed so as to focus inwardly more intently.
Muscle Testing	Also called applied kinesiology, it is a way of measuring the motor response of the central nervous system by asking for strong or weak responses from muscles. Some call it accessing the innate wisdom of the body.
Natural Healing	Healing is derived through nature's bounty, including common sense. The body is dealt with as a whole rather than through separate symptoms.
New Hope Clinic	A Mexican clinic that featured a unique five-pronged approach to cancer treatment: attack, alkalinize, enhance the immune system, balance emotionally, and upgrade nutrition. All of this was done simultaneously in a complex "dance."
Nutritional IV	Nutrition given intravenously.
Optimum Health Institute	A nondenominational Christian-based facility in California or Texas that provides a safe and sacred environment for healing. Clients take classes that teach optimal diet, optimal exercise, and optimal mental processes.
Potato Juice	Juiced raw potatoes benefit the digestive system to restore physical strength and to suppress tumor growth.
Prayer	An ancient practice, prayer helps a person find greater perspective in connecting with a higher power. It helps you feel that you're not alone. Joy, comfort, and solace are usually associated with prayer.
Prescriptions	Drugs are designed to decrease pain and alleviate other symptoms. Drugs are known for covering symptoms, while not getting at the root cause. A saying is "Once you start taking medicine, you're in 'disease care,' not healthcare." Every drug has a side effect.
Processing	Also called Three-Dimensional Therapy, change is achieved energetically instead of intellectually. It allows access to situations and beliefs deep within a person and then helps to release problems if the client chooses to release them.
Protocel	Previously called Entelev or Cancell, this formula (twenty-three or fifty) breaks down any anaerobic cells (i.e., cancer cells) by interfering with the production of ATP in the cell. The cell cannot produce enough energy to survive, so the cell membranes burst. It does not hurt normal, healthy cells, and is sold as a supplement.
Radiation Therapy	High-energy radiation is used to shrink tumors and kill cancer cells.

Raw Foods	Any food that is eaten raw or cooked under 105 degrees. The benefit is not cooking out nutrition or enzymes that the body needs to digest the food.
Reflexology	Also called zone therapy, this is an ancient method of healing. There are thirteen hundred nerve endings per square inch on the soles of the feet, and the nerves are connected to the organs of the body. Stimulating the nerves on the bottom of the feet stimulates the organs.
Resonance Repatterning	Method One: varying colors or light are shone into the eye. Method Two: Varying frequencies of sound are played through headphones worn by the patient.
Rife Machine	A complex machine that broadcasts frequencies toward a person. The machine weakens or destroys pathogens by energetically exciting destructive resonances. The vibrations only affect those for whom a particular resonance is set; therefore, the machine can't harm anyone else in the same vicinity.
Sports	Games and competitions help us enjoy the wonderful bodies we've been given as well as provide social and mental outlets. Occasionally, injuries or repetitive overuse may necessitate rest for a while.
Surgery	Arising out of triage or wartime use, those who have been through Western medical universities are experts at this. Western medicine looks at surgery as a first resort, whereas Eastern medicine looks at it as a last resort.
Toning	Also called bioresonance sound therapy, balance is restored by engaging sound and color at certain chakra points along the meridian.
Visualization	Imagining a new outcome creates and stimulates synapses in the brain that allow the new outcome to become a reality. Besides health, this is useful in all areas of life: emotional, relationships, financial, sports, goal setting.
Water	Besides air, the most fundamental of nutrients and needs is pure, clean water. Since every occurrence in the body happens in a liquid medium, water that is structured, energized, and slightly alkaline hydrates even better than just "clean" water. Water that is not desirable is contaminated, filled with chlorine and chemicals (like municipal tap water), or stripped of minerals (like reverse osmosis or distilled water).
Wheatgrass Juice	Cleanses, detoxifies, and feeds the body through ultra-high nutrition.

EMATOSOMA—LOCATION OF SPECIFIC EMOTIONS

Appendix 11: Ematosoma–Location of Specific Emotions

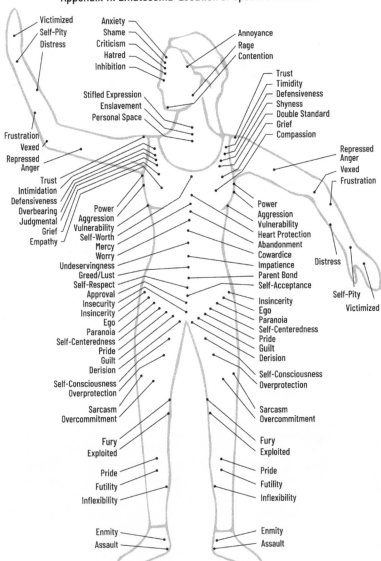

Ematosoma by Kelly Call. Used with permission.

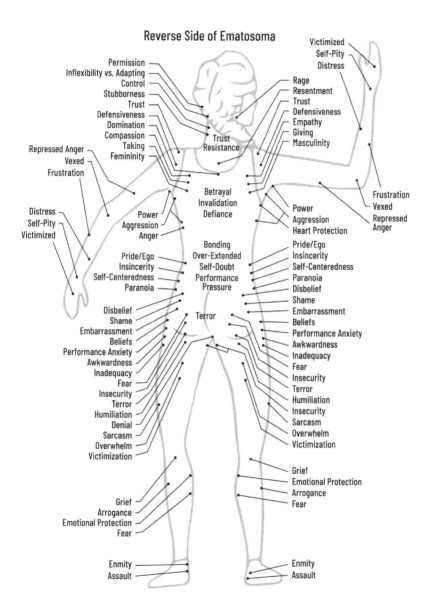

Reverse Side of Ematosoma

APPENDIX E

READING LISTS

1. DR. NEAL DEOUL'S READING LIST ON VIBRATIONAL/ENERGY HEALING METHODS (CHAPTER 5)

Activate Your Immune System, Leonid Ber and Karolyn A. Gazella

Arthritis & Cetyl Myristoleate, Chuck Cochran

The Body Electric: Electromagnetism and the Foundation of Life, Becker and Selden

Cross Currents: The Perils of Electropollution, The Promise of Electromedicine, Becker

Electromagnetism and Life, Becker and Andrew Marino

Enzymes and Enzyme Therapy, Anthony J. Cichoke

Healing with Magnets, Gary Null, Ph.D.

Magnetic Field Application Handbook, Walls

Magnet Therapy, The Pain Cure Alternative, Ron Lawrence and Paul J. Rosch, M.D.

Molecules of Emotion, Candace B. Pert, Ph.D.

Quantum Healing, Deepak Chopra, M.D.

Your Body's Many Cries for Water, F. Batmanghelidj, M.D.

2. DR. NEAL DEOUL'S PARTIAL
READING LIST ON CANCER RESEARCH
(CHAPTER 5)

Aloe Vera and the Human Immune System, Dr. Lawrence Plaskett

The Basic Science and Principles for the Use of Acemannan in Clinical Medicine by Harley R. McDaniel, M.D., Bill H. McAnalley, Ph.D. and Robert H. Carpenter, D.V.M

The Calcium Factor: The Scientific Secret of Health and Youth, Robert R. Barefoot and Carl Reich, M.D.

Cancer Doesn't Scare Me Anymore, Dr. Lorraine Day (cassette tape)

Cesium Therapy in Cancer Patients, Dr. Abdul-Hagg Sartori

Death by Diet, Robert Barefoot (Topic: cesium and potassium lower pH)

Epidemiologic Survey on Lung Cancer with Respect to Cigarette Smoking and Plant Diet, Ryoji Sakai

High-pH Cancer Therapy with Cesium, Dr. Aubrey Keith Brewer

The High-pH Therapy for Cancer Tests on Mice and Humans, Dr. Aubrey Keith Brewer

3. BECKY'S READING LIST
(CHAPTER 15)

Any books by these authors: Dr. Christopher, Norman Walker, Professor Arnold Ehret, Ann Wigmore

Blatant Raw-Foodist Propaganda, Joe Alexander

Cleanse and Purify Thyself, Dr. Rich Anderson

Conscious Eating, Dr. Gabriel Cousens

Diet Decisions for Latter-day Saints, Joyce Kinmot

Eating for Beauty, David Wolfe

Feelings Buried Alive Never Die, Karol Truman

Forgiveness, the Healing Gift We Give Ourselves, Cheryl Carson

The Perfect Body, Roe Gallo

The Roots and Fruits of Fasting, Dr. Mary Ruth Swope

Spiritual Nutrition and the Rainbow Diet, Dr. Gabriel Cousens

The Sunfood Diet Success System, David Wolfe

4. ELAINE'S READING LIST

Alkalize or Die, Dr. Theodore A. Baroody

All These Things Shall Give Thee Experience, Neal A. Maxwell

Becoming Supernatural, Dr. Joe Dispenza

Believing Christ, Stephen E. Robinson

Blood Never Lies, Ted Aloisio

Bonds That Make Us Free, C. Terry Warner

Cancer as a Turning Point, Lawrence LeShan, Ph.D.

Cancer Cover-Up, Kathleen Deoul

The Cost of Being Sick, Nicholas J. Webb

Dancing with Water, MJ Pangman and Melanie Evans

Earthing, Clinton Ober, Stephen Sinatra, M.D., and Martin Zucker

Energy Resources, Wendell H. Wiser, Ph.D.

Feelings Buried Alive Never Die, Karol K. Truman

The Healing Light, Agnes Sanford

The Heart of Health, Stephen Linsteadt, N.D., C.N.C., and Maria Elena Boekemeyer, N.D.

The Hidden Messages in Water, Masaru Emoto

If Thou Endure It Well, Neal A. Maxwell

Inflammation Nation, Floyd H. Chilton, Ph.D.

An Introduction to Young Living Essential Oils and Aromatherapy, D. Gary Young, N.D.

The Miracle of Pi-Water, Shinji Makino, Ph.D.

Molecules of Emotion, Candace B. Pert, Ph.D.

Outsmart Your Cancer, Tanya Harter Pierce

Quantum Healing, Deepak Chopra, M.D.

Questioning Chemotherapy, Ralph W. Moss, Ph.D.

Peace, Love & Healing, Bernie S. Siegel, M.D.

Reverse Aging, Sang Whang

School of Natural Healing, Dr. John R. Christopher

Super Simple Wellness, Connie Boucher, L.M.T.

Your Body's Many Cries for Water, F. Batmanghelidj, M.D.

The Water Puzzle and the Hexagonal Key, Dr. Mu Shik John

INDEX

Milk, 232
Mind-Body, 23, 132, 162, 168, 206, 216, 238, 376
Minerals, 127, 136
Miracle, 123, 156, 209–211, 217, 224, 233, 238, 331, 355, 365, 372, 375–376, 379
Mistakes, 156
Mom B and Lorin, 57, 214, 216, 219, 262, 271–272, 277, 292–293, 298, 301, 305, 311–314, 318
Money, 71, 77, 127, 141, 146–148, 154, 157, 163–164, 175, 190, 282, 301, 357, 367, 371
Monte, President, 209–211, 262
Morishita, Keiichi, M.D, 34
Morphine, 99, 322
Moss, Dr. Ralph, 142, 193
Motion for emotion, 348
Mountain, 110
Move forward, 197, 212
MRI, 9, 79, 159, 282, 283
M.S. (multiple sclerosis), 232
MS Contin, 338
MTA, 76
MTC, 89, 91
Multidisciplinary method, 154, 162, 274
Murray, Bill, 358
Muscle spasm, 65–66, 117, 279
Muscle testing, 23, 112–113, 284, 303
Musician, 120, 225

N

National Cancer Act of 1971, 142
Natural Energy Technologies from earth, air, sun, 1, 25, 45, 167
Natural fiber clothes, 205
Natural food stores, 154
Natural Healing, 10, 37, 38, 203, 206
Naughty, 303
Nausea, 139, 153, 223, 227, 253, 260, 294
Neal, physicist, 45–46, 97, 125, 140, 201, 407, 408
Negative, 371
Negative broadcast messages, 172, 176
Negative feelings/thoughts, 172, 218, 265
Negative release work, 228
Negative student comments, 173
Neighbors, 99, 183, 338, 358
Nelson, Dr. Bradley, 113–115, 177
Neutral, 302
New Hope in Tijuana, 263–264, 304, 358, 361
New methods, 203
New Year, 68, 69
Nicodemus, 29–30, 136
NIH (National Institutes of Health), 56
Nikken, 31

Nixon, President, 142
No medical personnel, 219
Nobel Prize, 299
Nola and Clyde, 183
Non-cancer admissions, 146
Noninvasive, 159
Norma, 351
Normalcy, 17, 98, 312, 324
North America, 28
Nutrition/nutrients, 48, 79, 161, 274, 344

O

Oak Ridge Boys, 76
Obesity, 232
Obey, 59
Oblation, radiofrequency, 164
Observation, 41, 64
Ogden, UT, 17, 61
Oils, essential, 1, 23, 205, 262, 345, 358
Old man, 337
Old Man Willow, 342
Olympic, 14, 285
Oncologists, 143, 148, 203
Opera, 13, 96
Operation, 87
Optimum Health Institute (OHI), 206–207, 213, 263, 284
Orange Blossom Special, 14
Out-of-pocket, 147, 282
Ovarian cancer, 202
OxyContin, 105, 163, 243, 266, 288, 290, 305, 318, 323, 341
Oxygen, 65, 128, 248, 253, 372
Ozone, 264, 341

P

Pac-Man, 241
Packer, Boyd K., 102
Packs: castor oil, garlic, 82–83, 85
Pain, 7, 10, 118, 153, 193, 243, 251, 260, 283, 293, 301, 305, 317–318, 345
Pain medication, 105
Pam, OHI Director, 216, 224, 273, 275, 279
Paradigms, 71, 169, 176
Parsley juice, 344
Path, 9
Pay It Forward, 253
Payoff, 226
Peace, 210, 212
Pearl, 352–354, 366
Pekar, Dr, 301
Penny whistle, 19